THE LIMITS POLICY CHANGE:

Incrementalism, Worldview, and the Rule of Law

Michael T. Hayes

GEORGETOWN UNIVERSITY PRESS/WASHINGTON, D.C.

Georgetown University Press, Washington, D.C.
© 2001 by Georgetown University Press. All rights reserved.
Printed in the United States of America

10 9 8 7 6 5 4 3 2 1   2001

Library of Congress Cataloging-in-Publication Data

Hayes, Michael T., 1949–
  The limits of policy change: incrementalism, worldview, and the rule of law /
by Michael T. Hayes.
    p. cm. — (Essential texts in American government)
  Includes index.
  ISBN 0-87840-834-7 (cloth: alk. paper)
1. Political planning—United States. 2. United States—Politics and government.
3. Rule of law—United States. I. Title. II. Series

JK468.P64 H38 2001
320'.6'0973—dc21   00-061017

Contents

Figures

Preface

In my experience, thinking is the most difficult of all human activities. Although I am a college professor and the author of two previous books, I find that I do not think very long or very productively unless I am stimulated by the works of other authors or prodded by the comments of colleagues, editors, or reviewers. The book you hold in your hands illustrates this thesis very well. Although I thought I had a clear idea what I wanted to do when I began, I needed three complete drafts over a two-year period to produce a manuscript worthy of publication.

This book had its origins several years ago in an inquiry from John Samples—who had recently become editor at Georgetown University Press—about whether I was working on any manuscripts. In the mid-1970s, he had been a graduate student in political science at Rutgers, taking a course on public policy with me. I remembered him as one of the very best students I had encountered during my years there and thought it would be fruitful to write a book under his direction—which definitely has proven to be true.

In considering whether to produce the book with Georgetown University Press, I read a volume by Michael W. Spicer—*The Founders, the Constitution, and Public Administration: A Conflict in Worldviews* (published in 1995)—that John had sent me as a sample of the kind of product the press was putting out under his direction. Exposure to that book profoundly influenced my thinking. Building on the earlier works of Friedrich Hayek and Thomas Sowell (both of whom I discuss in chapter 2 of this volume), Spicer identified two worldviews, which he termed "rationalist" and "anti-rationalist." Proponents of the rationalist worldview regard humans as potentially perfectible and place enormous faith in the capacity of human reason to design utopian reforms of social and economic systems; anti-rationalists regard humans as fallible and prone to self-interest in a way that warrants checks on political power.

Although I did not fully work out the implications of these two worldviews for my own argument for some years, I could see immediately that I needed to take them into account before I went any further. At a minimum, it seemed to me, they suggested that there can be no neutral or objective way of evaluating incrementalism as a form of policymaking. One's evaluation of incrementalism necessarily flows directly out of one's worldview—that is, the assumptions one makes about human nature. Although this insight eventually took the book in a radically different direction than I had envisioned initially, not until my third draft (in response to guidance from my editors, acknowledged below) did I finally move the discussion of worldviews to the beginning of the book.

My thinking also has been stimulated at key points by the works of several other authors whose influence on this book is readily apparent: Joseph Bessette, Lawrence J. Brown, James MacGregor Burns, Friedrich Hayek, Charles O. Jones, Willmoore Kendall, Frank Knight, Charles Lindblom, Theodore Lowi, Reinhold Neibuhr, Michael Oakeshott, Karl Popper, Thomas Sowell, David Spitz, Herbert Stein, and Aaron Wildavsky. My thinking also has been very much influenced by the late Frank S. Meyer, though I discovered his works too late to incorporate them fully into this work. Although I have not met most of these individuals, and some are no longer living, I am deeply indebted to them.

This book also has benefited enormously from the guidance of several people whose insights and criticisms I must acknowledge. First, John Samples was consistently encouraging and supportive as I radically revised the focus and the argument of this book more than once over a period of years. He also was very patient as my duties as department chair made it difficult for me to move very fast over much of this period. In addition, he made invaluable suggestions for revision in response to all three of my drafts.

Second, two anonymous reviewers made many valuable suggestions and pointed to serious deficiencies in the manuscript. Although they offered contradictory strategies for revision—and neither will be fully satisfied with how I have responded to their criticisms—the book is much better for their careful reading.

Third, because these two reviewers offered conflicting direction about how the manuscript should be revised, John Tierney was brought into the mix. As editor of the series in which this book appears, he reread the book and offered his own suggestions for reorganization of my argument. John Samples echoed Tierney's views. Reorganizing the book along the lines they suggested transformed it into a very different and much better volume, opening the door to new conceptual material and suggesting connections to my previous work that never would have occurred to me otherwise.

The book also benefited enormously from the insights of four of my colleagues in the political science department at Colgate—Bob Kraynak, Bob Rothstein, Barry Shain, and Joe Wagner—who gave me feedback on various chapters. In very different ways, each had a significant impact on a portion of my argument.

Finally, I am grateful to God for keeping the promise He made in Proverbs 3:6: "In all your ways acknowledge Him, and He will make your paths straight." By the time I began to work seriously on this project, I had become chairman of the political science department at Colgate. This new role, combined with various committee responsibilities I had taken on and my firm commitment to my primary roles as husband and father, led to enormous demands on my time. It became almost impossible to find time to *read* a book, let alone produce one of my own. Although my account of how this book evolved may appear to describe a path that was anything but straight, this book never would have been completed if God had not helped me in various ways to make efficient use of my time, exposed me to works of scholarship that profoundly shaped my thinking, and put so many people in my path who would challenge and guide me as I worked over a period of years to produce this book. Proverbs 3:5 tells us to trust in God rather than learning on our own understanding, and James 1:17 tells us that every good and perfect gift comes from God. My experience in writing this book has strengthened my faith and verified the truth of these two passages for me. I have accomplished nothing here on my own (*cf.* 1 Corinthians 4:7).

In conclusion, I would like to dedicate this book to my family—my wife, Candace, and to my two sons, Tim and Terry. They know better than anyone how focused I can become when I am engaged in a research project. They also know, however, how much I love them and delight in them. Without them I would doubtless be too maladjusted to produce anything of real value. I thank God above all for them, His good and perfect gifts to me.

Michael T. Hayes

CHAPTER ONE

Needed: A Realistic Theory of Policy Change

This is a book about the limits of policy change. Developing realistic expectations regarding the potential for policy change is critically important, as the late economist Frank H. Knight observed a half-century ago:

> Because reliable prediction, in terms of scientific laws, is impossible, because judgment is more important than rules, the way is open for the ignorant and romantic, the wishful thinkers, to picture political measures as working out any way they feel to be desirable. One of the most vital needs in the education of the citizen is a fair knowledge of the possibilities and limitations of democratic political machinery—of government by law, based on discussion, and responsible administration.[1]

Knight believed that democracies tend to breed an unrealistic sense of how the policy process works and just how much it is possible to achieve through politics: "Electorates educated in and by democracy tend to combine lack of respect for 'politicians' with the belief that elected officials will satisfy any craving by fiat, if only the right pressure is brought to bear."[2]

In this regard, opinion surveys show that many Americans have lost confidence in their government in recent years. They distrust politicians and Washington in general. They are impatient with gridlock, and they believe something happens to corrupt, or at least co-opt, good people once they get to Washington. They see an "Inside-the-Beltway" mentality that is out of touch with the people. Overwhelming majorities say in polls that government can no longer be trusted to do the right thing most of the time.[3]

This perspective carries over into a distrust of our primary institution of representative government: the Congress. Americans seldom give Congress a high approval rating, and when asked by pollsters to rank-order occupations in terms of overall trustworthiness, they almost always place members of Congress at or near the bottom. Americans judge Congress primarily by how well it is doing in passing the President's legislative program.[4] Although Americans appear to grasp the role of "checks and balances" within our system of government, and they recognize that Congress plays an important role in checking presidential power, under normal circumstances they evidently do not want Congress to do much more than briefly slow down the progress of presidential initiatives. The public has a hard time grasping the idea that public policy issues might be complicated, that disagreements among participants might be difficult or impossible to resolve, that the process of reaching consensus might take a long time, or that the result might be significant erosion or even defeat of the President's program. A piece of irreverent graffiti expresses this attitude well: "If pro is the opposite of con, then progress must be the opposite of Congress."

Nor is discontent with the American political system confined to the layperson. According to some reform-minded political scientists, our system of checks and balances cannot meet the serious challenges our nation faces today. James MacGregor Burns is the most prominent advocate of reforms that would make the U.S. political system more like the British parliamentary system.[5] Under such a system, the voters would be able to choose between two issue-oriented parties running on specific, programmatic platforms. The winning party would have an electoral mandate to enact its legislative program. Moreover, voters could hold the party in power accountable for performance in a way they cannot now. Although elimination of our system of checks and balances in favor of a pure parliamentary system is highly unlikely, given our constitutional tradition, such reformers still could achieve their objectives within our constitutional framework by enacting measures to weaken the independence of Congress vis-à-vis the executive—for example, by making House and Senate terms four years in length and having presidential and congressional candidates run together as teams.

The thesis of this volume, by contrast, is that there are inherent limits to policy change. Regardless of whether reforms designed to make our national government function more like a parliamentary system are a good idea (a topic I address in chapter 2), they would not bring an end to the need for bargaining and compromise among people who don't agree on what we should be doing as a nation or how to bring about the results we want. To the contrary, much of the time—as political science research overwhelmingly confirms[6]—public policies necessarily evolve gradually through a pluralistic and highly conflictual process that Charles Lindblom has termed "disjointed incrementalism." There are inherent reasons why this incremental process occurs that would not go away even if we made radical changes in our political institutions.

As advanced by Lindblom and various others, incrementalism advances three major empirical propositions about the policy process. First, policymaking necessarily involves bargaining and compromise ("partisan mutual adjustment") among a multiplicity of actors who possess different information, different personal or institutional interests, and different views of the public interest. Second, participants typically build on past policies, focusing almost exclusively on alternatives that differ only slightly (or "incrementally") from existing policies. Third, because the range of options under consideration typically is confined to proposals for incremental change and because compromise typically will be required to secure agreement even within this restricted range of alternatives, policy outcomes tend to be incremental as well. Lindblom regarded his model as descriptive of the policy process and prescriptive for policymakers. In his view, incrementalism is the prevalent form of policymaking precisely because it is the superior method of policymaking. In particular, the primary alternative to incrementalism—comprehensive, rational decision making—is unattainable in most instances because of conflicts over objectives or inadequacies of the available knowledge base. In short, expecting conflicts to be resolved easily and quickly is unrealistic. To the contrary, we should expect the policy process to be characterized by bargaining and the delays that go with it. Moreover, we should not be surprised when policy outcomes are compromises or even incoherent, and we should realize that major change is most likely to occur through a series of smaller steps.

This book explores whether incrementalism really is the best way to make public policies. Is Lindblom correct in asserting that comprehensive rationality is unattainable most of the time? Are there political or intellectual limits on policy change? When, if at all, is major change possible? Are major policy departures really desirable? Or is major change best attained through gradual evolution of policies, as Lindblom has argued? In short, this book attempts to meet the challenge set forth by Frank Knight more than 50 years ago:

If we are to keep our liberties, preserve peace, and make orderly progress, political science must—I do not know whether it can or not—teach the people, as well as specialists, the major realities of human behavior in relations of power and obedience, and must give them realistic notions as to how many problems, and of what degree of difficulty, can be solved at the same time by group deliberation, and at what speed.[7]

Three themes emerge from my analysis in the remainder of this volume. The first, which I explore in chapters 2 and 3, is that one's evaluation of incrementalism as a strategy for policymaking will turn on underlying assumptions about human nature and what is achievable through politics. Following Friedrich Hayek, chapter 2 begins by identifying two worldviews that are rooted in very different assumptions regarding human nature—particularly whether mankind is perfectible or inherently self-interested, with a capacity for evil. These two worldviews also differ significantly with regard to mankind's intellectual capacities and the potential for reason and analysis in the design of public policies. Chapter 3 expands Hayek's analysis to develop a typology of four distinct worldviews. It explores how proponents of these four worldviews differ in their attitudes toward incrementalism and policy change.

A second theme is that incrementalism derives from at least three distinct sources: the dispersion of important knowledge throughout the political system, checks and balances that are built into our system of government as a safeguard against tyranny, and various efficiencies that flow out of a focus on incremental alternatives. To the extent that incrementalism results from one or more of these three sources, it can be defended; in other words, incrementalism has distinct benefits that more than offset the costs in delay and incoherence that are an inherent consequence of the strategy.

Unfortunately, as chapters 4 through 8 show, incrementalism also can be the result of significant political inequalities that are an inherent part of any pluralistic approach to policymaking. In particular, many of the interests affected by pending legislation will fail to mobilize at all, and there will be major disparities in political resources among those that do succeed in mobilizing. The major drawback of policymaking in the United States is not that it is too incremental but that it departs from incrementalism too often, taking on a variety of pathological forms. If we want to make incrementalism work properly, we need *more* conflict, not less.

As chapter 9 shows, however, creating a balanced equilibrium among groups concerned only with their own narrow interests is not enough. We also must make it harder for organized interests and corporations to pursue narrow benefits at the expense of the general public. The best way to constrain organized interests is through a renewed commitment to the rule of law, as advocated by Theodore Lowi and Friedrich Hayek.[8] Good laws are clear and specific, limiting the discretion of administrators and making clear to the general public which behaviors are acceptable and which are subject to punishment. In addition, good laws are impersonal, applying equally to all citizens. Properly understood, the rule of law does not make for weak government but for government that is *limited* in the best sense: Where incrementalism is governed by a commitment to the rule of law, the arbitrary power of the state over individuals is minimized, and the potential for narrow interests to pursue discriminatory legislation is eliminated. Far from constituting weak government, in Lowi's view, the rule of law is the best defense of the powerless against the powerful.[9]

In sum, this volume argues that incrementalism is a superior form of policymaking, rooted in realistic assumptions about mankind's inherent nature and capacities. For incrementalism to work properly, however, we must strive for a fairer equilibrium of social interests. In addition, incrementalism must be constrained by overarching norms that specify the proper scope of politics. Thus, this book explores the limits of policy change in two distinct senses. First, there are distinct limits on policy change that any realistic theory of policymaking must recognize. Second, if policy change is to be consistently beneficial to the broader public, it must be further limited by a commitment to the rule of law.

NOTES

1. Frank H. Knight, "Economics, Political Science, and Education," in *Freedom and Reform: Essays in Economics and Social Philosophy* (Indianapolis: Liberty Fund, 1982), 395–96. (Originally published in 1947 by Harper & Brothers.)

2. Ibid.

3. For a particularly good study of American attitudes toward national institutions, see John R. Hibbing and Elizabeth Theiss-Morse, *Congress as Public Enemy: Public Attitudes Towards American Political Institutions* (New York: Cambridge University Press, 1995).

4. On public attitudes toward Congress, see Everett Carl Ladd, "Public Opinion and the 'Congress Problem,'" *Public Interest* 100 (summer 1990): 57–67; Herb Asher and Mike Barr, "Popular Support for Congress and Its Members," in *Congress, the Press, and the Public,* ed. Thomas E. Mann and Norman Ornstein (Washington, D.C.: American Enterprise Institute and Brookings Institution, 1994),

15–43; Karlyn Bowman and Everett Carl Ladd, "Public Opinion Toward Congress: A Historical Look," in Mann and Ornstein, 45–57.

5. See James MacGregor Burns, *The Deadlock of Democracy: Four-Party Politics in America* (Englewood Cliffs, N.J.: Prentice-Hall, 1963), and *Cobblestone Leadership: Majority Rule/Minority Power* (Norman: University of Oklahoma Press, 1990).

6. On incrementalism as a method of policymaking, see the following works by Charles E. Lindblom: "The Science of 'Muddling Through,'" *Public Administration Review* 19 (spring 1959): 79–88; *The Intelligence of Democracy: Decision-Making Through Mutual Adjustment* (New York: Free Press, 1965); "Still Muddling, Not Yet Through," *Public Administration Review* 39 (November/December 1979): 517–26; and *The Policy-Making Process*, 2nd ed. (Englewood Cliffs, N.J.: Prentice-Hall, 1980). For two particularly important works co-authored by Lindblom, see David Braybrooke and Charles E. Lindblom, *A Strategy of Decision: Policy Evaluation as Social Process* (New York: Free Press of Glencoe, 1963), and Robert A. Dahl and Charles E. Lindblom, *Politics, Economics, and Welfare: Planning and Politico-Economic Systems Resolved into Basic Social Processes* (New York: Harper and Row, 1953). Charles O. Jones develops a variation on this model that he terms "majority-building incrementalism" in three different works: "Speculative Augmentation in Federal Air Pollution Policy-Making," *Journal of Politics* 36 (May 1974): 438–64; *Clean Air* (Pittsburgh: University of Pittsburgh Press, 1975); and *An Introduction to the Study of Public Policy*, 3rd ed. (Belmont, Calif.: Brooks-Cole, 1984). Aaron B. Wildavsky pointed to incrementalism as a recurring characteristic of the budget process in *The Politics of the Budgetary Process*, 4th ed. (Boston: Little, Brown, 1984). The prevalence of incrementalism also is a recurring theme in Wildavsky's *Speaking Truth to Power* (Boston: Little, Brown, 1979). For a characterization of policymaking as a process of "least steps down the path of least resistance," see James E. Krier and Edmund Ursin, *Pollution & Policy: A Case Essay on California and Federal Experience with Motor Vehicle Air Pollution, 1940–1975* (Berkeley: University of California Press, 1977).

7. Knight, "Economics, Political Science, and Education," 396.

8. See Theodore J. Lowi, *The End of Liberalism: The Second Republic of the United States*, 2nd ed. (New York: W. W. Norton & Co., 1979), and various works by Friedrich A. Hayek, especially *The Constitution of Liberty* (Chicago: University of Chicago Press, 1960) and *Law, Legislation, and Liberty, Volume 3: The Political Order of a Free People* (Chicago: University of Chicago Press, 1979).

9. Lowi, *The End of Liberalism*, 298.

CHAPTER TWO

Incrementalism and Worldview: The Virtues of Systemic Rationality

Before we can properly evaluate incrementalism as a method of policymaking, we must ask how much policy change we can reasonably expect from politics most of the time. My central thesis in chapters 2 and 3 is that expectations about political change reflect certain underlying assumptions about human nature. In other words, one's view of incrementalism will depend on one's worldview.

In this chapter I begin by identifying two distinct worldviews, following on earlier work by Friedrich Hayek, Thomas Sowell, Michael Spicer, and Michael Oakeshott. These two worldviews are rooted in very different assumptions about mankind's basic nature and intellectual capacities. From very different starting points, these two worldviews arrive at divergent conclusions regarding the proper role of government; the definitions of concepts such as freedom, equality, and justice; and the extent to which solving public problems is even possible. Not surprisingly, these two worldviews also arrive at very different conclusions regarding the proper *pace* of policy change—a subject that is the primary focus of chapter 3.

Before taking up that topic, I focus on the implications of these two worldviews regarding the role of reason in designing public policies and the proper place of power in politics. In particular, the two worldviews differ over the extent to which rational decision making is possible or even desirable. Proponents of incrementalism—most notably Charles Lindblom—

suggest that attempts at rational-comprehensive analysis are misguided and doomed to fail. Better policies result when policymaking instead involves a process of deliberation and persuasion among a multiplicity of actors representing various interests and vantage points—a process Lindblom termed "partisan mutual adjustment."

My central thesis in this chapter is that partisan mutual adjustment produces better policy outcomes than any attempt at rational-comprehensive analysis. Partisan mutual adjustment is superior to rational analysis in two ways. First, partisan mutual adjustment draws on the dispersion of knowledge throughout the political system ("the social fragmentation of analysis," in Lindblom's terms), which makes centralized decision making inefficient.[1] Second, in distinct contrast to the rational-comprehensive ideal, partisan mutual adjustment recognizes the potential for tyranny that is inherent in the self-interested nature of individuals—and thus acknowledges the importance of checks on the arbitrary exercise of power by political officials.

❑ THE TWO WORLDVIEWS

Michael Spicer has convincingly demonstrated the critical importance of such worldviews, contrasting the worldview shared by most of the Framers of our Constitution with that characterizing the modern academic field of public administration.[2] The two worldviews he identified there (rationalist and anti-rationalist) are useful for the analysis in this volume as well. Drawing on the work of Thomas Sowell,[3] Spicer defines worldviews as pre-analytic cognitions or visions of how the world works. As such, they provide a frame of reference for interpreting human action on the basis of an almost instinctive set of prior assumptions regarding why people act the way they do.[4] Worldviews should not be understood as social science theories; they provide preconceptions on which such theories may be based. Worldviews do not derive from logic or reasoning; instead, "they shape the objects of our reason and the premises we use in reasoning."[5]

Spicer and Sowell built on the earlier works of Friedrich Hayek,[6] who identified two distinctive worldviews—which he labeled "rationalist" and "anti-rationalist." (Sowell identifies the same two worldviews but refers to them as "unconstrained" and "constrained.") These two worldviews embrace radically different visions of what constitutes a desirable and attainable political order. Although most thinkers may combine elements of both worldviews, the sharp differences between them help to explain "how often the same people line up on opposite sides of different issues."[7]

The Rationalist Worldview

The rationalist worldview regards mankind as fundamentally altruistic and ultimately perfectible. The rationalist places almost unlimited faith in the capacity of human reason to solve social problems. Michael Oakeshott captures this perspective well in his essay "Rationalism in Politics." According to Oakeshott, the rationalist

> can imagine a problem which would remain impervious to the onslaught of his own reason. But what he cannot imagine is politics which do not consist in solving problems, or a political problem of which there is no "rational" solution at all. Such a problem must be counterfeit. And the "rational" solution of any problem is, in its nature, the perfect solution. There is no place in his scheme for a "best in circumstances," only a place for "the best"; because the function of reason is precisely to surmount circumstances.[8]

In this worldview, the rational solution to any problem is identifiable through reason; indeed, it is identifiable only through reason—not through tradition or custom. Hayek refers to this decision-making method as "Cartesian rationality."[9] Sowell calls it "articulated rationality"—as distinct from its opposite, which he terms "systemic rationality."[10] Coherent, value-maximizing decisions require comprehensive analysis that is more likely to be the product of individual minds than of group decision making. For this reason, rationalists view reason as operating primarily through superior individuals who either gain power or persuade others to adopt their ideas. Thus, rationalists are much more likely than anti-rationalists to look to "experts" and intellectuals for guidance in designing and improving political, social, and economic systems.[11]

Rationalists place great confidence in the capacity of science and social science to uncover not only laws governing physical phenomena but also comparable laws governing human behavior. Even moral questions are considered amenable to expert analysis. Ethical systems are no longer regarded as fundamental and eternal truths emanating from God; they are subject to continual improvement through the application of scientific principles:

> There is also a faith in the power of education to mold the character of humanity and to free it from error and prejudice. The state in this sense is not

only reformist but also therapeutic in that it seeks to modify and improve the character of human beings.[12]

The Anti-Rationalist Worldview

By contrast, the anti-rationalist worldview regards mankind as fallible and self-interested and emphasizes the dispersion of knowledge throughout economic or social systems. Thus, to Hayek, the free market operates as a "discovery procedure." In contrast to most economists, Hayek does not base his case for free markets on the satisfaction of certain efficiency conditions such as perfect information or perfect competition. Instead, his case for markets is rooted in the superior capacity of free markets to acquire and utilize knowledge that by its very nature is dispersed throughout the system and thus unavailable to the central planner:

> The real issue is how we can best assist the optimum utilization of the knowledge, skills, and opportunities to acquire knowledge, that are dispersed among hundreds of thousands of people, but given to nobody in their entirety. Competition can be seen as a process in which people acquire and communicate knowledge; to treat it as if all this knowledge were available to any one person at the outset is to make nonsense of it.[13]

Anti-rationalists do not reject reason, but they see its role differently. Although individuals act rationally in pursuing their own ends, they are extremely fallible beings whose individual errors "are corrected only in the course of a social process" such as the market.[14] In Sowell's terminology, the anti-rationalist regards rationality as "systemic" rather than "articulated"; Sowell emphasizes the evolution of law, tradition, norms, and institutions. Hayek, in this regard, advances a theory of evolution that is similar to—but predates—Darwin's. Institutions, norms, or systems are subject to a kind of natural selection in which only superior systems survive. Thus, mankind makes progress less through great breakthroughs in the use of reason than by the steady evolution of institutions and practices.[15]

The ranks of the anti-rationalists include—in addition to Hayek— Adam Smith, Lord Acton, Alexis de Tocqueville, and Edmund Burke. Hayek distinguishes this "true individualism" from the "false individualism" of Rousseau, Descartes, and Condorcet, among others. Appropriation of the term "individualism" by these French writers and their descendants has introduced a great deal of conceptual confusion, in Hayek's view. Accordingly, he used the term "anti-rationalist" to refer to a school of thought that is identified more properly as individualist.[16]

☐ WORLDVIEWS AND THE PROPER ROLE OF GOVERNMENT

The two worldviews come to very different conclusions regarding the proper role of government and the extent to which solving social problems is even possible. Anti-rationalists emphasize amelioration of social problems—most of which never really go away—because genuine solutions are precluded by the twin problems of human fallibility and self-interest.

By contrast, rationalists believe the common good can be attained only if government acts as the chief agent of social cooperation. Ultimately, rationalists see no limits to the proper role of government and seek to expand the power and autonomy of the state:

> Rationalists place little faith in decentralized or spontaneous forms of human cooperation, such as markets, common law, or cultural norms and rules to advance human progress. They express disdain for any notion of an "invisible hand" in human affairs. From the rationalist perspective, only those institutions that can be consciously designed and controlled through the application of collective reason can really be expected to substantially promote the common good. Rationalists see government as the major instrument by which reason may be applied to human affairs for the enhancement of the common good. From the rationalist perspective, government is an instrument driven by common purposes. It is the embodiment of the collective will and reason.[17]

The two worldviews lead to two very different definitions of freedom, equality, and even justice. To the rationalist, *freedom* means freedom to attain personal goals. Differences between individuals in endowments or environments necessarily limit their ability to pursue happiness; such differences must be offset by government action. *Equality*, in this vision, means equalization of results; *justice* is defined as social justice—meaning attainment of the best or ideal distribution of incomes. This ideal distribution of income inevitably differs from that resulting from the free operation of the market; a major task of government (which, for the rationalist, is an attainable task) is the identification and achievement of this ideal income distribution.[18]

By contrast, anti-rationalists define *freedom* as the absence of coercion. Individuals are free to pursue happiness (however they define it) within a stable framework of general and impersonal laws. *Equality* means equality under the law: Impersonal and general rules apply equally to all—minimizing, if not completely eliminating, coercion and arbitrary actions by the state. Within this vision, *justice* requires equality of treatment. True equality of opportunity ultimately is unattainable, and equality of results could be attained only by violating the principle of equal treatment for all individuals:

> [A]ny policy aiming directly at a substantive ideal of distributive justice must lead to the destruction of the Rule of Law. To produce the same result for different people, it is necessary to treat them differently. To give different people the same objective opportunities is not to give them the same subjective chance. It cannot be denied that the Rule of Law produces economic inequality—all that can be claimed for it is that this inequality is not designed to affect particular people in a particular way.[19]

☐ THE RATIONALIST ATTITUDE TOWARD POWER

Because the rationalist worldview regards mankind as ultimately perfectible and considers government to be the primary instrument for achieving common purposes through the application of human reason, the rationalist sees no need to place checks on the exercise of political power. To the contrary, the rationalist seeks to concentrate power to facilitate decisive and coherent action.

The End of Politics?

The rationalist's faith in the power of reason to solve human problems inevitably gives rise to a utopian vision of politics—best captured by Oakeshott in his classic essay "On Being Conservative":

> [T]hey tell us that they have seen in a dream the glorious, collisionless manner of living proper to all mankind, and this dream they understand as their warrant for seeking to remove the diversities and occasions of conflict which distinguish our current manner of living. Of course, their dreams are not all exactly alike; but they have this in common: each is a vision of a condition of human circumstance from which the occasion of conflict has been removed, a vision of human activity co-ordinated and set going in a single direction and of every resource being used to the full.[20]

Ironically, as Kenneth Minogue has observed, if this kind of utopian vision were to be attained, it would lead to the end of politics because all occasion for politics would vanish in the new, perfect society:

> This single system would replace politics by moral judgment, and there would be a perfect society in the sense that there would be no crime, greed, or poverty because people would have been perfectly socialized. Since it would be a moral perfection without effort, we could describe it indifferently as either the triumph or extinction of morality.[21]

Unfortunately for the rationalists, the persistence of disagreement over human nature; the proper ends of politics; and the meaning of terms such as freedom, justice, and equality render the rational-comprehensive ideal unattainable, much as Lindblom suggested. Accordingly, rationalists are forced to resort to coercion to impose their particular vision on the polity as a whole; the proper objective of politics within the rationalist worldview, as Oakeshott observed, is "to turn a private dream into a public and compulsory manner of living."[22]

Burns on Four-Party Politics

This syndrome—the rationalist's frustration with disagreement and readiness to resort to coercion—is well illustrated in James MacGregor Burns's classic work, *The Deadlock of Democracy*.[23] Writing in the early 1960s, Burns had seen a series of liberal presidents take office, armed with an apparent "mandate" from the people, only to find themselves thwarted by a Congress that was responsive to local constituencies and narrow special interests. According to Burns, this situation was attributable to a peculiarly American system of "four-party politics" in which the Democratic and Republican parties are split by our constitutional structure into presidential and congressional wings, which are accountable to entirely different constituencies. The need to win a majority in the electoral college encourages the two presidential parties to compete for the votes of populous states. Throughout the 1930s, 1940s, and 1950s, this imperative led to the nomination of relatively liberal presidential nominees within both parties. Regardless of which party won the presidency, however, the president would face a Congress dominated by conservatives (southern Democrats as well as Republicans) who owed their election to rural, small-town constituencies.

Four-party politics clearly persists today, although the four parties have changed a great deal since 1963. Nowadays, the two presidential parties tend to produce moderate nominees (e.g., Clinton and Dole, or Gore and Bush). By contrast, the two congressional parties have become increasingly polarized in the wake of recent elections, with Democrats becoming increasingly liberal and Republicans becoming increasingly conservative. Whatever their ideological composition, however, the contention among the four parties inevitably leads to a kind of government by consensus—or, more accurately, of concurrent majorities—that is antithetical to utopian visions of all sorts. The defeat of President Clinton's health plan in 1993–94 provides one example; the rise and fall of the Contract for America provides another.

In distinct contrast to the American system of checks and balances, a parliamentary system centralizes power by unifying the executive and legislative branches of government. Where a parliamentary system is characterized by competition between two parties (as in Britain), the majority party will be able to pass its legislative program. Rank-and-file members of the majority party face compelling incentives to vote together within such a system. The party leadership controls career advancement in a way that majority party leaders in the American Congress do not, and failure by the majority to vote together on a major issue brings about a dissolution of the government and the need to face the people in a new election.[24] Accordingly, Burns advocated procedural reforms (an end to the seniority system, weakening of the Rules Committee, easing of the extraordinary majority required to close off a filibuster in the Senate, an end to staggered terms for Congress and the presidency) that were all aimed at subordinating Congress to the executive and reducing the need to develop a consensus before adopting new policies. Burns is still making very much the same argument in a contemporary work—calling (among other things) for four-year terms for members of the House and Senate, with congressional elections held contemporaneously with presidential elections.[25]

There can be no doubt that such a concentration of power would facilitate policy change. Even within the American context—in which the executive and legislative branches are constitutionally independent—transforming a private dream into a public and compulsory manner of living would be much easier if presidential elections were viewed as plebiscites and Congress acted as a rubber stamp. Although Burns couches his argument in terms of the virtues of majority rule, in reality he is advocating a form of minority rule in which any faction that is numerous enough to control the majority party could impose party discipline on the remaining members of the party caucus and thus control the entire legislative body.

◻ THE ANTI-RATIONALIST ATTITUDE TOWARD POWER

Whereas the rationalist embraces power as inevitable and necessary—something to be concentrated in the pursuit of desirable social ends—the anti-rationalist regards power as a potential source of tyranny. In Lord Acton's famous dictum, "Power corrupts, and absolute power corrupts absolutely." Indeed, the purpose of government, in the anti-rationalist view, is to establish the rule of law to limit the coercive power of the state over individuals.

As Spicer has demonstrated convincingly, the American system of checks and balances is deeply rooted in the anti-rationalist worldview.[26] Whereas the rationalist emphasizes "articulated rationality," the anti-rationalist looks to "systemic rationality" (in Sowell's terms): The mistakes of fallible individuals are corrected through a social process. In the economic realm, this social process is the market. Within the political realm, this process involves checks and balances—making ambition counteract ambition. Many interests are represented, and deliberation on the merits of various policy proposals is encouraged.

The Two Majorities in American Politics

Willmoore Kendall argued that subordinating Congress to the President (as Burns proposes) is only one way to pursue majority rule; the Framers embraced a rival conception of majority rule that is at least as legitimate as this "presidential majority." Within this vision—which Kendall termed "the congressional majority"—policy would be made by a deliberative assembly of uninstructed representatives. Elections should not be regarded as yielding mandates for action but as determining who will represent each district. Each constituency will select its most outstanding individual to represent its interests and to exercise independent judgment. Thus, for a proposal to be enacted into law, it must secure the approval of a congressional majority that represents America in all its diversity. The president, as representative of a national constituency, is only one participant among many in this process.[27]

Kendall's vision of the American political system as fundamentally deliberative rather than plebiscitary has been echoed in recent years by contemporary scholars. For example, Charles O. Jones has characterized the American system as one of "mixed representation and diffused responsibility"[28] that is sure to be "anathema to party responsibility advocates."[29] Similarly, Joseph Bessette has identified the various ways in which the American political system promotes reasoning on the merits of public policy proposals. Although the Framers distrusted aroused, passionate, and transient majorities, they sought to "refine and enlarge" public sentiments that were enduring and well-informed. Majority-building in the American system relies much more on persuasion and bargaining and much less on coercion than a parliamentary system such as Britain's. The Framers carefully considered how the size of the legislative assembly affected deliberation; in the same way, they considered the relationship between constituency size and effective representation. In addition, they deliberately promoted a concern with the larger public interest by designing a system in which legislative coalitions necessarily would be broad, requiring accommodation of a multiplicity of interests. This attention to broader interests is reinforced as politicians climb the ambition ladder within the American system; in moving from the House to the Senate and, ultimately, the presidency, aspirants must appeal to ever-larger constituencies.[30]

The Capacity to Say No to the Executive

The contrast between the rationalist and the anti-rationalist views of power is exhibited clearly in their respective attitudes toward the independence of Congress. The case for a majoritarian democracy can be traced back to Woodrow Wilson in the late 19th century. Wilson favorably contrasted the British parliamentary system with the American system of "congressional government." Like Burns, Wilson called for a strengthening of the presidency through a variety of measures designed to reduce the independence of Congress. He also called for a strong rhetorical presidency in which the president—as the sole elected official representing the entire nation—would champion the larger national interest against narrow special interests and local constituencies represented by individual legislators.[31]

Wilson's case rested on the assumption that the most to which any legislature realistically can aspire is to approve or withhold approval from initiatives emanating from the executive. Although this role may seem to be very limited and reactive, Parliament nevertheless performs a vital function, according to Wilson, by subjecting the government's proposals to open and principled debate on the issues, thus educating the public and legitimating government policy. By contrast, in Wilson's view the American system is inevitably dominated by strong committees and excessively responsive to narrow special interests. Consequently, it fails to educate voters via principled floor debates on the issues. It also fails to advance or debate any coherent program; to the contrary, the legislative program in any given Congress consists of the sum of the initiatives flowing out of the various committees. Finally, the constitutional division of power between Congress and the executive makes it harder for voters to hold anyone accountable for performance in office.

If legislatures are to be judged by their capacity to approve or withhold approval of initiatives originating with the executive, as Wilson suggests, the real question is which system actually permits the legislature to say no to the executive and prevail. Passage of the Cabinet's program is virtually automatic within two-party parliamentary systems such as that in Great Britain; indeed, this dynamic is the primary basis of its appeal to reformers such as Burns. If rank-and-file members must vote with the party to have any chance of advancing to leadership positions, and if defeat of a major government initiative forces dissolution of the government, the legislature will be extremely reluctant to say no to the executive.

Within the American system, by contrast, Congress is well-positioned to block the president's program, even if both houses of Congress are under the control of the president's party; the defeat of President Clinton's health plan is only one of many such instances. The government does not fall when Congress defeats a presidential initiative, and members of Congress are nominated and elected locally, outside the effective control of the president or party leaders. Moreover, the president has no monopoly on the legislative initiative. The president's program is only one part of Congress's agenda, albeit an important part; Congress typically has its own agenda, and much legislation originates outside the party leadership, with individual members.[32]

Kendall emphasized this capacity of Congress to say no to the executive, pointing to the existence of a "congressional majority" with normative claims that are at least equal to those of the "presidential majority."[33] In a debate with Burns on the question of whether the 1963 "deadlock" in Washington should be deplored, Kendall argued that President Kennedy's legislative program was stalled not because an obstructionist Congress persisted in thwarting the will of the majority but because liberals had failed to create a genuine consensus in favor of their agenda. If Congress's primary function is to say yes or no to the president's program, as Wilson argued, it must have the effective power to say something besides yes.

❏ THE SUPERIORITY OF THE CONGRESSIONAL MAJORITY

Even if we accept Burns's contention that decisions should be made through a process of majority rule, the case for the "presidential majority" is weaker than it appears. Presidential elections do not necessarily yield clear policy mandates. The candidates may take ambiguous positions on major issues or run on general themes (e.g., emphasizing character, good feelings, or the need for change). Even if the candidates do make the election a referendum on one or more key issues, voters remain free to vote on other grounds. Each individual has only one vote to cast. Some of those voting for the winning candidate may focus on a peripheral issue of paramount importance to them; others may decide on the basis of factors that are totally unrelated to issues, such as character or party identification. Inferring a mandate for any of the winning candidate's issue positions is unwarranted; indeed, the winner may have failed to attract a majority of voters on every issue.[34]

Even if a clear mandate can be identified (as, for example, in 1980, when Ronald Reagan made a proposal for major tax cuts and a defense buildup the central themes of his campaign), the electoral mandate will necessarily be discontinuous or evanescent: It exists at a moment in time and then disappears. Elections serve as crossroads within this vision; a decision by the electorate to turn right rather than left binds elected officials until the next election. There is no room for the exercise of discretion between elections within the responsible party model.[35]

As Kendall argues, the "congressional majority" circumvents each of these difficulties. First and foremost, the congressional majority does not depend on the existence of mandates at all. To the contrary, the purpose of elections within this vision is to produce a government—more specifically, to identify outstanding individuals who will sit in Congress to exercise independent judgment in deliberating on policy proposals. The relationship between legislator and constituency is continuous; it is not limited to the period immediately preceding elections. Moreover, communication between the representative and his or her constituency goes in two directions. By contrast, in the responsible party vision, the parties communicate to the voter, who can respond only with a vote for one party or the other.[36]

Finally, majority-rule systems of the sort Burns advocates make no provision for the rights of intense minorities. To the contrary, in a straightforward system of majority rule, each citizen has one vote; there is no provision for differences in intensity among voters. In this regard, recent comparative research on Western democracies distinguishes between *majoritarian* systems and *consensualist* systems. Majoritarian systems emphasize accountability to voters by making it easier for the majority party to enact its legislative program. The British parliamentary system provides a classic example of a pure majoritarian system. Because Britain's first-past-the-post electoral system gives rise to two major parties, the majority party in Parliament is free to ignore objections from the minority party in passing its legislative program.

Although such a system makes it easier for voters to hold the in-party accountable for performance in office, it has not worked well historically in societies characterized by severe religious or ethnic differences. The high levels of mutual distrust that characterize such societies suggest the need to encourage responsiveness to minority interests through a more consensualist political system. For example, where parliamentary systems are combined with some form of proportional representation, multi-party systems and coalition governments are the norm. Minority elements within the governing coalition tend to be accommodated in such systems so the party in power can avoid the defeat of government initiatives, which may result in a vote of no confidence and lead to a new election. Where ethnic or religious divisions are particularly intense, the system may need to go even further—for example, establishing definite levels of representation for different groups or providing for alternation in power between major parties.

The case for strong party government, as defined by Burns and others, holds great appeal for American political scientists because it appears to enhance popular control over public policy via elections. From a cross-national perspective, however, the case for majoritarian systems is far from self-evident.[37]

By contrast, the most frequently cited strength of the Madisonian system is its protection of intense minorities. In this regard, Spicer emphasizes the role of multiple veto points in forcing policymakers to take into account information and preferences throughout the political system.[38] Moreover, the congressional majority by its very nature represents the nation in all its diversity, encouraging responsiveness to local interests of various sorts; by contrast, the presidential majority regards such group affiliations and local interests with suspicion, instead treating citizens as isolated voters whose preferences will be aggregated to determine an electoral mandate.[39]

In this regard, Jane Mansbridge has identified two distinct conceptions of democracy. *Unitary* democracy emphasizes common interests among participants, face-to-face relations, equal respect for various points of view, and decision making by consensus. By contrast, *adversary* democracy emphasizes the inevitability of conflicting interests, the need for equal protection of various interests, and decision making by majority rule. Although majority rule, in some form, characterizes decision making within most large-group settings (such as elections and legislatures), consensus characterizes decision making in many small-group settings (such as faculty committees).[40]

As Ross Baker has demonstrated, the American political system combines elements of both of these democratic forms, facilitating movement back and forth between adversary and unitary democracy. The House, with its large membership, is characterized by adversary democracy. Two-year terms for Representatives guarantee that the House will be quick to reflect popular sentiments of all sorts. With 435 members, moreover, the House must be managed in a way the Senate is not; debate is limited by a Rules Committee, and floor activity is controlled by majority party leaders. By contrast, the smaller Senate embodies unitary democracy. With its six-year terms and larger constituencies, the Senate emphasizes discussion and deliberation; its smaller membership permits unlimited debate, and the filibuster protects intense minorities. Although the Senate has become more adversarial in recent years, Senators are much more likely than Representatives to know all of their colleagues. Face-to-face relationships, mutual respect, and civility are more important in the Senate than in the House, and decision making is more likely to be by unanimous consent.[41]

❏ THE VIRTUES OF SYSTEMIC RATIONALITY

In this chapter I introduce two worldviews: rationalist and anti-rationalist. The rationalist worldview is utopian in every respect; it regards mankind as ultimately perfectible and places great confidence in the role of reason (or "articulated rationality") in making policy decisions. Because rationalists think in utopian terms, they do not see any need for checks on power. To the contrary, the exercise of power is regarded as natural and inevitable in imposing a coherent vision on the whole society. Of course, the very need to do this is testimony to the breakdown of the rational-comprehensive ideal because there is no need for coercion where there is agreement on ends and means.

Because genuine consensus usually is unattainable, rationalists invoke an idealized conception of majority rule as a prescriptive model for policy-making. Strengthening the presidential majority as Burns proposes, however, fails to deliver on its promises. This approach entails no need to protect the interests of minorities, and under a troubling variety of circumstances, it cannot even claim to deliver majority rule. What responsible party reforms *would* accomplish is to make it easier for rationalists to get their way—"to turn a private dream into a public and compulsory manner of living."

By contrast, the anti-rationalist vision is more realistic in its treatment of human nature and its recognition of inherent limitations on the use of reason. Where knowledge is dispersed throughout the economic system, free markets operate as a kind of "discovery system." Knowledge is dispersed throughout the political system in the same way; a deliberative process encourages representation of various interests and vantage points. Moreover, to the extent that mankind is fallible and self-interested, checks on the exercise of political power are prudent.

Whether one ultimately advocates a parliamentary system or the American system of checks and balances, the choice among political systems should not be based on naive, utopian visions of human nature. The real question is not whether to place checks on political power but what forms of checks are most effective. Although parliamentary systems often fail to yield clear electoral mandates, there is no question that they make it easier for voters to hold the party in power accountable for performance in office. The American system of checks and balances places greater weight on persuasion, and less on coercion, than the British system—but at the expense of accountability. The policy process in the United States is complex and difficult to follow, and the dispersion of power among three branches of government makes it difficult for the average voter to hold anyone accountable for performance. As Woodrow Wilson noted a century ago, the need to stand for reelection serves as a check on power. This check is most effective where accountability is centralized. The larger question is whether this check is sufficient by itself or whether "auxiliary precautions" are necessary.

There can be no doubt that adoption of a parliamentary system in the United States—or some combination of reforms that effectively subordinate Congress to the presidency, along the lines Burns suggests—would facilitate nonincremental policy change. Determining whether such reforms are desirable requires us to address the very different issue of the optimal *pace* of policy change (see chapter 3). I draw two conclusions with some confidence from the discussion in this chapter, however. First, some degree of incrementalism stemming from the mutual adjustment of diverse interests and vantage points is an inevitable and desirable feature within any democratic political system. Second, our system places a high premium on persuasion rather than coercion, encouraging deliberation—defined as reasoning on the merits of public policy. Ultimately it may be better, as Oakeshott observed, "for a society to move together than for it to move either fast or far."[42]

NOTES

1. Partisan mutual adjustment and the social fragmentation of analysis are discussed most fully in Charles E. Lindblom, *The Intelligence of Democracy: Decision-Making Through Mutual Adjustment* (New York: Free Press, 1965).

2. Michael W. Spicer, *The Founders, the Constitution, and Public Administration: A Conflict in Worldviews* (Washington, D.C.: Georgetown University Press, 1995).

3. Thomas Sowell, *A Conflict of Visions: Ideological Origins of Political Struggles* (New York: William Morrow, Quill Books, 1987). For further development of these ideas, see Thomas Sowell, *The Quest for Cosmic Justice* (New York: The Free Press, 1999).

4. Spicer, *The Founders, the Constitution, and Public Administration,* 9.

5. Ibid.

6. F. A. Hayek, "Individualism: True and False," in *Individualism and Economic Order* (Chicago: University of Chicago Press, 1948), 1–32.

7. Sowell, *A Conflict of Visions,* 13.

8. Michael Oakeshott, "Rationalism in Politics," in *Rationalism in Politics and Other Essays* (Indianapolis: Liberty Fund, 1991), 10.

9. Hayek, "Individualism," 4–5 and 9–10.

10. Sowell, *A Conflict of Visions,* 49–58.

11. Ibid., 43–49. See also Thomas Sowell, "The Anointed Versus the Benighted," in *The Vision of the Anointed: Self-Congratulation as a Basis for Social Policy* (New York: Basic Books, 1995), 104–142.

12. Spicer, *The Founders, the Constitution, and Public Administration,* 15.

13. Friedrich A. Hayek, *Law, Legislation, and Liberty, Volume 3: The Political Order of a Free People* (Chicago: University of Chicago Press, 1979), 68.

14. Hayek, "Individualism," 8–9.

15. F. A. Hayek, *The Fatal Conceit: The Errors of Socialism* (Chicago: University of Chicago Press, 1988), 23–28.

16. Hayek, "Individualism," 6–10. An excellent example of the rationalist worldview, identified by Sowell, is William Godwin.

17. Spicer, *The Founders, the Constitution, and Public Administration,* 14.

18. For an excellent example of this kind of thinking, see John E. Schwarz, "Is There Another Bottom Line?" in *Illusions of Opportunity: The American Dream in Question* (New York: W. W. Norton and Company, 1997), 41–55.

19. Friedrich A. Hayek, *Road to Serfdom* (Chicago: University of Chicago Press, 1994), 87–88. For the most complete development of this argument, see Friedrich A. Hayek, *Law, Legislation and Liberty, Volume 2: The Mirage of Social Justice* (Chicago: University of Chicago Press, 1976).

20. Oakeshott, "On Being Conservative," in *Rationalism in Politics and Other Essays,* 426.

21. Kenneth Minogue, *Politics: A Very Short Introduction* (New York: Oxford University Press, 1995), 110.

22. Oakeshott, "On Being Conservative," 426.

23. James MacGregor Burns, *The Deadlock of Democracy: Four-Party Politics in America* (Englewood Cliffs, N.J.: Prentice-Hall, 1963). See also Steve Allen et al., *Dialogues in Americanism* (Chicago: Henry Regnery Co., 1964), 106–111.

24. Philip Norton, *The British Polity,* 3rd ed. (New York & London: Longman, 1994).

25. James MacGregor Burns, *Cobblestone Leadership: Majority Rule/Minority Power* (Norman: University of Oklahoma Press, 1990). See also G. Calvin Mackenzie, *The Irony of Reform: Roots of American Political Disenchantment* (Boulder, Colo.: Westview Press, 1996), 182–97, for a strikingly similar set of reform proposals.

26. Spicer, *The Founders, the Constitution, and Public Administration,* 34–40.

27. In addition to Willmoore Kendall, "The Two Majorities in American Politics," in *The Conservative Affirmation in American Politics,* ed. Willmoore Kendall (Lake Bluff, Ill.: Regnery Gateway, 1985), 21–49, see James Burnham, *Congress and the American Tradition* (Chicago: Henry Regnery Company, 1959), for a defense of Congress as representative of the full diversity of the nation in a way the president is not.

28. Charles O. Jones, *The Presidency in a Separated System* (Washington, D.C.: Brookings Institution, 1994), 19.

29. Ibid., 17.

30. Joseph M. Bessette, *The Mild Voice of Reason: Deliberative Democracy and American National Government* (Chicago: University of Chicago Press, 1994).

31. Woodrow Wilson, *Congressional Government: A Study in American Politics,* 15th ed. (Boston: Houghton, Mifflin and Company, 1900), and *Constitutional Government in the United States* (New York: Columbia University Press, 1921). On Wilson's conception of the rhetorical presidency, see Jeffrey Tulis, *The Rhetorical Presidency* (Princeton, N.J.: Princeton University Press, 1987).

32. Jack L. Walker, "Setting the Agenda in the U.S. Senate: A Theory of Problem Selection," *British Journal of Political Science,* 7 (October 1977), 423–45.

33. Kendall, "The Two Majorities in American Politics." A contemporary and debating rival of Burns, Kendall was a political conservative as defined by Michael Oakeshott in his classic essay. Kendall's conservatism was less an ideology than a disposition; he was skeptical of utopian visions of all sorts—and thus inclined to gradual change designed to remedy specific defects in a system that drew its justification from tradition and experience. Kendall was anathema to liberals; he also had a very difficult personality that made him something of a maverick even within the nascent conservative movement of his day. In addition to the essays in *The Conservative Affirmation,* see also Nellie D. Kendall (ed.), *Willmoore Kendall Contra Mundum* (Lanham, Md.: University Press of America, 1994).

34. Kendall, "The Two Majorities in American Politics," 41*ff.* Jones echoes Kendall's skepticism regarding electoral mandates; see Jones, "Presidents, Mandates, and Agendas," in *The Presidency in a Separated System,* especially 149–64. See also

Leon D. Epstein, "Electoral Decisions and Policy Mandate: An Empirical Example," *Public Opinion Quarterly* 28 (winter 1964): 564–72.

35. Kendall, "The Two Majorities in American Politics," 41; Robert A. Dahl, *A Preface to Democratic Theory* (Chicago: University of Chicago Press, 1956), 71.

36. Kendall, "The Two Majorities in American Politics," 41–42.

37. See R. Kent Weaver and Bert A. Rockman (eds.), *Do Institutions Matter? Government Capabilities in the United States and Abroad* (Washington, D.C.: Brookings Institution, 1993), and Arend Lijphart, *Parliamentary Versus Presidential Government* (New York: Oxford University Press, 1992).

38. Spicer, *The Founders, the Constitution, and Public Administration,* 50–52. See also Willmoore Kendall and George W. Carey, "The 'Intensity' Problem and Democratic Theory," *American Political Science Review* 62 (March 1968): 5–24. For an acknowledgment that majority rule cannot deal with intensity, see Dahl, *Preface to Democratic Theory*, 125.

39. Burnham, *Congress and the American Tradition*, 317*ff.*

40. Jane J. Mansbridge, *Beyond Adversary Democracy* (Chicago: University of Chicago Press, 1980).

41. Ross K. Baker, *House and Senate*, 2nd ed. (New York: W. W. Norton and Company, 1995).

42. Oakeshott, "On Being Conservative," 396–97.

CHAPTER THREE

Incrementalism as Meliorative Liberalism

In chapter 2 I focus on one element of Lindblom's normative case for the incremental model, making a case for the superiority of partisan mutual adjustment over misguided attempts at rational, comprehensive decision making. In this chapter I focus on the remaining component of Lindblom's defense of incrementalism: his argument that policymaking works best when attention is largely confined to incremental policy alternatives.

The desirability of nonincremental policy change should not be taken for granted. As the discussion in chapter 2 shows, the two worldviews start from very different assumptions regarding mankind's basic nature and capacity for reason—which lead naturally to radically different conclusions regarding the proper pace of political change. In the first section of this chapter, I argue that rejection of the rationalists' utopian notions of political change does not necessarily imply acceptance of the anti-rationalists' limited conception of the proper role of government. I identify a third school of thought, which I term "meliorative liberalism"; this perspective shares the rationalists' emphasis on the need for social and economic reforms yet espouses incremental or piecemeal change as the best strategy for addressing social problems. In the second section of this chapter, I clarify this concept of meliorative liberalism by placing it within the larger context of a typology of four distinct worldviews. Although meliorative liberalism is not the only worldview that embraces gradual political change, the most prominent advocates of incrementalism—Karl Popper and Charles Lindblom—are both meliorative liberals as defined here. In succeeding sections of this chapter, I review their main arguments; I suggest that incrementalism is best understood as a strategy for pursuing meliorative liberalism. I conclude the chapter with a summary of the virtues of incremental policy change and a brief discussion of strategies for making incrementalism work better.[1]

❏   MELIORATIVE LIBERALISM VERSUS CLASSICAL LIBERALISM

The anti-rationalists I review in chapter 2 (particularly Hayek, Sowell, Oakeshott, and Burke) emphasize the organic nature of the state and the importance of tradition, consensus, and gradual evolution of institutions as well as policies. For these authors, politics involves a covenant between generations as well as a bargain among contemporary interests; to borrow a phrase from Joseph Cropsey, their main emphasis is on "conserving the inheritance."[2]

The anti-rationalists expect progress to occur through the slow evolution of culture and institutions. For example, Oakeshott expresses a preference for "slow, small changes which have behind them a voluntary consensus of opinion"[3] and defines the key task facing policymakers as identification of "the next step dictated or suggested by the character of the society in contact with changing conditions." The key principles guiding policymakers should be *continuity*—which recognizes a diffusion of power between past, present, and future—and *consensus*, which acknowledges the need to recognize the various interests that possess legitimacy in the present.

Not surprisingly, this school of thought tends to advocate a minimalist role for the state. Hayek is an exception in stressing a significant role for the state in regulating and maintaining competitive markets, but advocacy of a vigorous state is not really his central project.[4] Although the anti-rationalist philosophy was known as liberalism in the 19th century, it bears little resemblance to contemporary liberalism, with its advocacy of a strong central government and extensive regulation of the economy. Hayek believed this earlier meaning of *liberalism* has been irretrievably lost; he devoted a postscript to *The Constitution of Liberty* to explaining why he is better understood as a classical liberal rather than a conservative.[5]

The fact that the *liberal* label has been appropriated by the rationalists in the 20th century does not mean that all contemporary liberals may be characterized as rationalist or utopian. Utopian thinkers are not confined to the political left. Moreover, one of the defining characteristics of genuine liberals is a belief in human fallibility. Precisely because liberals see all knowledge as tentative and thus view error as inevitable, they favor political arrangements that facilitate the peaceful correction of error. In particular, liberals have consistently favored democratic forms over monarchies or systems that preserve the power of any self-proclaimed aristocracy, such as the mercantilist economic policies that were prevalent in the 19th century. Thus, liberalism, properly understood, is committed to the principle of experimentalism and the open-ended negotiation of differences.[6]

There are therefore two distinct strains within the anti-rationalist worldview: The anti-rationalists we met in chapter 2 must be contrasted with a second and more reformist school that I call "meliorative liberalism." Although meliorative liberals are anti-rationalist in their skepticism regarding the possibility of attaining absolute knowledge or absolute truth, they share with the rationalists an emphasis on the need for reform to address serious social or economic problems:

> Generations and individuals who respect the improved or who incline toward reform defer to no reason but their own. . . . They wish to examine each age and situation as it is, that is to say, as it differs from other ages and situations; and they wish to prescribe for the age and situation by the light of what they understand for themselves, by acts of reason, rather than by the light of other men's agreement as to the good. To refuse the authority of conventions, and to investigate the nature of each thing—each age and situation—by the light of reason seems congenial to the spirit of reform and thus to the spirit of liberalism.[7]

L. T. Hobhouse has convincingly accounted for the evolution of liberalism in theory and practice from a 19th-century focus on limiting government intervention in the economy to the modern liberal conception of a powerful state role as regulator and stabilizer. On one level, liberalism's early emphasis on the benefits to be gained via a self-regulating market was replaced by a more sophisticated recognition of the various ways in which competition could be unfair—giving giant firms market power over unorganized workers, for example.[8] In addition, Hobhouse regarded property as having a social and a private component. This insight implied an ambiguous but nevertheless positive role for the state in striking the proper balance between private and public in every sphere.[9]

At the same time, Hobhouse made explicit the anti-rationalist and experimental essence of meliorative liberalism. Because the balance between public and private is impossible to specify with any precision—and in any case will be subject to change over time—gradual policy evolution is preferable to grandiose policy changes in pursuit of what is inherently an elusive target:

> [T]he manner in which the State is to exercise its controlling power is to be learnt by experience and even in large measure by cautious experiment. . . . [T]he teaching of history seems to be that progress is more continuous and secure when men are content to deal with problems piecemeal than when they seek to destroy root and branch in order to erect a complete system which has captured the imagination.[10]

☐ A TYPOLOGY OF WORLDVIEWS

The essence of meliorative liberalism may be further clarified by making explicit its defining elements and contrasting it with a broader range of alternative worldviews. Figure 3-1 identifies four distinct worldviews derived from the interaction of two underlying dimensions. The first dimension, drawn from chapter 2, distinguishes utopian thinkers from anti-utopian or meliorative thinkers. In essence, this dimension represents a distinction between visions that are process-oriented and visions that are oriented toward a knowable end or "solution." Anti-rationalists believe that identifying absolute truth through reason is impossible; thus, they regard the development of a good process (systemic rationality) as the best way to alleviate concrete problems. Rationalists believe that identifying truth is possible and thus stress progress toward (or a return to) a knowable, desirable end-state.

The second dimension, drawn from this chapter, distinguishes proponents of social change or reform from those who would "conserve the

FIGURE 3-1. Typology of Worldviews

	Meliorative: Process-Oriented	Utopian: End- or Solution-Oriented
Progressive vision: reformers	Meliorative liberals	Utopian visionaries (Hayek's rationalists)
Nostalgic vision: preservers	Adaptive conservatives (Hayek's anti-rationalists)	Nostalgic conservatives

inheritance." In effect, this dimension represents a distinction between progressive and nostalgic visions.

The resulting four categories or schools of thought are the utopian visionaries, the adaptive conservatives, the nostalgic conservatives, and the meliorative liberals.

Utopian Visionaries

I introduced the utopian visionaries in chapter 2; they are Hayek's rationalists, advancing utopian visions of social or economic reform. Utopian visionaries will be impatient with incrementalism. Because they are drawn to large-scale policy experiments, and because they place a premium on logical coherence, they naturally resent any political institutions that force them to settle for one piece at a time. They are in a hurry to get where they are going, and they distrust any process, like incrementalism, that tends to produce watered-down, compromised, and seemingly incoherent outcomes. Because the task of government, within this worldview, is to identify the perfect solution to problems (e.g., to optimize) subject to ever-changing conditions, they tend to place a premium on flexibility. Thus, rules or laws cannot be binding on the state where they begin to impede this process of optimization. Policymakers must have complete freedom to override existing laws or rules whenever the circumstances warrant. Parliamentary sovereignty—as it operates within the British system—is one way to guarantee this flexibility; in the British system, Parliament can make or unmake any law it wants and cannot be overturned by the courts.

Another way of achieving this flexibility is to delegate vast discretion to bureaucrats. This solution is very much in keeping with the rationalist stress on the role of experts. For example, utopian visionaries often distrust free markets, believing that central planning of an economy is possible. For this reason, they are willing to vest judges and bureaucrats with the responsibility for determining what is "fair" or "reasonable" with regard to various actions.[11]

Adaptive Conservatives

Adaptive conservatives essentially are Hayek's anti-rationalists (as described in chapter 2)—a group that would include Burke, Tocqueville, Lord Acton, and Michael Oakeshott. (Hayek would place himself in this category as well, but as I argue in a subsequent section of this chapter, he is better understood as a nostalgic conservative.) Although Hayek refers to this group as classical liberals, characterizing them as adaptive conservatives would be more accurate inasmuch as they grudgingly accept adaptation to social and economic developments as necessary to preserve an inheritance that is basically sound.

The essence of the adaptive conservative worldview was best captured by the late Frank Meyer, a prominent conservative writer of the 1950s and 1960s and one of the original editors of *National Review* magazine:

> In any era the problem of conservatives is to find the way to restore the traditions of the civilization and apply it in a new situation. But this means that conservatism is by its nature two-sided. It must at one and the same time be reactionary and presentist. It cannot content itself with appealing to the past. The very circumstances that call conscious conservatism into being create an irrevocable break with the past.[12]

For example, the Great Depression posed a real threat to the survival of capitalism. Capitalism survived because it adapted. The real legacy of this adaptation, according to Herbert Stein, is a new form of capitalism that combines free enterprise, elements of a welfare state, managed economic stabilization, and a substantial amount of regulation of economic activity. This *mixed* economy is what has triumphed, and it has triumphed "in the sense that there is no serious alternative in the countries that have it and that it is envied in all the countries that do not."[13]

Stein—chairman of the Council of Economic Advisors under President Nixon—is a particularly good contemporary example of an adaptive conservative. Stein is an adaptive conservative rather than a meliorative liberal by virtue of his recognition of a valuable inheritance that needs to be preserved through adaptation to changing conditions. For Stein, this inheritance is capitalism; it is worth preserving, however, because it places a high value on human freedom without treating freedom as an absolute:

> Capitalism is not a blank slate upon which anything can be written; it has a central core that must be preserved if it is to remain capitalism. But the large penumbra around that core can change without ending capitalism, and it has to change from time to time if capitalism is to survive.
>
> The central core of capitalism, without which a society would not be capitalist, is freedom. But absolute freedom is impossible, and no one has satisfactorily defined the amount and kind of freedom that is essential to qualify as capitalism. Undoubtedly, the adaptations of American capitalism in the past 60 years have rearranged freedoms, redistributed them among individuals, and changed their character. People are no longer free, for

example, to spend as large a part of their incomes as they formerly were. If some of the leading figures of 1929 were to be confronted with the picture of American society as it is now, they would say that this society is neither free nor capitalist. But very few Americans living today would doubt that we qualify as both free and capitalist, nor would there be much doubt that countries as diverse as, say, Sweden and Singapore qualify.[14]

Nostalgic Conservatives

Where adaptive conservatives recognize a need to adapt to changing circumstances to preserve as much as possible of what was valuable in the past, nostalgic conservatives long to return to the values and practices of an earlier age. In distinct contrast to meliorative liberals, nostalgic conservatives believe in the existence of an absolute, knowable truth—a truth that was identified at some earlier point in time and subsequently lost. This absolute truth may be revealed in Scripture, history and tradition, the ideas of ancient philosophers, natural law, the self-regulating market, or some other source. The important thing for nostalgic conservatives is that this truth be identified and preserved—or, if necessary, restored.

The Christian Right is the most striking contemporary example of such a group. Often, however, the emphasis is not on religious values but on economics—particularly the need to return to an earlier era in which the federal government played a much smaller role and the market was largely self-regulating. This phenomenon is a recurring theme within American politics. The conservative movement of the 1950s and early 1960s, which culminated in the Goldwater movement, may be understood in these terms inasmuch as it represented a longing to return to the period before the New Deal, when the federal government's involvement in the economy and social policy was much more limited and the states exercised more autonomy vis-à-vis the federal government. A more recent variation on this theme has been advanced by Newt Gingrich, former Speaker of the House and a prominent leader of the New Right within the Republican Party. Gingrich advocates what can only be characterized as a utopian vision of America's future in the global economy of the third millennium. Gingrich wants to facilitate the development of new technologies to ac-celerate the transition into what Alvin and Heidi Toffler call "the third wave."[15]

Gingrich's attraction to futuristic ideas can easily obscure the extent to which he is really a nostalgic conservative. Much as the conservatives of the 1950s wanted to overturn the economic policies of the New Deal, Gingrich's goal is to dismantle the welfare state and recreate a self-regulating market in the new global economy. Although Gingrich's futuristic spin on this very old idea is designed to make nostalgic conservatism appear very up-to-date, the fundamentally utopian nature of the self-regulating market was recognized by Karl Polanyi in the 1940s. According to Polanyi, the development of capitalism in 16th-century Britain was not a natural evolution but the result of deliberate policy decisions by Parliament—particularly legislation that encouraged the enclosure of what had previously been open lands. In Polanyi's view, this policy represented a misguided attempt to impose a utopian ideal: a "self-regulating market"—a disastrous mistake that eventually spawned a host of countermeasures as various groups within society sought to buffer the brutal effects of capitalism.[16]

Nostalgic conservatives are not committed to conserving everything, only "the good." As a consequence, they emphasize the need to resist false doctrine and do not ultimately share liberals' commitment to an open society:

> To permit the unrestrained expression of such falsehoods may lead to their widespread acceptance. Then error, not truth, will govern mankind. Since it is the business of government according to conservatives, to apply justice and achieve virtue, not speech but "good" speech, not conflicting ideas but "right" ideas, should be tolerated. The idea of an open society, in which men are free to utter and debate diverse opinions, including the wrong opinions, is from this standpoint both evil and absurd. What is vital is the inculcation of right attitudes, right habits, right conduct; and this can only be achieved if men who know what is right teach and control those who would not otherwise understand or do what is right.[17]

This emphasis on the need for people who know what is right to teach and control those who otherwise would not recognize "the right" accounts for the common tendency among nostalgic conservatives to advocate a hierarchical social system. Within this worldview, there is a natural order of things—and people need to know and accept their place in it. Throughout history, conservatives have resisted the encroachment of egalitarianism in all forms, defending instead the idea of an aristocratic order.[18] Not surprisingly, nostalgic conservatives differ from adaptive conservatives in their attitude toward political change. Although adaptive conservatives are cautious about initiating change themselves, they are prepared to accommodate social change to the extent that it is inevitable within a developing industrial society.[19] By contrast, the attitude of nostalgic conservatives toward political change will be a function of circumstance. They will resist change where the social order conforms to their preconceptions of the good society—where it is characterized by hierarchy and widespread acceptance of "correct" doctrines. Where a society has strayed away from this ideal state, however (as the contemporary United States has, in the view of the Christian Right), nostalgic conservatives can become a force for fundamental social or economic change. Of course, the kind of reactionary change that nostalgic conservatives advocate will be very different from the futuristic reforms advocated by utopian visionaries, who believe reason can be used to improve social or economic institutions. Moreover, nostalgic conservatives do not necessarily agree among themselves on which doctrines are correct. At any given point in time, different nostalgic conservative factions may have very different agendas for reactionary change. Within the contemporary Republican party, for example, the Christian Right wants America to return to Judeo-Christian religious values; Gingrich and other economic conservatives seek a return to unregulated markets—albeit updated for the global economy and a new millennium. This factionalism represents an enduring tension within conservatism as a contemporary political movement.[20]

Nostalgic conservatives' attitude toward political *power* will vary with circumstances in this same way. Checks and balances impede change, thereby aiding those who would conserve traditional institutions or values. Such obstacles quickly lose their appeal, however, when nonincremental change is necessary to restore the values of a previous age. The recent struggle over the Contract for America provides a particularly good example.[21]

Friedrich Hayek as Nostalgic Conservative

As I noted, Friedrich Hayek characterized himself as a classical liberal, claiming affinity with a variety of thinkers (Alexis de Tocqueville, Edmund Burke, Lord Acton, Michael Oakeshott) that I have classified as adaptive conservatives. On the basis of a simple, dichotomous distinction between rationalist and anti-rationalist worldviews, Hayek does indeed belong in the same category with these adaptive conservatives; doubtless, his case for the free market as a kind of discovery system would be accepted without much hesitation by any of the members of this group.

Hayek departs from the adaptive conservatives, however, in his emphasis on the need for a return to the rule of law. Where rules are general and impersonal, true liberty is maximized, according to Hayek, because individuals are not subject to coercion by the arbitrary will of any other actor or institution.[22] "Man is free if he needs to obey no person but solely the laws."[23] Within a framework of laws or rules, individuals are free to pursue happiness however they define it:

> The formal rules tell people in advance what action the state will take in certain types of situation, defined in general terms, without reference to time and place or particular people. . . . The knowledge that in such situations the state will act in a definite way, or require people to behave in a certain manner, is provided as a means for people to use in making their own plans.[24]

Although rules do constrain behavior, and thus limit absolute freedom, they will be *predictable*—and thus not arbitrary—to the extent that they are specific. Individuals can take the rules into account in planning their own activities and pursuing their own ends.

One might expect Hayek to join with the adaptive conservatives in embracing incrementalism as a method of policymaking, inasmuch as it retards the rate of policy change, thereby facilitating a degree of relative stability. For Hayek, however, incrementalism is defensible only as long as it operates in accordance with the rule of law. In this regard, Hayek sought to reverse what he saw as a drift away from a free society:

> [G]radually and by almost imperceptible steps, our attitude toward society has changed. What at every stage of this process of change had appeared a difference of degree only has in its cumulative effect already brought about a fundamental difference between the older liberal attitude toward society and the present approach to social problems. The change amounts to a complete reversal of the trend we have sketched, an entire abandonment of the individualistic tradition which has created Western civilization.[25]

Although incrementalism may delay the arrival of an all-powerful state, where it is unconstrained by a firm commitment to the rule of law it represents a "road to serfdom."

In Hayek's view, the drift away from rule of law in Western democracies has been going on for so long that few people can any longer even define what the concept involves, and almost no one recognizes that anything important has been lost. Hayek's central project, articulated over 30 years in a variety of works, is not merely a defense of the market but a return to the rule of law. This desire to restore the practices of a bygone era clearly marks Hayek as a nostalgic conservative.[26]

In making his case, Hayek clearly exhibits the nostalgic conservative's ambivalent attitude toward political change. To get where he wants to go, one must take the radical step of enacting an absolute prohibition on all special interest legislation as part of a new constitution. Once the rule of law is secured by rewriting the political constitution, it will be preserved by replacing existing legislative bodies with a new bicameral parliament. The lower house will manage the day-to-day affairs of government, but it will be prohibited from taking any actions that violate general rules of conduct to be established by the upper house. Although members of the lower house would be expected to be responsive to voters—much like the U.S. Congress or the British Parliament—the members of the upper house would be expected to exhibit experience and detachment. In Hayek's model constitution, the upper house would consist of men and women between the ages of 45 and 60, elected for 15-year terms, with one-fifteenth replaced each year. Thus, although nonincremental change—in the form of a complete constitutional overhaul—clearly would be required to restore the rule of law, once the new system was in place it would be preserved by constraints on political action that would be much more severe than those operating in the American system of checks and balances.[27]

Meliorative Liberals

The typology of worldviews developed in Figure 3-1 helps to clarify the central elements of meliorative liberalism. Meliorative liberals are true liberals: Although they share utopian visionaries' emphasis on social reform, they regard mankind as fallible and all knowledge as necessarily incomplete. Whereas adaptive conservatives believe that fallible people can do little to improve on tradition and thus should adapt to changing conditions only as necessary to preserve traditional institutions and values, meliorative liberals regard inherited institutions and policies as the product of fallible people and always subject to question.

Thus, meliorative liberals consistently view social and economic change as potentially beneficial but ordinarily see that change as best pursued via a series of incremental steps. Where utopian visionaries regard politics as an exercise in *solving* problems once and for all through the application of *articulated rationality*, meliorative liberals regard politics as a means to *ameliorate* problems gradually through a process of *systemic rationality*. We may confidently characterize the two most important proponents of incrementalism in policymaking, Karl Popper and Charles Lindblom, as meliorative liberals.

☐ KARL POPPER ON PIECEMEAL SOCIAL CHANGE

A critically important forerunner of Charles Lindblom,[28] Karl Popper is known primarily as a philosopher of science with a particular interest in the nature of knowledge and the ways in which human beings acquire knowledge. This interest shaped his writing on politics and policymaking, particularly *The Poverty of Historicism* and *The Open Society and Its Enemies*.[29]   In both of these works, Popper characterized utopian efforts at social reform as inherently at odds with the ways in which human beings learn.

Social Engineering and the Scientific Method

Like Hayek, Popper conceded that most social institutions are more the product of gradual evolution or adaptation than any conscious design.[30] Nevertheless, from a functional or instrumental perspective, institutions may be redesigned to more efficiently attain desired ends. Efforts to reform human institutions therefore may be regarded as social engineering.[31]

According to Popper, social engineering can take on two distinct forms, which he termed "holistic social engineering" and "piecemeal social engineering." Holistic social engineering "aims at remodeling the 'whole of society' in accordance with a definite plan or blueprint" by taking control of key positions and extending the power of the state until it becomes commensurate with society. From these key positions, the state can arrest the course of historical forces or foresee their course and adjust society to them.[32]

By contrast, although piecemeal social engineers may cherish certain ideals that apply to society as a whole—social justice, for example, or the general welfare—they will reject as impractical any attempt to remodel society as a whole: "Whatever his ends, he tries to achieve them by small adjustments and readjustments which can be continually improved upon."[33]

Popper's distinction between piecemeal and holistic social engineering clearly anticipates Lindblom's analysis of incremental and nonincremental change. Lindblom, however, defined this important distinction differently at different times. In his early works, Lindblom treated the distinction as a matter of degree rather than kind, envisioning policy changes as taking place along a continuum, with incremental change at one end and nonincremental change at the other.[34] In his later work on corporate power, by contrast, Lindblom equated nonincremental change with systemic transformation. This later definition is much closer to what Popper termed "holistic social engineering"—remodeling the whole of society in accordance with a definite plan or blueprint. Under this second definition, however, policy departures that most scholars and journalists would characterize as significant (e.g., the Clean Air Act of 1970, the Civil Rights Act of 1964, the passage of Medicare in 1965) would qualify as incremental, or piecemeal, inasmuch as they failed to challenge the capitalist system.[35]

Popper's advocacy of piecemeal social engineering reflected his view of the scientific method. According to Popper, although we learn by induction, we can never verify hypotheses with complete confidence. We can only be conclusive in disconfirming hypotheses through counterexamples. Generalizations that have held up under a wide variety of cases may be held with considerable confidence, but they may nevertheless be disconfirmed at any point by the occurrence of a counterexample.[36]

The heart of the scientific method, in Popper's view, is trial and error: setting up experiments and then learning from the inevitable mistakes. Piecemeal social engineering is preferable to holistic social engineering primarily because it is rooted in the reality of how human beings acquire knowledge:

> The piecemeal engineer knows, like Socrates, how little he knows. He knows that we can learn only from our mistakes. Accordingly, he will make his way, step by step, carefully comparing the results expected with the results achieved, and always on the look-out for the unavoidable unwanted consequences of any reform; and he will avoid undertaking reforms of a complexity and scope which make it impossible for him to disentangle causes and effects, and to know what he is really doing.[37]

In short, piecemeal social engineering may be understood as the application of the scientific method to the solution of political or social problems.[38]

By contrast, the holistic approach to social engineering is ill-equipped to learn from mistakes and thus violates the scientific method. Sweeping attempts to transform society as a whole introduce a multiplicity of small changes at one time, so tracing unwanted consequences to their particular causes becomes impossible. Where the whole society is transformed, we can only attribute the sum of the consequences to the sum of the changes. Therefore, holistic social changes can be characterized as experiments only in the sense that they constitute actions whose outcomes are uncertain. They are not experiments in the scientific sense of actions that are set up so that we can learn from them.[39]

Holistic social engineering is ultimately unworkable. Although holists reject the piecemeal approach as too modest, they cannot avoid reliance on the method when their grand schemes crash—as sooner or later they must. The greater the scope of the policy change attempted, the greater the unintended and unanticipated consequences, forcing the holistic engineer to engage in what Popper termed "piecemeal improvisation" or "unplanned planning."[40]

Popper as Meliorative Liberal

Although Popper clearly is anti-rationalist in his rejection of holistic social engineering, he is just as clearly a meliorative liberal in his emphasis on using piecemeal social change to pursue social reform:

> This method can be used, more particularly, in order to search for, and fight against, the greatest and most urgent evils of society, rather than to seek, and to fight for, some ultimate good (as holists are inclined to do). But a systematic fight against definite wrongs, against concrete forms of injustice or exploitation, and avoidable suffering such as poverty or unemployment, is a very different thing from the attempt to realize a distant ideal blueprint of society. Success or failure is more easily appraised, and there is no inherent reason why this method should lead to an accumulation of power and to the suppression of criticism. Also, such a fight against concrete wrongs and concrete dangers is more likely to find the support of a great majority than a fight for the establishment of a Utopia, ideal as it may appear to the planners.[41]

Clearly, piecemeal social change is not as modest as it sounds. Popper cites constitutional reforms and significant changes in the class structure of society as ambitious in scope yet compatible with the piecemeal approach. Major change is particularly likely where a series of piecemeal reforms aim at a common objective—for example, toward a greater equalization of incomes.[42] Ultimately, the real difference between the two approaches is not in the scope or scale of initiatives but in their capacity to learn from unavoidable surprises.[43]

Utopianism and Tyranny

Although it is relatively easy for the holistic reformer to centralize power, knowledge tends to be widely dispersed over many individual minds. To the extent that any attempt at comprehensive social reform must necessarily inconvenience large numbers of people, dissent will be inevitable. Although there will always be unfounded objections to the plan that should be ignored, there is no way to suppress these objections without suppressing reasonable criticisms as well.[44]

In distinct contrast to the piecemeal engineer, the holist has a closed mind regarding the desirable scope of reform: Nothing short of a complete reconstruction of society will do.[45] The real danger is the conclusion the holist draws when such visions fail to produce the desired results. At that point, the goal is no longer building a new society fit for men and women to live in; it becomes necessary to mold men and women to fit into the new society. To the holist, the transformation of society ultimately requires the transformation of mankind.[46]

❑ THE MELIORATIVE LIBERALISM OF CHARLES LINDBLOM

Where Popper saw piecemeal social change as preferable to holistic attempts at social transformation, Lindblom advanced his method of disjointed incrementalism as an alternative to rational, comprehensive decision making. This method of decision holds great appeal for students of the policy process—including many who would not characterize themselves as utopian dreamers—because it forces policymakers to specify objectives and engage in a rigorous analysis of options before proceeding. In an ideal world, policies would result from a thorough examination of all relevant alternatives, culminating in a value-maximizing choice.

According to Lindblom, however, comprehensive rationality is simply out of the question for most policy areas. The method is extremely demanding because it requires high levels of consensus and knowledge that are unlikely to be attained very often. (I examine whether these conditions are satisfied as rarely as Lindblom suggests in more depth in chapter 7.)

Like Popper, Lindblom is clearly anti-rationalist in orientation but cannot be characterized as a classical liberal. Lindblom's meliorative liberalism—his emphasis on the desirability of social and economic reform—becomes especially evident in his later writings, which sharply criticize the "privileged position of business" in capitalistic societies. The failure of any capitalistic society to experiment with central planning of the economy led Lindblom to question whether corporate power prevented the proper operation of incrementalism in Western democracies.[47] According to Lindblom, our reliance on free markets to produce goods and services constrains policymakers to reject out of hand virtually all policy proposals that are detrimental to business. Within capitalistic economies, any attempt to alter fundamental institutions automatically triggers punishment in the form of unemployment or a sluggish economy.[48]

If Lindblom's meliorative liberalism is evident in his later works on corporate power, his earlier works on incrementalism consistently emphasized the potential for significant policy change over time via a succession of small steps. In a 1979 reexamination of the merits of incrementalism, for example, Lindblom observed, "A fast-moving sequence of small changes can more speedily accomplish a dramatic alteration of the status quo than can an only infrequent major policy change."[49] For Lindblom, incrementalism offers a feasible way to pursue social and economic reform where comprehensive rationality is unattainable; incrementalism must be understood as a clearly formulated strategy for pursuing meliorative liberalism.

Incrementalism as a Strategy

Incrementalism, as advanced by Lindblom, has several key elements. First, public policies are not a product of conscious choice but the political results of interaction among a multiplicity of actors who possess different information and adhere to different values. The need to make concessions to gain adherents reinforces the incrementalism already present in the tendency to focus on alternatives that differ only peripherally from the status quo. This process of mutual adaptation, which Lindblom terms partisan mutual adjustment, virtually guarantees incremental policy outcomes.

Problems are brought to government by affected publics rather than through a rational analysis of the decision makers' environment. Lindblom terms this phenomenon the social fragmentation of analysis. No single actor is required to possess comprehensive information. Instead, each actor brings important knowledge to bear in analyzing the problem. In distinct contrast to decision making under the rational-comprehensive ideal, all actors need not define the problem in the same way. Problems may be acted on without ever being fully defined, and disagreements among participants can be accommodated through bargaining and compromise.[50]

To the extent that constraints on time and information preclude a comprehensive examination of all alternative solutions, policymakers must somehow limit their attention to a manageable number of options—and do so in a way that screens out alternatives that are unlikely to be adopted. In practice, they accomplish this goal by limiting their focus to alternatives that differ only incrementally from existing policies.

Moreover, policymakers compare alternatives by focusing on the increments by which various proposals differ from each other and from past policies. Lindblom terms this process margin-dependent choice. In the budgetary process, for example, legislators normally make no attempt to comprehensively evaluate the performance of the vast range of federal policies. Instead, they focus on the increments by which spending will go up or down for various programs under different proposals. Focusing on the margins permits intelligent comparison of proposals where comprehensive analysis would be virtually impossible.[51]

Policy Change in the Incremental Model

Although building on past policies enables administrators to learn through experience, policy evaluation is not a straightforward process of learning through trial and error. The same actors who disagree over values, tradeoffs, and even problem definition initially will be central participants in the process of policy analysis and change. Thus, policy evaluation is necessarily a political process—characterized by fragmentation, conflict, and imperfect knowledge. Problems may be considered unsolved as long as some publics continue to express dissatisfaction with existing policies. By contrast, a problem may be regarded as solved when it finally disappears from the agenda, crowded off by other problems that now are considered more pressing.[52]

In practice, incrementalism often means inadequate statutory powers and limited appropriations for agencies, making implementation difficult. Ambiguous legislative mandates typically will fail to resolve all conflicts, leaving important terms undefined and passing controversial questions on to administrators for resolution. Often, a long series of inadequate measures—which in hindsight may seem to be senseless experiments yielding predictable results—must be taken before any real progress is made.[53] In California, for example, the initial reliance on counties to deal with air pollution was doomed to fail in the long run given the large number of mobile sources of pollution (e.g., automobiles) and the tendency for wind and weather to carry emissions far away from their sources.

Fortunately, however, policymakers need not make a single, comprehensive decision that will solve a problem once and for all. To the contrary, policies can always be modified as necessary in subsequent iterations of the policy cycle: "Policymaking is a process of successive approximation to some desired objectives in which what is desired itself continues to change under reconsideration."[54]

❑ THE VIRTUES OF INCREMENTALISM

Meliorative liberals make a very strong case for incrementalism. As a strategy for policymaking, incrementalism offers several important advantages. (The term *incrementalism* may be considered synonymous with *piecemeal social change* in the discussion that follows.)

First, incrementalism facilitates action where the rational ideal is paralyzed, often yielding no guidance whatever to policymakers. Incrementalism is much less demanding than the rational method; it requires neither comprehensive information nor agreement among policymakers on objectives. It combines the reformism of rationalists with the realism of anti-rationalists.

Second, incrementalism reduces the costs of analysis by providing a defensible basis for confining attention to some alternatives over others. The costs of analysis, in time and money, must be taken into account in any attempt to make value-maximizing decisions. Analyzing all conceivable options is neither possible nor desirable. Incrementalism restricts attention to alternatives that are most realistic and for which policy analysis is most likely to be accurate.

Third, incrementalism facilitates learning from mistakes. Popper stressed the incompatibility of holistic social engineering with the scientific method. Attempts to remodel the whole of society change many things at one time; when things go wrong (as they inevitably will), it is impossible to determine which of the many changes involved in the holistic reform are responsible for the undesirable consequences of social reform. By contrast, incremental or piecemeal policy proposals make changes at the margins of existing policy, enabling policy analysts to trace consequences to their true causes.

Fourth, incrementalism facilitates majority-building by minimizing disruption to established practices. As Popper observed, any political reform will strengthen opposing forces in rough proportion to the scope of the reform.[55] Therefore, minimizing the scope of the reform will minimize opposition. In the air pollution case, for example, minimalist initiatives—although transparently inadequate when considered after the fact—had the virtue of avoiding the kinds of draconian intervention into lifestyles (restrictions on car travel, lawn mowing, and so on) that would have aroused intense and widespread opposition.

Fifth, the failure of any given step to solve a particular problem often makes the best case for taking the next step.[56] Krier and Ursin emphasize the near-inevitability of periodic crises in this process. At the state and federal levels, air pollution policymaking has been driven at times by dramatic focusing events, particularly smog disasters. Although policy change is not always a response to crisis, occasional crises are inevitable in a system that by its nature produces minimal responses to steadily worsening problems.[57] Such crises can at times force the issue on the agenda—or, where the issue already is on the agenda, provide leverage to policy entrepreneurs who are seeking the strongest possible bill. Dramatic performance failures make a powerful case for moving on to the next step, however unpalatable it may have seemed previously.

❑ MAKING INCREMENTALISM WORK BETTER

In chapter 2, I demonstrate the superiority of systemic over articulated rationality and made a strong case for checks on political power to encourage deliberation on the merits of public policy proposals. In effect, chapter 2 embraces the anti-rationalist worldview on the basis of its greater realism. In this chapter I show that we can accept the anti-rationalists' views on human nature and the limits of reason in policymaking without necessarily embracing the classical liberals' minimalist conception of the state. Meliorative liberalism occupies a middle ground between the rationalists' utopian visions of reform and the classical liberals' emphasis on evolutionary change in institutions that are basically sound. Karl Popper and Charles Lindblom, the foremost proponents of incrementalism in policymaking, clearly fall within this school of thought. As we have seen, incrementalism (or piecemeal social engineering) is properly understood as a clearly conceived strategy for pursuing meliorative liberalism.

The real question is not whether incrementalism is the best method of policymaking; if Lindblom and Popper are correct, there is no viable alternative. The question we should be asking is whether incrementalism works as well as it should. As Lindblom observed:

> Many critics of incrementalism believe that doing better usually means turning away from incrementalism. Incrementalists believe that for complex problem solving it usually means practicing incrementalism more skillfully and turning away from it only rarely.[58]

In other words, if good policymaking is a lot like walking—if a series of small steps is superior to periodic lurches, as Lindblom suggests—are there elements in our system that make it hard to walk properly? We can identify at least three impediments to the proper functioning of incrementalism.

First, although a focus on incremental alternatives does limit information costs by providing a rationale for looking at some alternatives rather than others, policymakers may still neglect some important incremental alternatives because of prejudices or biases that cannot really be defended. According to Krier and Ursin, for example, the long history of air pollution policymaking in California was constrained throughout—channeled in some directions rather than others—by certain preoccupations or "fixations." Examples include a fixation with the requirements of existing law, a fixation with the division of powers under federalism, and a tendency to place the burden of proof on actors who would challenge the wisdom of ongoing technological change.[59]

The two most important biases affecting air pollution policymaking, however, were a fixation with technological solutions and a fixation with regulatory solutions. Technological solutions were attractive because they appeared to offer quick, easy, and predictable solutions—in distinct contrast to the kinds of lifestyle restrictions policymakers wanted to avoid.[60] Similarly, regulatory solutions appeared to be dramatic actions that would guarantee substantial reductions in pollution by imposing direct controls of one sort or another. Although policymakers may prefer regulatory solutions because they are more likely to produce real results, regulation also serves as a symbolic reassurance to mass publics concerned about air pollution. Legislating ostensibly health-based, technology-forcing standards in the Clean Air Act of 1970 enabled elected officials to satisfy a pre-formed majority on the air pollution issue (see chapter 5). Certainly, such standards appear more adversarial—and thus more forceful—than a tax on emissions that seems to let industry get away with polluting.[61]

Meliorative liberals are particularly vulnerable to a fixation with the federal government as a positive agent for social change. (I develop this point at greater length in chapter 8.) This bias leads them to focus almost exclusively on the rate of change in government policies, when government sometimes plays its most important role in facilitating or impeding change that originated in other social forces. Polanyi made this observation in discussing the devastating effects of the nonincremental movement toward a self-regulating economy in Great Britain in the 16th century. Although he conceded that this deliberate decision to adopt a market economy eventually led to an overall rise in the standard of living for most Britons, in the short run the number of paupers increased and the factory system exploited unskilled labor.[62] Attempts to set a floor under incomes through the Speenhamland law were incompatible with the new self-regulating market for labor that came into being as soon as labor was treated as a commodity, producing at least two perverse effects: greatly expanding the number of laborers supported entirely or primarily by government payments and depressing wage rates for workers employed by private firms below the subsistence level. For all its faults, the Speenhamland experiment, while it lasted, mitigated the worst effects of the sharp transition to a market economy on the rural poor. Accordingly, we need to recognize that sometimes, the most important thing government can do may be to *slow down* the rate of change fostered by social, economic, or technological developments.[63]

Second, as we saw in chapter 2, the American political system by design contains multiple veto points. Although these veto points force proponents of policy change to engage in persuasion by limiting the potential for coercion, they can make doing anything at all difficult much of the time. As our periodic struggles over gun-control legislation illustrate, all too often incrementalism in the United States is characterized less by periodic lurches than by small steps a generation or more apart, as the defensive power of opposing interests combines with multiple veto points to preclude the succession of small steps Lindblom envisioned.[64]

Finally, incrementalism works well, in Lindblom's view, only to the extent that most interests affected by any given issue are represented in the decision process. In his early writings on incrementalism, Lindblom was optimistic on this point:

> Almost every interest has its watchdog. Without claiming that every interest has a sufficiently powerful watchdog, it can be argued that our system often can assure a more comprehensive regard for the values of the whole society than any attempt at intellectual comprehensiveness.[65]

In his later work (as we have seen), Lindblom concluded that excessive corporate power within capitalist societies precludes policymakers from even considering policies that are threatening to business as a class. Ralph Miliband had made a similar argument a decade earlier. More recently, Thomas Ferguson has added a new dimension to this argument, demonstrating that control over access to campaign money by "major investors" (such as corporations) translates into control over the agenda.[66] To the extent that some groups fail to mobilize while others wield disproportionate power, incremental outcomes will reflect a skewed group equilibrium.

In conclusion, a certain amount of incrementalism is inevitable and desirable within any political system because of the dispersion of knowledge throughout the political system and the need to learn from experience with policies. Moreover, gradual policy change can be defended where it results from checks and balances that are built into the system to guard against tyranny and encourage deliberation. By contrast, incrementalism that arises from inequalities among groups cannot be defended on intellectual grounds. In chapter 4, I show how disparate resources and the failure of some groups to mobilize do in fact lead to distortions in the operation of partisan mutual adjustment.

NOTES

1. In addition to Popper and Lindblom, this section draws on the work of two contemporary scholars, James E. Krier and Edmund Ursin. After examining air pollution policymaking in California from 1940 to 1975, Krier and Ursin characterized policymaking as a process of "least steps taken down the path of least resistance—steps, that is, quite consciously designed to disturb the existing situation as little as possible." Although Krier and Ursin derived their model of policymaking independently, without reference to Lindblom's various works on incrementalism, their analysis provides strong support for his contention that incrementalism in policymaking is both inevitable and desirable under normal circumstances. See James E. Krier and Edmund Ursin, *Pollution & Policy: A Case Essay on California and Federal Experience with Motor Vehicle Air Pollution, 1940–1975* (Berkeley and Los Angeles: University of California Press, 1977), 252.

2. Joseph Cropsey, "Conservatism and Liberalism," in *Left, Right, and Center: Essays on Liberalism and Conservatism in the United States,* ed. Robert A. Goldwin (Chicago: Rand McNally, 1965), 43. For more on the distinction between conservatism and classical liberalism, see Kenneth Minogue's discussion of Edmund Burke as the founder of modern conservatism in *Politics: A Very Short Introduction* (Oxford and New York: Oxford University Press, 1995), 79–80.

3. Michael Oakeshott, "The Political Economy of Freedom," in *Rationalism in Politics and Other Essays* (Indianapolis: Liberty Fund, 1991), 396–97.

4. See, for example, Henry C. Simons, "A Positive Program for Laissez Faire: Some Proposals for a Liberal Economic Policy," in *Economic Policy for a Free Society* (Chicago: University of Chicago Press, 1948), 40–77. Milton Friedman, a Simons student at the University of Chicago, also takes pains to characterize himself as a classical liberal, as distinct from a conservative, in *Capitalism and Freedom* (Chicago: University of Chicago Press, 1962). Similarly, although Oakeshott is well known for his essay on what it means to be a conservative, he embraces classical liberalism in his enthusiastic review of Simons's *Economic Policy for a Free Society*; see "The Political Economy of Freedom," in *Rationalism in Politics and Other Essays*, 384-406.

5. F. A. Hayek, "Postscript: Why I Am Not a Conservative," in *The Constitution of Liberty* (Chicago: University of Chicago Press, 1960), 395–411. On the problems in arriving at a meaningful name for what used to be known as classical liberalism, see pages 407–411.

6. See David Spitz, "A Liberal Perspective on Liberalism and Conservatism," in *Left, Right, and Center*, ed. Robert A. Goldwin, 25–26. For a fuller development of these arguments, see also David Spitz, *The Liberal Idea of Freedom* (Tucson: University of Arizona Press, 1964). Although I have cited Spitz on this point, my colleague at Colgate, Joe Wagner, was the first to call these essential characteristics of liberalism to my attention. For a good discussion of the meaning of conservatism, see Joseph Wagner, "Hollow at the Core: The Poverty of Conservatism as Political Philosophy," paper presented at the annual meeting of the American Political Science Association, Atlanta, September 1999.

For another example of the liberal's commitment to experimentalism—and rejection of utopian visions of all kinds—see Arthur M. Schlesinger, Jr., *The Vital Center: The Politics of Freedom* (Cambridge, Mass.: Riverside Press, 1962), 159–61. See also Schlesinger's contrast between the "empirical temper" of American liberalism and the "millennial nostalgia" of the American right and the European left (page xvi of the same volume).

7. Cropsey, "Conservatism and Liberalism," in *Left, Right, and Center*, 44.

8. L. T. Hobhouse, "Laissez-Faire," in *Liberalism* (London, Oxford, and New York: Oxford University Press, 1964), 44–55.

9. Hobhouse, "Economic Liberalism," in *Liberalism*, 88–109.

10. Ibid., 108.

11. F. A. Hayek, *The Road to Serfdom*, Fiftieth Anniversary Edition (Chicago: University of Chicago Press, 1994), 86.

12. Frank S. Meyer, *In Defense of Freedom and Related Essays* (Indianapolis: Liberty Fund, 1996), 188. For more examples of Meyer's thought, see Frank S. Meyer, *The Conservative Mainstream* (New Rochelle, N.Y.: Arlington House, 1969).

13. Herbert Stein, "The Triumph of the Adaptive Society," in *On the Other Hand: Essays on Economics, Economists, and Politics* (Washington, D.C.: American Enterprise Institute, 1995), 53.

14. Ibid., 27–28.

15. For a good discussion of the utopianism of Gingrich's third wave vision, see E. J. Dionne, *They Only Look Dead: Why Progressives Will Dominate the Next Political Era* (New York: Simon & Schuster, 1996), 206–209. In Dionne's view, just as Mark Hanna and William McKinley chose to embrace the rising forces of industrialism—writing off "backward" rural regions and mobilizing the new capitalists as the Republican Party's financial base—Gingrich would embrace the new global, information age economy. By identifying and subsidizing the emerging forces of the information age, Gingrich would secure a stable financial advantage for the GOP while "forcing the scale of change necessary to be successful in the twenty-first century." See also Newt Gingrich, *To Renew America* (New York: HarperCollins, 1995).

16. Karl Polanyi, *The Great Transformation: The Political and Economic Origins of Our Time* (Boston: Beacon Press, 1957; first published in 1944).

17. Spitz, *The Liberal Idea of Freedom,* 33.

18. Spitz, *The Liberal Idea of Freedom,* 27. See also James Burnham, *The Suicide of the West: An Essay on the Meaning and Destiny of Liberalism* (Washington, D.C.: Regnery Gateway, 1985), for one conservative's acknowledgment of the importance of hierarchy in society. For a particularly good example of this worldview, see Richard Weaver, *Ideas Have Consequences* (Chicago: University of Chicago Press, 1948), and *The Southern Tradition at Bay: A History of Postbellum Thought* (Washington, D.C.: Regnery Gateway, 1989; originally published in 1968). In *Ideas Have Consequences,* Weaver explores the implications of the widespread loss of faith in God and emphasizes the critical role well-educated gentlemen play in preserving civilization. In *The Southern Tradition at Bay,* Weaver offers a defense of the traditional Southern way of life, with its hierarchical relations and subordinate place for blacks.

19. In addition to works already cited, my typology of worldviews was influenced by two earlier efforts to categorize Republican politicians. See A. James Reichley, *Conservatives in an Age of Change: The Nixon and Ford Administrations* (Washington, D.C.: Brookings Institution, 1981), 1–37, and Nicol C. Rae, *The Decline and Fall of the Liberal Republicans from 1952 to the Present* (New York: Oxford University Press, 1989), 7–9. Here I am paraphrasing A. James Reichley's characterization of Republican moderates in *Conservatives in an Age of Change* (Washington, D.C.: Brookings Institution, 1981), 29.

20. The continued presence of these rival factions is evident in Douglas L. Koopman, *Hostile Takeover: The House Republican Party, 1980–1995* (Lanham, Md.: Rowman & Littlefield, 1996). Koopman analyzes shifts over time in the relative strength of various factions within the Republicans in the U.S. House of Representatives.

21. See Nicol C. Rae, *Conservative Reformers: The Republican Freshmen and the Lessons of the 104th Congress* (Armonk, N.Y.: M. E. Sharpe, 1998).

22. Hayek, *The Constitution of Liberty,* 11.

23. Hayek cited Immanuel Kant and Voltaire in defining freedom in this way; see *Road to Serfdom,* 90.

24. Hayek, *Road to Serfdom,* 82–83.

25. Ibid., 24.

26. The contrast between Stein's adaptive conservatism and Hayek's nostalgic conservatism comes into sharp focus on this point. See Stein, "The Triumph of the Adaptive Society," 48–52, for Stein's critique of Hayek's thesis that we are on a road to serfdom.

27. Friedrich A. Hayek, "A Model Constitution," in *Law, Legislation, and Liberty, Volume 3: The Political Order of a Free People* (Chicago: University of Chicago Press, 1979), 105–127.

28. For an explicit acknowledgment of Lindblom's debt to Popper, see Robert A. Dahl and Charles E. Lindblom, *Politics, Economics, and Welfare: Planning and Politico-Economic Systems Resolved into Basic Social Processes* (New York: Harper & Row, Harper Torchbooks, 1963), 82ff.

29. Karl Popper, *The Poverty of Historicism* (London and New York: Routledge and Kegan Paul, 1994; first published in 1957), and *The Open Society and Its Enemies* (Princeton, N.J.: Princeton University Press, 1950; 5th ed., 1966).

30. Popper, *The Poverty of Historicism*, 65.

31. Ibid., 58–59.

32. Ibid., 67.

33. Ibid., 66.

34. David Braybrooke and Charles E. Lindblom, *A Strategy of Decision: Policy Evaluation as a Social Process* (New York: Free Press of Glencoe, 1963), 66–79.

35. Charles E. Lindblom, *Politics and Markets: The World's Political-Economic Systems* (New York: Basic Books, 1977).

36. See David Miller, "The Problem of Induction," in *Popper Selections* (Princeton, N.J.: Princeton University Press, 1985), 101–117.

37. Popper, *The Poverty of Historicism*, 67.

38. For an explicit statement of this point, see Popper, *The Poverty of Historicism*, 88:

> [T]he only way to apply something like the scientific method in politics is to proceed on the assumption that there can be no political move which does not have its drawbacks, no undesirable consequences. To look out for these mistakes, to find them, to bring them into the open, to analyze them, and to learn from them, this is what a scientific politician as well as a political scientist must do.

39. Popper, *The Poverty of Historicism*, 88–89.

40. Ibid., 68–69.

41. Ibid., 91–92.

42. Ibid., 68. Here again, Lindblom echoes Popper's argument, suggesting that major change is not only possible but more likely to be effective through a succession of incremental steps. On this point, see Charles E. Lindblom, "Still Muddling, Not Yet Through," *Public Administration Review* 39 (November/December 1979): 520.

43. Popper, *The Poverty of Historicism*, 69.

44. Ibid., 89.

45. Ibid., 69.

46. Ibid., 69–70.

47. See Lindblom, "Still Muddling, Not Yet Through," 520–21 and 525 for an explicit defense of the connection between Lindblom's later emphasis on corporate power and his earlier writings on incrementalism.

48. Charles E. Lindblom, "The Market as Prison," *Journal of Politics*, 44 (May 1982): 324–25. See also *Politics and Markets* for a fuller development of the argument.

49. Lindblom, "Still Muddling, Not Yet Through," 520.

50. Friedrich Hayek regarded this phenomenon—which he referred to as the decentralization of knowledge—as perhaps the most serious obstacle to rational decision making. In distinct contrast to Lindblom, however, Hayek concluded that efforts by legislators to improve on the functioning of free markets were doomed to failure in most instances. Hayek's case for free markets did not rest on any assumption that markets could be made to work perfectly, although he did see an active role for government in policing the operation of markets. Instead, his point was that markets act as discovery mechanisms that do a better job of identifying and making use of decentralized knowledge than any attempt at centralized, rational decision making by government. See Hayek, *The Political Order of a Free People*, 67–70.

51. Aaron Wildavsky, *Speaking Truth to Power: The Art and Craft of Policy Changes* (Boston: Little, Brown, 1979).

52. Ibid., 60.

53. Krier and Ursin, *Pollution & Policy*, 252.

54. Lindblom, "Science of Muddling Through," 86.

55. Popper, *The Poverty of Historicism*, 62. Popper regards natural laws as essentially impossibility statements in the sense that they can all be expressed by asserting that "such and such a thing cannot happen." For example, it is impossible, in an industrial society, to organize consumers' pressure groups as effectively as producers' pressure groups. (This assertion is a restatement of what economists term "the free rider problem.")

56. Krier and Ursin, *Pollution & Policy*, 255.

57. Ibid., 265–77.

58. Lindblom, "Still Muddling, Not Yet Through," 517.

59. Krier and Ursin, *Pollution & Policy*, 256–63.

60. Ibid., 277–78.

61. Ibid., 286.

62. Polanyi, *The Great Transformation*.

63. Ibid., p.37.

64. For Lindblom's own critique of the American constitutional system as an obstacle to the efficient functioning of incrementalism, see "Still Muddling, Not Yet Through," 520–21.

65. Lindblom, "Science of Muddling Through," 85.

66. Thomas Ferguson, *Golden Rule: The Investment Theory of Party Competition and the Logic of Money-Driven Political Systems* (Chicago: University of Chicago Press, 1995).

CHAPTER FOUR

The Unequal Group Struggle

I argue in chapter 2 that partisan mutual adjustment yields good public policies—better, in any event, than would be produced by a misguided attempt at rational decision making. The normative case for Lindblom's model, however, rests on two unrealistic assumptions: that almost every social interest will have its watchdog and that competition among social interests will be "atomistic"—that is, no single actor or coalition will possess political market power.

To the contrary, certain kinds of groups will be consistently underrepresented in the policy process. In the first section of this chapter, I identify three distinct ways in which the interest group universe is biased in favor of some interests over others. In the second section, I identify the primary resources available to interest groups as they seek to influence public policy; these resources are distributed unequally among different groups. In the third section, I argue that corporations tend to have more of these various resources than any other groups, to the extent that they occupy a "privileged position" within capitalistic societies—as suggested by Ralph Miliband as well as by Lindblom in his later writings.

In the fourth section of this chapter, I examine the implications of these inequalities for policymaking. In particular, I argue that normal incrementalism—defined as a process of partisan mutual adjustment among a multiplicity of interests—is only one of six common policy processes. In short, there is no guarantee that partisan mutual adjustment will feature a reasonable balance of groups representing a variety of viewpoints. Nor is there any reason to expect that contending interests will have anything like equal power. Although none of this analysis implies that we should throw out meliorative liberalism in favor of utopian attempts at rational decision making or, alternatively, a sharply restricted conception of the state, it does serve as a sober reminder that policymaking is, at best, a continual effort to ameliorate problems that will never fully go away.

☐ THREE BIASES TO THE GROUP UNIVERSE

The major group theorists—Arthur Bentley, Earl Latham, Bertram Gross, and David Truman—all characterize the group struggle model as a particularly realistic and unsentimental description of how the policy process actually works. In this model, politics is a struggle to determine who gets what, and the distribution of active groups and mobilized political resources is the fundamental variable that determine the group equilibrium.[1] Far from arguing that the group struggle would automatically produce outcomes that are in the public interest, group theorists see the public interest as virtually impossible to define in the abstract and seldom, if ever, clearly identified for specific issues.[2] In point of fact, group theorists identify three distinct biases to the group universe: a bias in favor of small groups over large, diffuse groups; a bias in favor of wealthy interests over the poor; and a bias in favor of institutions of all sorts over membership groups.

The Free Rider Problem

In a seminal contribution to group theory, political economist Mancur Olson observed that all potential groups must first overcome a "free rider" problem if they are to organize at all.[3] Because the benefits of interest group activity typically are available to potential members regardless of whether they join the group, self-interested individuals will find it rational not to contribute, hoping instead to benefit from the efforts of others.

This free rider problem is particularly severe for large, diffuse interests—consumers, taxpayers, or environmentalists, for example—because the larger the size of the group, the less likely any one individual's contribution will make a difference to the group's success; as a result, large groups will have particular difficulty mobilizing. In very small groups (such as the three major domestic automobile manufacturers), by contrast, the importance of each member's contribution to the group's success is so apparent—and the individual's personal stake in the outcome so much larger—that collective action is much more likely.

Well before Olson identified the free rider problem as an obstacle to group formation in 1971, earlier group theorists had recognized the distinct advantages that formal organizations possess in dealing with the more numerous unorganized interests. For example, although David Truman often is cited for his contention that unorganized "potential groups" could not be ignored by policymakers, he nevertheless acknowledged that there would always be greater incentive to respond to the pressures of the effectively mobilized. According to Truman, formal organization provides evidence that a group has attained a threshold level of cohesion and shared values and suggests a degree of permanence, implying that the group is an important element in the environment whose wishes will have to receive some consideration.[4] Similarly, Earl Latham regarded organized groups as "structures of power" in the struggle to determine policy—structures that were designed to "concentrate human wit, energy, and muscle for the achievement of received purposes."[5] In Latham's words:

> In this group struggle, there is an observable balance of influence in favor of organized groups in their dealings with the unorganized, and in favor of the best and most efficiently organized in their dealings with the less efficiently organized. . . . Or, to put it another way, organization represents concentrated power, and concentrated power can exercise a dominating influence when it encounters power which is diffuse and not concentrated, and therefore weaker.[6]

The Class Bias to the Group Universe

Moreover, interest groups are hardest to form during economic downturns—when they are most needed. As Robert Salisbury has shown, group membership is an economic transaction; entrepreneurs such as Ralph Nader offer potential members a mix of tangible and intangible benefits in exchange for dues. To survive in the long run, the group eventually must reach a point at which income from member dues exceeds the costs of servicing the membership. Group membership is at best more of a luxury than a necessity, and collective benefits pursued by most groups are vulnerable to the free rider problem. Thus, interest groups are most likely to form in prosperous times and most likely to fail (or at least lose members) in times of group hardship—when they might make a greater difference in members' lives.[7]

By extension, this analysis implies a socioeconomic bias to all forms of political participation, including interest group membership. Entrepreneurs who seek to mobilize poor persons face particularly serious difficulties inasmuch as potential members have little income or leisure time to spend on group memberships that typically will yield benefits only in the distant future, if at all. As E. E. Schattschneider observed, in the interest group struggle, "the heavenly chorus sings with a strong upper-class accent."[8]

The Permanence of Institutions

Finally, institutions tend to be much more permanent than membership groups.[9] The free rider problem never goes away for membership groups; once a group has gotten off the ground, it still must motivate members to remain in the group over the long haul.

Corporations provide the best example. Lobbying as individual organizations, they do not face a free rider problem in getting off the ground. Where membership groups are vulnerable to economic cycles—with membership rolls rising in good times and falling in hard times—institutions are much more likely to have surplus profits to devote to lobbying regardless of economic circumstances.

In this regard, a comparative study of the group universe in 1960 and 1981 found the vast majority of corporations active in the earlier period still on the scene two decades later. By contrast, most citizen groups in the 1960 sample were no longer in existence in 1981, and most of the citizen groups in the 1981 sample were born over the preceding 10–15 years—suggesting that the recent explosion of new citizen groups may have accomplished little more than to replace a whole generation of earlier groups that failed to survive, with the net effect that the group universe is not significantly more balanced today than it was two decades ago.[10]

❑ UNEQUAL RESOURCES AND THE BALANCE OF FORCES

According to the group struggle model, policy will be a function of the balance of forces active on the issue. Specifically, the group equilibrium will depend on the resources available to the various participants and the extent to which each participant can translate these resources into effective influence.[11]

Money is not the only resource available to interest groups in this regard. In 1970, environmental groups were able to arouse public opinion to push Congress into passage of a much stronger Clean Air Act than political observers originally anticipated. Similarly, nuclear freeze groups successfully forced the arms control issue onto the agenda in 1981 through grassroots mobilization of public opinion even though they were operating on a shoestring budget. (See chapter 5 for a discussion of these two issues.)

The pollution and nuclear freeze cases suggest that intangible resources at times can be as important to a group's success as money and staffing. For example, a group's influence will depend in part on its reputation as a reliable source of information or *expertise*. Interest groups often act as "service bureaus" for legislators who already are sympathetic to their cause, providing information on alternative policies and, in turn, educating their members on the need to accept compromises emerging from the bargaining process. A reputation for honesty and accuracy is essential, lest groups forfeit access to policymakers.[12]

A second intangible resource is the group's prestige or *legitimacy*. In part, legitimacy refers to the esteem in which the public holds a group's membership; doctors, church leaders, and heads of major corporations will be more "legitimate" than welfare recipients, for example.[13] Legitimacy also reflects the conformity of the group's goals and tactics to values held by policymakers and the broader public. Senior citizens' groups possess extraordinary legitimacy, for example, partly because the serious problems they face (large medical bills in their retirement years) are widely regarded as not of their own making and partly because all of us eventually must confront problems associated with aging. In effect, Medicare and Social Security have come to be perceived not as largess for a segment of the population but as universal entitlements that sooner or later are available to all. By contrast, welfare recipients are readily characterized (rightly or wrongly) as failures who are living off the toil of others: men too unskilled or irresponsible to hold a steady job, women abandoned by their husbands or having children out of wedlock, "welfare queens" taking advantage of the system by collecting multiple benefits. The contrast is striking, and it helps to explain why seniors were relatively insulated from major program cuts during President Reagan's term in office, whereas Aid to Families with Dependent Children (AFDC) and the food stamp program were cut repeatedly.[14]

Finally, a group's *strategic position* in society can be a critically important resource. A group has leverage to the extent that society depends on the goods or services it routinely provides. For example, Charles Lindblom has argued recently that corporations occupy a "privileged position" in capitalistic societies (see chapter 5).[15] Because prosperity helps government officials remain in office, these officials are naturally solicitous of the needs of business. Business leaders receive automatic access, whereas other groups must compete to make their views heard. Even if business groups are inactive on an issue, they may exercise indirect influence as policymakers take into account the effects of proposed policies on economic growth, plant location, or incentives to invest.

☐ CORPORATIONS AS A SPECIAL CASE: THE MARKET AS PRISON

There can be little doubt that business as a class exercises disproportionate power within capitalist societies. To the extent that all actors within the system need prosperity—which only business can provide, and which it also can withhold—business acquires a kind of veto power over proposals that threaten capitalist interests.

Ironically, Charles Lindblom—originator of the theory of disjointed incrementalism—is the most influential theorist in this regard.[16] Because Lindblom's earlier model was so optimistic regarding the potential for attaining the public interest through the interplay of contending groups, his conversion to the ranks of elite theorists had a magnified impact within the discipline.

According to this view, the free market constrains policymakers to reject out of hand virtually all policy changes that are detrimental to business. Within capitalistic economies, any attempt to alter fundamental institutions automatically triggers "punishment," in the form of unemployment or a sluggish economy:

> Do we want business to carry a larger share of the nation's tax burden? We must fear that such a reform will discourage business investment and curtail employment. Do we want business enterprises to reduce industrial pollution of air and water? Again we must bear the consequences of the costs to them of their doing so and the resultant declines in investment and employment.[17]

More fundamental reforms, such as worker participation in management or public involvement in corporate decision making, cannot be raised at all, according to Lindblom, lest they undermine business confidence.

Ralph Miliband advances a variation on this theme.[18] Whereas Lindblom characterizes the market as a kind of prison, precluding any reforms that threaten business interests, Miliband sees the problem as one of "imperfect competition" among social interests.[19] In distinct contrast to

Lindblom, Miliband explicitly acknowledges that business groups do not always dominate policymaking:

> Had business predominance been absolute, it would be absurd to speak of competition at all. There *is* competition, and defeats for powerful capitalist interests as well as victories. . . .[20]

According to Miliband, the advantage to business in this competition among interests is rooted in the extraordinary degree of commitment to capitalism within advanced industrial democracies. Disagreements among the viable contenders for elective office typically are confined to secondary issues, leaving the fundamental question of the form of economic organization unaddressed. Thus, debate is confined to the proper degree of state intervention in an economy that all agree will remain capitalistic.[21]

❏ SOURCES OF BUSINESS POWER

In Lindblom's view, business is a qualitatively different kind of actor that occupies a special place within capitalist systems: On economic issues, policymaking is imprisoned by the need to induce business performance. At best, policy accurately may be regarded as an equilibrium of a multiplicity of contending groups only for a highly restricted, unimprisoned zone of policymaking.[22] Thus, there is little point in assessing the relative advantages of different actors in the group struggle.

If the policy process is characterized instead as an imperfect competition among social interests—as Miliband suggests—then business can be treated as only one of many actors in the system, albeit an arguably advantaged one. In this light, what is striking about the arguments of Lindblom and Miliband is how well they fit into the framework of the group struggle model advanced in this chapter. Although the group theorists recognized the importance of tangible resources (such as money), they placed greater emphasis on a variety of intangible factors—particularly strategic position, legitimacy, and expertise.[23]

The Strategic Position of Business

Both Lindblom and Miliband play down business's substantial advantage in financial resources over other actors in the system. In short, their argument is that business derives extraordinary legitimacy, expertise, and strategic position within any capitalistic society, giving it an almost insurmountable advantage over any other actor in the system. Whether business is merely the strongest actor in an ongoing group struggle (a Goliath among Davids, in Miliband's formulation)[24] or a qualitatively different kind of actor that renders the whole concept of group struggle meaningless for most issues is simply a matter of how far one wants to push the argument. The sources of business power are essentially the same for both authors.

Foremost among the intangible resources available to business is strategic position. As I argue above, a group will possess leverage to the extent that society depends on goods or services it routinely provides. In this vein, according to Lindblom, business managers in effect serve as a second set of public officials in capitalist economies insofar as a wide range of activities that affect the entire public are delegated into their hands: decisions regarding what is to be produced, how labor and other factors of production will be allocated to different lines of production, what technologies will be employed, where plants will be located, and so on. Although all of these activities are defined as "private" by the market (and by most economists), they have momentous consequences for the average citizen, affecting the overall level of economic growth and the prospects for employment in different locations and lines of work.[25]

In this regard, some scholars have emphasized the power this dynamic gives to a relatively small number of giant corporations to affect the performance of the economy. From this perspective, the real problem is the "corporate revolution" in American capitalism in the 20th century that gave rise to an economy dominated by giant (and generally uncompetitive) firms.[26] The result is not so much a single power elite as a system of multiple elites in which the leading corporations wield excessive power.[27]

That is not Lindblom's argument, however. To Lindblom, the central problem is the delegation of properly public functions into private hands—and with it the forfeiture of command as a means of control. This delegation makes the performance of the economy dependent on the response of business managers to changes in the business climate, regardless of whether the economy is dominated by a few large firms or is atomistically competitive. Relations between the state and business managers are not hierarchical; corporations must be induced to perform the functions on which society depends. This characterization is where the "market as prison" analogy comes into play: In making public policies, government officials must always take into account the effects of their proposals on the incentives facing business managers.

The Business Advantage in Expertise

This dependence of the state on business for the maintenance of prosperity gives rise to a second significant advantage. Government officials need reliable information when they formulate public policies—all the more so when the subject matter is highly technical, as is typically the case with business regulation. Business managers typically possess a near-monopoly on expertise relating to production processes; for example, until the late 1970s the U.S. government relied on the petroleum industry for estimates of available oil and gas reserves.[28] Possession of such information guarantees businessmen automatic access to policymakers, whereas other groups in society must compete to make their voices heard.

A 1983 study of interest group involvement in energy policymaking verified the critical importance of expertise. Under the Ford administration, industry groups (e.g., nuclear, oil and gas) had virtually monopolized access to the energy bureaucracy. President Carter sought to reverse this pattern and made clear his commitment to environmental protection—even appointing environmental activists to many positions. Despite this major change in personnel and top-level attitudes, the vast majority of contacts between bureaucrats and clientele groups still involved industry representatives, and most of these contacts were initiated by the agencies themselves. The need for technical information—and for a sense of how proposed regulations would affect business performance—overrode the administration's very real commitment to move policy in a new direction.[29]

The Unparalleled Legitimacy of Business

A final advantage to business stems from the extraordinary legitimacy granted to business managers in a capitalist society. Part of this advantage follows from the delegation of public functions into private hands. To the extent that corporate executives serve as a second set of public officials in such societies, they are responsible for decisions of great consequence to all citizens; as a result, they naturally are accorded high status.

Another important aspect of legitimacy, however, is the degree to which a group's demands are compatible with the values held by policymakers and the larger society. In this regard, business possesses an enormous advantage. Because capitalism is so entrenched within Western democracies, the narrow class interests of business come to be equated with the broader national interest. By comparison, all other groups—particularly organized labor—are perceived as narrow sectoral interests:

[I]f the national interest is in fact inextricably bound up with the fortunes of capitalist enterprise, apparent partiality towards it is not really partiality at all. On the contrary, in serving the interests of business and in helping capitalist enterprise to thrive, governments are really fulfilling their exalted roles as guardians of the good of all.[30]

Money as a Source of Business Power

Although Lindblom and Miliband minimize the importance of tangible resources as a source of business power, the financial advantage of business over other actors is very large and growing steadily larger. With the legalization of political action committees (PACs) in the mid-1970s, the total amount of business contributions to candidates had grown dramatically—much faster than the contributions of any other group. By the early 1980s, corporate and trade association PACs had amassed a better than two-to-one dollar advantage over organized labor, business's closest competitor on this dimension. Even more impressive, this total for all business groups exceeded the combined resources of all the other groups in the system, including labor.[31]

This remarkable monetary advantage to business interests enables corporations and trade associations to gain access to a broader range of legislators than almost any other group. Although most PAC contributions do not make a significant difference in determining the outcome of a given race, single-issue groups typically focus on close races where they can at least claim to have affected the election. Organized labor limits its contributions to Democratic candidates, who tend to be more receptive to labor issues. By contrast, business can afford to reward its friends and to neutralize its potential opponents. Business PACs tend to favor incumbents over challengers, regardless of which party controls the Congress. The net result is that the average Republican candidate receives a relatively homogeneous pot of contributions from business groups and sympathetic conservative and New Right groups. By contrast, the contributions going to Democrats show a rough balance between liberal groups (including organized labor) and business PACs.[32]

☐ EFFECTIVE INFLUENCE

Such resource advantages, however impressive in the abstract, cannot be equated with influence. Whether such resources are translated into effective influence ultimately will depend on at least two additional variables: internal cohesion and the political skill of the group's leadership.

Internal Cohesion

Internal cohesion is a critically important intervening variable. Internal divisions reduce a group's credibility in claiming to speak for its constituency and may prevent the group from taking any position at all. For example, peak associations organized to represent the shared class interests of American business (e.g., the Chamber of Commerce or the National Association of Manufacturers) have difficulty acting on many economic issues because such issues tend to divide the business community. Because these groups typically require near-unanimity among their members before they take a stand, they are much more likely to lobby on issues that affect business only peripherally, such as farm price supports or welfare reform.[33]

Lindblom plays down internal cohesion as a significant problem for business groups, arguing instead that business largely avoids the free rider problem because of its prior organization for the purpose of producing and marketing economic goods.[34] Although Miliband concedes the existence of internal divisions within the business community, his main line of defense is to distinguish between grand issues that affect business as a class and secondary issues that affect individual industries.[35] This distinction between grand and secondary issues plays a major role in the theory of corporate power. It not only responds to objections stemming from the persistence of internal divisions within the business community on a broad range of issues; it also provides a way to reconcile a theory of corporate predominance with the substantial evidence of business defeats on secondary issues. In short, business uses its control of the agenda to suppress any significant assault on the grand issues of capitalism, private property, and corporate autonomy in making production and investment decisions.

Political Skill of the Group's Leadership

In this same vein, the political skill of the group's leadership should not to be taken for granted. In a case study of tariff lobbying in the 1950s, many business lobbyists were found to be timid and poorly informed. They were afraid that efforts to persuade unsympathetic legislators would be perceived as unreasonable "pressure," so they focused most of their attention on congressmen who already were sympathetic to their cause. These same lobbyists were found to lack even the most rudimentary data about which legislators remained undecided—and thus potentially persuadable—on the issue.[36]

Although such timidity no longer is the norm for business lobbyists in this era of expanded corporate involvement in politics, it nevertheless is a reminder that seemingly overwhelming resource advantages do not translate automatically into effective influence. Skilled leadership must be understood as a variable rather than a constant, differing across groups and over time.

❏ A TYPOLOGY OF POLICY PROCESSES

Although internal divisions or an unskilled leadership can prevent the translation of business resources into effective influence, all groups are vulnerable to these limitations. The larger point is that political resources—particularly strategic position, expertise, legitimacy, and money—are distributed unevenly among groups. Although groups such as the nuclear freeze movement or the environmental movement may triumph on an issue (or, more often, during one stage of an issue), there is little reason to expect politically weak groups to triumph over stronger groups with any regularity.

The implications of political inequality for incrementalism are developed in Figure 4-1, which presents a typology of common policy processes.[37] The three biases to the group universe identified in the first part of

FIGURE 4-1. Typology of Policy Processes

Supply Pattern	Consensual Demand Pattern	Conflictual Demand Pattern
Nondecision supply pattern: Inaction; Congress fails to pass any legislation at all	**Nondecision: Barrier I** No overt challenge to prevailing values: Apparent consensus masks privileged position of elites	**Nondecision: Barrier II** Initial success by challenging group forces successful counter-mobilization by entrenched interests
Delegative supply pattern: policy without law	**Self-regulative issues** Delegation of public power to private groups	**Normal incrementalism** Partisan mutual adjustment of many groups
Allocative supply pattern: rule of law	**Distributive issues** Active group or coalition seeks and receives subsidies	**Nonincremental change** Balance of forces tips in favor of challenging groups

this chapter make clear that an expectation that all groups will be repre-sented in the workings of partisan mutual adjustment all of the time is unrealistic. More specifically, I identify two distinct configurations of de-mands (or "demand patterns"), which constitute the columns in the typology in Figure 4-1. Where various groups are active, representing many (if not all) sides of an issue, the demand pattern is characterized as conflictual; by contrast, where all or most of the active groups are aligned on one side of an issue because of the free rider problem or imperfect information, the demand pattern is characterized as consensual.

The second dimension of the typology refers to what I term "supply pattern." Here, Congress may respond to mobilized interests with no bill at all; a vague bill that delegates broad discretion to the bureaucracy; or a clear-cut, specific decision (an allocative outcome).

Nondecision Making: Barriers I and II

The first supply pattern—the failure to pass any bill at all—corre-sponds to what Bachrach and Baratz termed *nondecision making*.[38] The term *nondecision making* fails to convey the meaning originally intended by the authors and has come in for a great deal of criticism inasmuch as nondecisions turn out to be a form of decision.[39] What Bachrach and Baratz really meant by this concept is better expressed by the notion of institutional gatekeeping.[40] Essentially, their hypothesis is that some elite groups (corpo-rations or other powerful groups within society) control access to the agenda, preventing issues that threaten their fundamental interests from arising at all; in effect, they control a gateway to the agenda, which they can open or close at will. Nondecisions may take two distinct forms, according to Bachrach and Baratz: Barrier I and Barrier II nondecisions. With Barrier II nondecisions, challenging groups[41] have mounted an overt challenge to powerful groups that benefit from the status quo; these powerful groups use their power to defeat the challenge—often, though not always, before it gets very far. Because Barrier II nondecisions are overt, students of the policy process can observe them. Various examples (often testifying to corporate power) can be cited.

By contrast, Barrier I nondecisions are impossible to observe. All we can see, as we study a given issue, is the lack of sentiment for change—an apparent consensus on the virtues of the status quo. Although this consen-sus may be genuine, it also may reflect elite power over public attitudes or the expression of dissenting attitudes. This dynamic is what Lindblom and Miliband are describing when they refer to the "privileged position of business within capitalist societies" or the tendency for policymakers to equate the class interests of business with the broader public interest. Tom Ferguson has identified another way Barrier I nondecisions may occur. Running for office requires candidates to raise large sums of money. These sums are very large relative to the average person's income, and candidates are forced to seek funds from individuals or groups with large sums of money, whom Ferguson terms "major investors." Because these major investors will not finance candidates who advocate issues that threaten their fundamental interests, the need to raise large sums of money to mount campaigns necessarily excludes some issues from public debate. The failure of these issues to arise constitutes a Barrier I nondecision that easily can be mistaken for widespread public satisfaction with things the way they are.[42]

For example, the corporate income tax as a share of all federal income tax revenues has fallen dramatically over the past few decades, to about half its share in the Eisenhower years.[43] Major-party presidential candidates seldom highlight this marked shift away from corporate taxation, although there has certainly been no shortage of proposals for tax reform of one kind or another. Ferguson's theory would point to the dependence of candidates on corporate contributions to explain the relative neglect of this important issue.

Legislation in Response to Consensual Demand Patterns

Issues that do result in the passage of legislation fall under two headings. Often, Congress fails to resolve contentious issues, choosing instead to delegate broad discretion to the bureaucracy. (In recent years, devolution of federal authority to the states has become an increasingly popular form of legislative delegation.) Theodore J. Lowi called this delegation "policy-without-law" in his critique of the modern interest group state, *The End of Liberalism*.[44] By contrast, Congress may choose instead to make clear-cut, specific allocations, which Lowi termed "rule-of-law." For example, tariff bills prior to 1934 set specific tariff levels for individual products in particular industries; this legislation would represent an allocative supply pattern. (Even today, import quotas—as distinct from tariffs—set specific limits on the amounts of different products that may be imported from particular countries: another allocative outcome.) Beginning in 1934, however, Congress chose instead to delegate broad authority to the president to enter into negotiations with foreign countries aimed at lowering as many tariff levels as possible; this policy represents a delegative supply pattern.

Where the demand pattern is consensual, the balance of forces discussed above does not come into play because the active groups are overwhelmingly aligned on the same side of the issue. Under such circumstances, elected officials will rationally give mobilized interests whatever they are seeking. Sometimes these interests seek subsidies from the government; farm price supports for various commodities provide a classic example. Following Lowi, I term such policies "distributive policies." They are distributive rather than redistributive to the extent that all of the active groups can benefit together—usually at the expense of taxpayers, who have failed to mobilize because of some combination of imperfect information and the free rider problem.

The Sugar Act, in effect for several decades with only a brief interruption in the mid-1970s, provides a good example. Major sugar producers and refiners (typically less than a half dozen firms) wanted to stabilize the price of sugar above the level that would be operative in a free market. (Note here two disadvantages of the free market to such firms: The market price is not as high as they would like, and it is not stable; it depends on fluctuations in demand and supply.) To stabilize the price at a desirable level, the sugar producers and refiners approached Congress with a plan that would set an overall figure for the amount of sugar to be sold within the United States in the coming year; this amount would fix supply at an amount that would yield the price they sought, given their best estimate of the likely demand for sugar. This amount would then be divided up among domestic and foreign producers through the allocation of specific production quotas. These quotas served, in effect, as licenses to produce sugar; companies could not enter the market to produce and sell sugar within the United States without first securing such a license, which would entitle them to sell a specific amount and no more. This arrangement looks a lot like socialism because it is—although it represents a socialism that is designed to protect the narrow interests of sugar producers and refiners at the expense of the general public.

Sometimes autonomy is more attractive to special interests. Oligopolistic industries (i.e., industries characterized by only a few sellers) would like to form stable cartels. Although the economic theory is a bit more complex than this, in effect a cartel consists of a group of sellers combining to act as one—agreeing on a single price and the share of overall production to be granted to each firm within the industry. This arrangement enables the members of the cartel to benefit from monopolistic pricing practices rather than competing with one another through destructive price wars. There are three problems with forming a cartel, from the viewpoint of the oligopolistic firms. First, the members of the cartel have to bear the costs of policing the agreement (e.g., enforcing the agreement against cheaters).

Cartels are notoriously unstable; they break down when individual members try to do better for themselves by offering goods below the cartel price and thus expanding their market share. Second, there is no way to prevent new entrants attracted by the high profit levels within the industry from coming in to compete with the cartel members, offering comparable goods at slightly lower prices. This dynamic represents a second reason why cartels tend to be unstable. Third—and perhaps most important—cartels constitute a clear violation of the antitrust laws, subjecting participants to serious fines or even imprisonment.

The solution to this problem, for the oligopolistic firms, is to seek governmental regulation of their industry. Although asserting that all business regulation is a response to such efforts by oligopolistic industries to shore up unstable cartels would be inaccurate, a great deal of business regulation does reflect this motive. Under a regime of government regulation, cartels are legalized; the antitrust laws are suspended to permit a regulatory agency to regulate prices and entry. In fact, the government takes on the burden of enforcing prices and market shares, effectively stabilizing the cartel. New entrants are excluded by requiring them to obtain licenses; the decision to grant or withhold licenses is made by the regulatory agency, which typically is highly protective of the regulated industry that constitutes, after all, its main supportive constituency when it returns to Congress for periodic appropriations or reauthorizations.[45] Where Congress responds to a consensual demand pattern with a delegative supply pattern, the result may be termed self-regulative policies.

Legislation in Response to Conflictual Demand Patterns

By contrast, where the demand pattern is conflictual, the balance of forces—which groups are active and with what specific resources—will determine the precise equilibrium among the contending groups. Most of the time, this balance will fail to favor one side or another enough to permit a clear-cut resolution of the issues. The policy process will be characterized by partisan mutual adjustment, as envisioned by Lindblom, whereby conflictual demand patterns give rise to delegative supply patterns.[46] Policy outcomes within this cell will be incremental in nature, with vague delegations of authority to the bureaucracy (or the states) typically granting implementing agencies appropriations and statutory authority that are inadequate to the tasks facing them.

Nonincremental change, in which Congress responds to a conflictual demand pattern with an allocative supply pattern, will not occur under normal circumstances. Instead, nonincremental change (within the confines of this typology) will result only when the balance of forces shifts, for one reason or another, in favor of challenging interests—for example, the rise of environmental groups seeking effective regulation of air pollution, water pollution, and strip mining.[47] The mobilization of new groups that challenge the interests of previously dominant groups will necessarily shift the demand pattern from a consensual to a conflictual configuration. If challenging groups gain strength over time (which is by no means inevitable), the result would be movement down the right-hand side of the typology, from Nondecision Barrier II through normal incrementalism to nonincremental change.[48]

Nonincremental policy changes typically will prove to be short-lived. For example, mass public concern over air pollution combined with the mobilization of new environmental groups to produce a bandwagon effect in 1970, leading to a significant strengthening of the Clean Air Act (see chapter 5). The response was clearly allocative and dramatic: Congress identified nine criteria pollutants and set specific, technology-forcing, health-based standards for ambient air quality in each instance. Progress in meeting these unusually specific targets was uneven and incremental at best, however, as public arousal waned and the energy crisis gave renewed legitimacy to the concerns of automakers as well as coal and oil interests.

☐ INEQUALITY AND INCREMENTALISM

Clearly, partisan mutual adjustment among a multiplicity of contending interests is the exception rather than the rule. Organized interests in general, and corporations in particular, often will triumph against little or no opposition in the distributive and self-regulative arenas. Where challenges to their power do arise, the defensive power of such groups will confine many issues to the realm of Barrier II nondecisions. Where legislation is passed, the results typically will be incremental, with implementors receiving unclear policy mandates and limited statutory authority and appropriations.

Thus, inevitable obstacles to mobilization and inequalities in political resources among groups constitute forces for incrementalism in policy *outcomes* that are as important as the limits on rationality emphasized by Lindblom. If all groups were politically active and if political resources were distributed more evenly among groups, the mix of policy outcomes across a wide range of issues would look very different than it does now.

A certain amount of incrementalism is inevitable and desirable within any political system because of the dispersion of knowledge throughout the political system and the need to learn from experience with policies. If the market serves as a discovery process in this regard—as Hayek suggests—the same thing surely can be said for political markets. Even where political markets fail to satisfy efficiency conditions that are analogous to those governing economic markets (in particular, perfect information and perfect competition), they still may be the best mechanisms available for identifying critically important information on policy consequences and the viewpoints of myriad political interests. In the same way, a certain amount of incrementalism can at least be defended where it results from checks and balances that are deliberately built into the system to guard against tyranny and encourage an emphasis on persuasion rather than coercion in the deliberative process.

By contrast, although a good deal of political inequality probably is inevitable within any political system, incrementalism arising from such inequalities cannot be defended on intellectual grounds. All one can argue here (as Lindblom does) is that no other method of policymaking—including attempts at comprehensive rationality—would do a better job of responding to weak or unmobilized interests.[49] The one silver lining in this cloud, if the analysis in this chapter has any value, is that policymakers who are concerned with weak or unrepresented interests can at least predict, with reasonable confidence, which interests are most likely to be weak or go unmobilized.

NOTES

1. See Arthur F. Bentley, *The Process of Government: A Study of Social Pressures* (Chicago: University of Chicago Press, 1908), 300. Another early group theorist made very much the same point: "What may be called public policy is actually the equilibrium reached in the group struggle at any given moment, and it represents a balance which the contending factions are constantly striving to shift in their favor." See Earl Latham, "The Group Basis of Politics: Notes for a Theory," *American Political Science Review.* 46 (June 1951): 390. See also Latham's *The Group Basis of Politics: A Study of Basing Point Legislation* (Ithaca, N.Y.: Cornell University Press, 1952), and David B. Truman, *The Governmental Process: Political Interests and Public Opinion* (New York: Knopf, 1951).

2. To Norman Wengert, for example, we need not define and agree on the public interest; the need for all groups to justify their demands in terms of some broader conception of the public interest tempers the group struggle. See Norman Wengert, *Natural Resources and the Political Struggle* (Garden City, N.Y.: Doubleday, 1955), 66. Here, too, Wengert echoes Truman. Of the original group theorists, Truman and Wengert come closest to equating the group equilibrium with the public interest. Over the past two decades or more, the thrust of interest group theory and empirical research has been to emphasize obstacles to group mobilization and inequalities in resources across groups.

3. Mancur Olson, Jr., *The Logic of Collective Action: Public Goods and the Theory of Groups* (New York: Schocken Books, 1970), 1–52. See also James Q. Wilson, *Political Organizations* (New York: Basic Books, 1973).

4. Truman, *The Governmental Process,* 112–15.

5. Latham, "The Group Basis of Politics: Notes for a Theory," 382.

6. Ibid., 387.

7. Robert H. Salisbury, "An Exchange Theory of Interest Groups," *Midwest Journal of Political Science* 8 (1969): 1–32.

8. E. E. Schattschneider, *Semi-Sovereign People: A Realist's View of Democracy in America* (New York: Holt, Rinehart and Winston, 1960), 35. See also Wilson, *Political Organizations*; and Salisbury, "An Exchange Theory of Interest Groups."

9. Robert H. Salisbury, "Interest Representation and the Dominance of Institutions," *American Political Science Review* 78 (March 1984): 64–77.

10. Kay Lehman Schlozman and John T. Tierney, *Organized Interests and American Democracy* (New York: Harper and Row, 1986), 58–87.

11. This list of group resources is drawn from David Truman's insightful discussion in *The Governmental Process*, 506–507.

12. Raymond A. Bauer, Ithiel de Sola Pool, and Lewis Anthony Dexter, *American Business and Public Policy: The Politics of Foreign Trade*, 2d ed. (Chicago: Aldine-Atherton, 1972), 350–57.

13. Roger W. Cobb and Charles D. Elder, *Participation in American Politics: Dynamics of Agenda-Building* (Baltimore: Johns Hopkins University Press, 1983), 89–91.

14. Theodore R. Marmor, *The Politics of Medicare* (Chicago: Aldine, 1973).

15. Charles E. Lindblom, *Politics and Markets: The World's Political-Economic Systems* (New York: Basic Books, 1977).

16. Lindblom, *Politics and Markets.* See also Lindblom's "The Market as Prison," *Journal of Politics* 44 (May 1982): 324–36.

17. Lindblom, "The Market as Prison," 324–25.

18. Ralph Miliband, *The State in Capitalist Society* (New York: Basic Books, Inc./Harper Colophon Books, 1969).

19. Ibid., Chapter 6, "Imperfect Competition," 146–78.

20. Ibid., 164–65.

21. Ibid., 68–69.

22. Lindblom, "The Market as Prison," 334–35.

23. Truman, *The Governmental Process,* 506–507. See also S. E. Finer, "The Political Power of Private Capital," Part I, *Sociological Review* 3 (December 1955): 279–94, and Part II, *Sociological Review* 4 (July 1956): 5–30. For an excellent review of corporate political resources, see also Edwin M. Epstein, *The Corporation in American Politics* (Englewood Cliffs, N.J.: Prentice-Hall, 1969), 187–242.

24. Miliband, *The State in Capitalist Society,* 165.

25. Lindblom, *Politics and Markets*, 171–75. See also Miliband, *The State in Capitalist Society*, 147–55. Finer termed this same phenomenon "surrogateship." See Finer, "The Political Power of Private Capital," Part I, 285.

26. See Gardiner C. Means, *The Corporate Revolution in America: Economic Reality vs. Economic Theory* (New York: Collier Books, 1964); Adolph A. Berle, *The 20th Century Capitalist Revolution* (New York: Harcourt, Brace, and World, 1954); Adolph A. Berle, *Power Without Property: A New Development in American Political Economy* (New York: Harcourt, Brace, and World, 1959); Morton S. Baratz, "Corporate Giants and the Power Structure," *Western Political Quarterly* 9 (June 1956): 406–415; and Peter Bachrach, *The Theory of Democratic Elitism* (Boston: Little, Brown, 1967).

27. Baratz, "Corporate Giants and the Power Structure."

28. Walter A. Rosenbaum, *Energy, Politics, and Public Policy*, 2nd ed. (Washington, D.C.: Congressional Quarterly Press, 1987), 45–48 and 73–75.

29. John E. Chubb, *Interest Groups and the Bureaucracy: The Politics of Energy* (Stanford, Calif.: Stanford University Press, 1983).

30. Miliband, *The State in Capitalist Society*, 75.

31. Lindblom, *Politics and Markets*, 194–96. See also Kay Lehman Schlozman and John T. Tierney, *Organized Interests and American Democracy*, 249, Table 10.5.

32. Thomas Byrne Edsall, *The New Politics of Inequality: How Political Power Shapes Economic Policy* (New York: W.W. Norton, 1984).

33. Bauer, Pool, and Dexter, *American Business and Public Policy*, 332–40.

34. Charles E. Lindblom, *The Policy-Making Process*, 2nd ed. (Englewood Cliffs, N.J.: Prentice-Hall, 1980), 81; *Politics and Markets*, 196–197.

35. Miliband, *The State in Capitalist Society*, 157.

36. Bauer, Pool, and Dexter, *American Business and Public Policy*, 341–57.

37. Figure 4-1 revises a typology I developed earlier; see Michael T. Hayes, "The Semi-Sovereign Pressure Groups: A Critique of Current Theory and an Alternative Typology," *Journal of Politics* 40 (February 1978): 134–61. For a fuller discussion of that typology, see Michael T. Hayes, *Legislators and Lobbyists: A Theory of Political Markets* (New Brunswick, N.J.: Rutgers University Press, 1981). That typology, in turn, was a modification of a typology developed by Theodore J. Lowi in "American Business, Public Policy, Case Studies, and Political Theory," *World Politics* 16 (July 1964): 677–715.

38. See Peter Bachrach and Morton S. Baratz, *Power and Poverty: Theory and Practice* (New York: Oxford University Press, 1970).

39. Richard M. Merelman, "On the Neo-Elitist Critique of Community Power," *American Political Science Review* 62 (June 1968): 451–61. For a response by Bachrach and Baratz and a reply by Merelman, see *American Political Science Review* 62 (December 1968): 1268–69.

40. The term "institutional gatekeeping" is from Cobb and Elder, *Participation in American Politics*.

41. I use the term "challenging groups" here in very much the same way that Cobb and Elder speak of "readjustors." To Cobb and Elder, readjustors are groups that initiate an issue because they perceive an unfavorable bias in the distribution of positions or resources within society. Thus, readjustors are distinct from "do-gooders," who initiate issues to make good public policy, and "exploiters," who manufacture issues for their own personal gain. See Cobb and Elder, *Participation in American Politics*, 82–83.

42. Thomas Ferguson, *Golden Rule: The Investment Theory of Party Competition and the Logic of Money-Driven Systems* (Chicago: University of Chicago Press, 1995).

43. See Donald L. Bartlett and James B. Steele, *America: Who Really Pays the Taxes?* (New York: Touchstone Books, 1994), 23–24.

44. Theodore J. Lowi, *The End of Liberalism: The Second Republic of the United States*, 2nd ed. (New York: W. W. Norton, 1979).

45. See George J. Stigler, "The Theory of Economic Regulation," *Bell Journal of Economics and Management Science* 2 (spring 1971): 359–65.

46. In the original version of this typology, I built on Lowi's seminal threefold classification of policies as distributive, regulative, or redistributive. (See "American Business, Public Policies, and Case Studies.") Accordingly, I built on Lowi's terminology in labeling this cell "regulative." Lowi termed such policies regulative because so many policies exhibiting these characteristics involve the regulation of business. There is no reason to assume, however, that all policies that fall within this cell involve business regulation.

47. Here again, in the original version of this typology I built on Lowi's terminology in labeling this cell "redistributive." Redistributive policies, to Lowi, occur when winners and losers are aware of the stakes involved in an issue and are successfully mobilized. Under such circumstances, both sides cannot gain together; for such zero-sum issues, one must lose for the other to win. The idea of nonincremental change is implicit in this category, as is the notion that to qualify as redistributive, a policy outcome must involve gains by challenging groups at the expense of previously dominant interests.

48. This is what Bruce Oppenheimer, using somewhat different terminology, found as the oil industry found itself under challenge on two different issues in the late 1960s and early 1970s: the oil depletion allowance and water pollution. Oppenheimer's continuum of three distinct policy types corresponds to the right-hand side of my typology, and the issue movement he observed—from nondecision through symbolic politics to material policies—is equivalent to what I describe as moving from nondecision Barrier II through normal incrementalism to nonincremental change. See Bruce I. Oppenheimer, *Oil and the Congressional Process: The Limits of Symbolic Politics* (Lexington, Mass.: Lexington Books, 1974).

49. Charles Lindblom, *The Intelligence of Democracy: Decision-Making Through Mutual Adjustment* (New York: Free Press, 1965), 265–90.

CHAPTER FIVE

Dramaturgical Incrementalism

In chapter 4, I suggest that nonincremental policy change will occur only where the balance of forces shifts in favor of challenging groups. This situation is the culmination of a process of issue movement in which issues would begin as Barrier II nondecisions, move through a period of normal incrementalism, and eventually produce nonincremental change. I also suggest that such issues may not remain very long within this cell; the conditions tipping the balance of forces in favor of challenging groups typically would be short-lived.

Charles O. Jones's case study of the Clean Air Act of 1970 provides an excellent example of such an issue. Jones concluded that nonincremental outcomes can result where mass public opinion is aroused on an issue, forcing policymakers to satisfy a "pre-formed majority." Although "majority-building incrementalism" does a very good job of accounting for policymaking under normal circumstances—including air pollution policymaking from 1941 to 1967—Jones developed an alternative model, which I call the "public-satisfying model," to characterize the distinctive pattern of policymaking he observed from 1967 to 1970. The increased salience of the air pollution issue produced a very different kind of policy process that departed from majority-building incrementalism on all points.[1]

By contrast, my own research on the evolution of the nuclear freeze issue from 1981 to 1983 suggested that mass public arousal does not yield nonincremental outcomes in every instance. To account for the distinctive pattern of events I observed in the nuclear freeze case, I developed a third model, which I termed "dramaturgical incrementalism."[2]

In the first section of this chapter I review the elements of Jones's model of majority-building incrementalism. In the second section I show how well that model fit air pollution policymaking prior to 1970. In the third section I review the elements of the public-satisfying model that Jones developed to account for the distinctive events surrounding passage of the Clean Air Amendments of 1970. In the fourth section I briefly analyze the evolution of the nuclear freeze issue in the early 1980s as an example of Jones's public-satisfying model, and in the fifth section I show that the nuclear freeze issue is better understood as an example of dramaturgical incrementalism. I conclude the chapter by arguing that the Clean Air Act of 1970, like the nuclear freeze issue, is better understood as an example of dramaturgical incrementalism.

❏ MAJORITY-BUILDING INCREMENTALISM

The majority-building incrementalism model developed by Jones to account for air pollution policymaking prior to 1970 highlights four dimensions: characteristics of issue areas, institutions, decision-making patterns, and policy outcomes.[3]

Issue Areas: Low Salience and Multidimensional Complexity

According to Jones, most issues are characterized by "multidimensional complexity." In other words, there is no consensus about what constitutes the public interest. Instead, a multiplicity of narrow interests is mobilized on various sides of the issue, seeking to influence policy. Mass public opinion typically is quiescent, leaving the field to these organized interest groups.[4]

Institutions: Policy Communities Dominate Policy Development

Policy communities develop to accommodate the multiplicity of special interests that are active on recurring national issues. These communities consist of (at a minimum) congressional committees or subcommittees with jurisdiction over particular issues, executive agencies with responsibility for enforcing legislation within the policy area, and clientele groups with a stake in the policies these governmental institutions make.

For most issues most of the time, policy development is centered within these policy communities. Most (if not all) of the participants who take a strong interest in a given issue are members of the relevant policy community; on many issues, active involvement is limited to a small number of members of this policy community. Thus, in the normal case policy proposals are formulated within these policy communities and then ratified (and often amended) within the broader political system (through floor action in the House and Senate, the President's decision to sign or veto, etc.).[5]

To clarify the relationships among these actors, which vary from one model to another, imagine a series of concentric circles in which the innermost circle consists of the policy community. These policy communities may be narrow subgovernments, or iron triangles, in which a small number of active participants have a symbiotic relationship with one another. Alternatively, these communities may be much more pluralistic and conflictual issue networks. In either case, this circle refers to the relatively narrow set of players who constitute the attentive public for the issue. Within Jones's majority-building incrementalism model—which almost surely captures most cases of policymaking—policy development takes place within this inner circle.

The second circle represents the broader political system (the President, the full House and Senate, other congressional committees or executive agencies, etc.). Under our Constitution, bills become law when they are passed in identical form by both houses of Congress and signed by the President; alternatively, they may be passed over a presidential veto by a two-thirds vote of both houses. Although policy development may be centered within the policy community, passage requires policymakers to build a majority within the full House and Senate and secure presidential approval or an extraordinary majority in Congress (if a presidential veto is anticipated).

The outermost of the three circles represents mass public opinion, which normally exerts little constraint on policymaking. On issues that are resolved through majority-building incrementalism, the issue area is characterized by multidimensional complexity, and public opinion is quiescent. Although public opinion does establish broad boundaries or parameters within which policymakers must operate, ordinarily there is a great deal of room for maneuver within these parameters. Because policymakers typically do not challenge these boundaries, in most cases of policymaking one can easily draw the erroneous conclusion that public opinion plays no role at all. The boundaries come into play only where they are called into question—for example, when President Reagan broke with previous presidents by abandoning ongoing efforts at arms control in 1981 (see discussion below). Under such circumstances, the role these boundaries play in the policy process becomes quite visible. The fact that they are invisible under normal circumstances does not mean they are not there.

Decision Making: The Importance of Tapering Down

Because most issue areas are characterized by disagreement over the content of the public interest and a good deal of conflict among organized interests, policy proposals normally have to be modified for proponents to build a majority that is sufficient to secure passage. Students of the policy process, including Jones, typically employ the term "legitimation" to refer to this process of majority-building. Policy formulation refers to the development of policy proposals that are aimed at solving, or at least ameliorating, social or economic problems. Because policy proposals must be formulated with an eye toward political feasibility, the line between formulation and legitimation can be thin at times; in Jones's terms, a perfect plan for solving a problem combined with an imperfect strategy for passage isn't worth very much.[6] For the purposes of this discussion, the important point is that formulation precedes legitimation in the normal case. This pattern is reversed in the public-satisfying model.

The need for legitimation is particularly acute within the American political system, with its genuinely bicameral legislature and strong committee system that creates multiple veto points along the way. Accordingly, decision making typically is characterized by what Jones termed "tapering demands from the optimal down to the acceptable."[7]

Policy Outcomes: The Inevitability of Incrementalism

Policy outcomes normally are incremental. That is, they represent fairly small changes from existing policy. These incremental policy changes typically take "the form of an indefinite sequence of policy moves"[8] that ameliorate problems without really solving them. The need to taper proposals from the optimal to the acceptable virtually guarantees incremental outcomes under normal circumstances. Accordingly, policy entrepreneurs often eschew nonincremental policy proposals as unrealistic—although sometimes proposing a major policy change may be good strategy to provide bargaining leverage going into this process of tapering down. All realistic participants recognize, however, the near-inevitability of incremental policy outcomes unless exceptional circumstances (such as an aroused public opinion) make pushing for something stronger possible.

❑ AIR POLLUTION POLICY PRIOR TO 1970

According to Jones, air pollution policymaking exhibited majority-building incrementalism at the local, state, and federal levels from 1941 to 1967. When the issue reached the federal agenda in the early 1960s, it was unambiguously characterized by multidimensional complexity. The issue had no salience at all for the mass public most of the time, and interest groups representing electric utilities and other point sources of pollution, automakers, and so on were active. The environmental movement did not really mobilize until the late 1960s and early 1970s; the air pollution issue initially was raised in Congress by a Republican legislator from California who was concerned with the growing problem of smog.[9] Little was known regarding the effects of various emissions on human health, so the federal government had to encourage research on these effects before moving toward a strong enforcement role. Indeed, although there was some controversy over provisions for pollution abatement in the Clean Air Act of 1963, the main effect of the proposed legislation was to provide federal categorical grants to states and localities that were willing to create executive agencies focused on the environment and then engage in research.[10]

Policymaking was centered within the policy community in 1963. Air pollution policy was not a high priority for President Kennedy, who had to be maneuvered into taking a position in favor of the legislation.[11] The issue was dominated instead by Senator Edmund Muskie of Maine, chair of the subcommittee on air and water pollution of the Senate Interior Committee. Prior to Muskie's ascension to that position, no one was really willing to push the issue in Congress, and for the remainder of the decade there was no one on the House side with a comparably strong interest in the issue.[12]

The struggle over the legislation also was characterized by tapering down from the optimal to the acceptable. Groups representing major sources of pollution were well represented in Congress, and the President was uninterested in pushing the issue. The federal agency that would be charged with enforcing the statute's relatively weak provision on pollution abatement—the National Air Pollution Control Administration (NAPCA), within the Public Health Service (which, in turn, was a part of the Department of Health, Education, and Welfare [HEW])—did not really want the proposed enforcement authority. The Public Health Service played an advisory role vis-à-vis the states and localities on a wide variety of health issues and did not want to upset these existing relationships by taking on a more adversarial posture in this new policy area.[13]

Not surprisingly, the eventual policy outcome was quintessentially incremental. Although a cumbersome and weak provision for enforcement by NAPCA was included in the final legislation, the main provision provided federal money to states and localities to encourage research on the effects of emissions on human health. By 1967, when the Air Quality Act was before Congress for consideration, the enforcement provision had seldom been invoked, but the number of states and localities conducting research on air pollution through agencies newly created for that purpose had increased dramatically.[14] As a first step, the legislation was a striking success, creating the foundation for an increase in the knowledge base in the policy area.

The Air Quality Act of 1967 also conformed to the model. As in 1963, the issue lacked salience with the mass public, and the interest group universe for the issue was skewed toward representatives of affected industries. There was no consensus regarding the public interest on the issue beyond a shared commitment to pass some kind of air pollution legislation in 1967.[15]

There was a slight departure, however, from the domination of policy development by the policy community that had characterized the clean air issue in 1963. President Johnson had become involved in the issue, calling for national air quality standards. His involvement was not triggered by public interest in the issue, however, but stemmed from his need—as a strong president bent on legislative activism—to find policy proposals that would expand the federal government's authority while shifting monetary costs as much as possible onto private actors. In the wake of Johnson's landslide victory over Barry Goldwater in 1964, Congress had passed all of the President's major initiatives in the preceding Congress. At the same time, the war in Vietnam was escalating rapidly, creating severe pressures on the federal budget. The President was forced to look around for new policy areas in which to propose legislation at a time when the federal government had little money to pay for new programs. National standards for air quality would cost the federal government nothing because compliance costs would be borne by industry.[16]

Senator Muskie opposed the President on the issue, partly because of his own longstanding commitment to primacy for the states in stand-ard-setting and partly out of a desire to protect his own turf. Prior to President Johnson's sudden interest in the issue, air and water pollution control issues had been Senator Muskie's exclusive domain; he had become known as Mr. Pollution and did not relish sharing credit with the president on the issue.[17]

Tapering down from the optimal to the acceptable was inevitable in the wake of this clash between Johnson and Muskie. The eventual outcome was incremental and ambiguous. The states retained formal authority for setting air quality standards, as preferred by Muskie, but these standards would have to conform to air quality criteria set by the federal government. NAPCA was charged with creating a multiplicity of air quality control regions that would not correspond to state boundaries. Air quality criteria would then be developed for each region separately.[18]

By the time the Air Quality Act expired in 1970, not a single state had completed all of the requirements of the 1967 Act involving the setting and enforcing of air quality standards. The states were reluctant to waste time and resources setting air quality standards before the federal air quality criteria were developed. Because no additional money was provided to hire additional staff within NAPCA to create the air quality control regions and develop the criteria that the Act called for, nothing was happening at the federal level. Federal implementors repeatedly urged the states to move ahead without them, but the states refused to move until the air quality criteria (to which their standards had to conform) were established.[19] The result was paralysis as the Act came up for renewal in 1970. The stage was set for another round of incremental policy adjustments; in particular, there was a clear need to clarify where the real responsibility lay for setting air quality standards.[20]

❑ THE PUBLIC-SATISFYING MODEL

Whereas air pollution policymaking exhibited all the characteristics of majority-building incrementalism during the 1960s, the legislative process departed from that model on all four points in 1970 in response to a significant increase in mass public concern with air pollution (as measured by public opinion polls). As a result, the Clean Air Act of 1970 marked a substantial increase in federal capability that could justifiably be characterized as a nonincremental policy departure. Because the events of 1970 departed so completely from majority-building incrementalism, Jones developed an alternative model of policymaking to describe what had occurred. This "public-satisfying" model suggests a very different set of expectations regarding issue areas, institutions, decision making, and policy outcomes.

Issue Area: A Pre-Formed Majority

Under majority-building incrementalism, most issues lack salience with the general public, and there is no agreement regarding the content of the public interest. In 1970, however, the air pollution issue was highly salient; various polls indicated a dramatic rise in public concern over the issue. This apparent rise in mass public concern was accompanied by the proliferation of new groups representing environmental interests. There was something approaching a consensus on the public interest—or at least on the need for some form of strong federal action on this issue.[21] There was no need to build a majority on the clean air issue in 1970; the majority was "pre-formed."[22] The pressing need for policy-makers was to satisfy this pre-formed majority.

Although the existence of this pre-formed majority did not eliminate the tradeoffs that normally characterized the issue (e.g., environmental protection versus economic growth and jobs), and it did not make industry groups disappear, the depth and intensity of public concern over the environment threw industry groups off balance. With the mass public so attentive to the legislative process, industry groups had difficulty proposing weakening amendments without seeming to be in favor of air pollution.[23] In short, although the issue still involved multidimensional complexity, bargaining and compromise were difficult in an atmosphere of public arousal.

Institutional Change and a Bandwagon Effect

Most recurring policies fall clearly enough within the jurisdiction of established policy communities. Occasionally, however, new issues may emerge that fail to fit neatly within these existing structures. Because new policy communities do not develop quickly or easily, these new issues initially are assigned to the existing policy community with the most plausible claim to expertise in the policy area. New issues that demonstrate real staying power, such as environmental protection, eventually generate institutional adaptation—for example, via reorganization of congressional committee structures or creation of new executive agencies.[24]

Increased public concern over air pollution from 1969 onward contributed to at least three important institutional developments. First, the National Environmental Policy Act of 1969 (NEPA) created the Council on Environmental Quality (CEQ). A presidential staff agency comparable to the president's Council of Economic Advisers, CEQ was given authority to conduct studies and make an annual report to Congress on the state of the environment. It also was required to review the environmental impact statements that would now be required before any new federal construction or water projects could be undertaken. A year later, President Nixon, by executive order, significantly enhanced the power of the agency in charge of air pollution. NAPCA had been part of the Public Health Service, buried several layers within HEW. Nixon's Reorganization Plan No. 3, approved by Congress in September 1970, consolidated NAPCA with a wide variety of federal pollution programs scattered throughout the executive branch into a newly created and much more powerful agency: the Environmental Protection Agency (EPA). Finally, the Clean Air Act of 1970 clearly placed responsibility for setting air quality standards at the federal level for the first time, giving this authority to the newly created EPA.[25]

Institutional changes within Congress did not keep pace with these changes in the executive branch. The air pollution policy community remained unchanged; hearings on the clean air legislation took place in the House Committee on Interstate and Foreign Commerce and the Senate Interior Committee. The sharply increased public salience of the issue, however, created a kind of bandwagon effect, as policymakers who were not normally associated with the issue saw the electoral potential of this motherhood issue. NEPA owed its existence in large part to Senator Henry Jackson's desire to link himself to this increasingly popular issue in advance of his planned run for the presidency in 1972. Similarly, President Nixon (never considered a friend of environmental causes previously) made the environment one of the four major themes of his State of the Union address in 1970 and sent clean air legislation to Congress "with virtual wartime urgency." The president's newfound concern over the issue had much to do, almost surely, with Senator Muskie's emergence (as perceived by pundits of the period) as his most likely Democratic opponent in 1972; Senator Muskie's long-time advocacy of environmental causes suddenly looked like very smart politics indeed, and the president wanted to steal some of the senator's thunder on this increasingly popular issue.[26] In sum, although the congressional policy community had not been changed in any formal way by the sudden emergence of mass public concern over the environment, new and significant players outside that community were now asserting jurisdiction over the issue.

Decision Making by Policy Escalation

The existence of a pre-formed majority on the clean air issue obviated the normal need to taper from the ideal down to the acceptable. Instead, policymakers in 1970 were forced to scramble to satisfy this highly aroused and pre-formed majority. In distinct contrast to the normal majority-building process, in 1970 air pollution legislation was *strengthened* as it moved through the process. NEPA not only placed responsibility for setting air pollution standards at the federal level for the first time, it also set specific standards for nine "criteria pollutants" that in fact were technology-forcing inasmuch as they could not be attained within the deadlines specified by the new law given technologies in existence at the time. This decision to spur the development of new and better technologies by setting ambitious, health-based standards was made purposefully and with full awareness of its potentially adverse implications for economic growth. Jones termed this process "policy escalation"—in distinct contrast to the normal process of "tapering down."[27]

Nonincremental Policy Outcomes: Legislating beyond Capability

Public arousal in 1970 gave rise to a process of public-satisfying via policy escalation that eventually produced a significant increase in federal authority and technology-forcing, health-based air pollution standards. Various new institutions were created to address environmental problems, and—in a provision that would turn out to be much more important than anyone probably understood at the time—the Clean Air Act granted citizen groups sweeping new rights to bring class action suits not only against polluters but also against federal agencies that were neglecting important responsibilities under the law.[28]

Jones did offer one important caveat in evaluating the dramatic policy changes of 1970. Major policy change in the air pollution case was driven by the need to satisfy an aroused mass public; it was *not* triggered by any corresponding increase in the scientific knowledge base on the issue. Given the slow growth in scientific understanding of causes of air pollution, the consequences of exposure to various pollutants in different degrees, and technology for reducing emissions, an incremental increase in federal capability was called for in 1970. Although Jones advocated an aggressive strategy of policy change via "large increments," he did not actually regard the events of 1970 as validating nonincremental policy change. To the contrary, he characterized the 1970 Act as an instance of "legislating beyond capability."[29]

☐ THE NUCLEAR FREEZE AS A TEST CASE OF JONES'S MODEL

The nuclear freeze issue, which occupied policymakers early in President Reagan's first term, bore a striking resemblance to the clean air case, inasmuch as policymakers once again appeared to face the need to satisfy a pre-formed majority on a highly salient policy issue. A straightforward application of Jones's model yields a surprising result, however. Although the pre-formed majority generated a bandwagon effect very much like the one Jones observed in 1970, the legislative process was characterized by multiple instances of tapering from the ideal down to the acceptable, and the eventual outcome could only be characterized as incremental.[30]

Issue Area: A Pre-Formed Majority

The first two-and-a-half years of the Reagan administration saw a sharp increase in concern over nuclear issues on the part of attentive and mass publics. These developments were fueled, in large part, by the president's own actions and rhetoric. Early in his first term, President Reagan opposed any attempt to ratify the SALT II treaty that had been negotiated by President Carter and saw little point in new arms control negotiations with the Soviet Union. Reports in the press suggested that the administration considered winning a limited nuclear war at least theoretically possible, and the president speculated during a press conference that it might be possible to contain a limited nuclear conflict to the European theater. Moreover, the president sought to close what he termed a "window of vulnerability" by building up the U.S. nuclear arsenal. Authorizations were requested for acquisition of the B-1 bomber and the MX missile, and the deployment of intermediate-range Pershing II missiles went forward in Europe.

These events triggered a sharp increase in public concern over nuclear war, as measured in a variety of public opinion polls. In another striking similarity to the clean air issue, the nuclear freeze issue spawned the rapid rise of a broad-based social movement in support of nuclear arms limitation. This new peace movement drew from the mainstream of American life. In addition to traditionally pacifist groups, such as the American Friends Service Committee, a plethora of new groups representing scientists, businessmen, professionals, housewives, and clergymen, among others, were formed. Many religious denominations that were not traditionally associated with peace issues also became involved, and in several cities and towns, local churches were in the forefront of efforts to pass resolutions calling for an end to the nuclear arms race.

By June 1982, nuclear freeze resolutions had passed one or more houses of 12 state legislatures, 125 city councils, and a variety of New England town meetings, and nuclear freeze referenda were approved in several states in November. There is little question that members of Congress voting on nuclear freeze resolutions in 1982 and 1983 saw themselves as responding to a genuine grassroots movement of unusual breadth and intensity.

Issue Area: A Classic Bandwagon Effect

As with the clean air issue, mass public arousal produced a bandwagon effect, expanding the circle of participants beyond the normal confines of the existing policy community. At the national level, more than 40 nuclear freeze resolutions were introduced in Congress in 1982, ultimately centering around a resolution sponsored by House Foreign Affairs Committee Chairman Clement Zlabocki (D-Wisc.). In the Senate, a similar measure was co-sponsored by Edward Kennedy (D-Mass.) and Mark Hatfield (R-Ore.). Because there was never any real prospect that a nuclear freeze resolution would pass the Republican-controlled Senate, freeze proponents placed most of their hopes on the House of Representatives, where the Democrats retained a comfortable majority.

The dramatic rise in public concern forced opponents of a nuclear freeze to pay lip service to the issue. In the Senate, Henry Jackson (D-Wash.) sponsored a resolution calling for a nuclear freeze to come only after the United States had achieved rough nuclear parity with the Soviet Union. In the House, William S. Broomfield (R-Mich.) sponsored an administration-backed resolution calling for a freeze at "equal and substantially reduced levels."

Most important, President Reagan took an increasingly active role on the issue. Faced with growing public concern over nuclear war and the very real prospect of passage of some form of freeze resolution in the House, the president reversed his earlier opposition to new arms control negotiations. In November 1981, the president unveiled his "zero option" initiative in which he offered to cancel deployment of 572 intermediate-range Pershing II and cruise missiles in Western Europe if the Soviets agreed to dismantle 600 comparable missiles already deployed in Eastern Europe. Reagan also called for new talks with the Soviets aimed at reducing strategic nuclear weapons to "equal and verifiable levels." In May 1982, he proposed deep cuts in the strategic nuclear arsenals of both sides, which eventually would reduce both arsenals by one-third and produce a rough equality in throw-weight levels. In June, the president followed with a proposal for significant mutual reductions in conventional force levels in Europe.

Thus, exactly as predicted by Jones's model, the rise in public concern stimulated policymakers at a variety of governmental levels to address the arms control issue. By 1982, arms control had acquired an almost irresistible political appeal, making it attractive for a wide variety of political actors all across the policy spectrum to seek identification with the issue.

Decision Making: Tapering Down from the Optimal to the Acceptable

Within the public-satisfying model, the existence of a pre-formed majority removes any need for normal majority-building. Policymakers strive to satisfy the aroused mass public through a process of "policy escalation" in which bills get progressively stronger as they move through the legislative process. On the nuclear freeze issue, by contrast, bargaining and compromise were necessary throughout; freeze proponents were forced to weaken their resolution considerably in the course of the two-year legislative struggle. Freeze proponents lacked the votes necessary to pass a strong resolution that would actually bind the president to negotiate a comprehensive nuclear freeze. Several moderate Democrats sought to distance themselves from the administration's arms buildup and initial indifference to new arms control negotiations; at the same time, however, this group favored modernization of the aging U.S. nuclear force, which would be precluded by a binding freeze resolution. To attract this group, freeze supporters made a variety of important concessions in wording. One amendment stipulated, for example, that a freeze would "not unilaterally preclude any defense program proposed by the Reagan administration"; another permitted the president to pursue "complementary" arms control proposals while pursuing a nuclear freeze. These amendments enabled legislators to symbolically repudiate the president without really tying his hands.

Administration supporters countered with a substitute resolution sponsored by Rep. Broomfield that highlighted the president's dramatic new arms control initiatives by calling for a nuclear freeze at "equal and substantially reduced levels." The president's vigorous lobbying averted an embarrassing defeat by a perilously narrow two-vote margin; more than 50 Democrats joined with the Republicans to provide the margin of victory.

In the wake of this defeat, freeze activists shifted their attention to the upcoming midterm elections, in which 30 to 40 seats were considered vulnerable on the freeze issue. Although the ultimate impact of the freeze movement on the 1982 elections is difficult to gauge, substantial Democratic gains in the House made passage of a freeze resolution appear more likely in 1983.

Despite these electoral gains, freeze proponents were forced to make additional concessions during the 1983 debate. The resolution now merely called for negotiations "in search of" a freeze; ongoing U.S. weapons development would continue in the meantime. Moreover, the freeze would no longer be across-the-board; it would apply only to weapons systems agreed to by both sides and would be contingent on verifiability.

The House finally passed a nuclear freeze resolution on May 4, 1983. The resolution had been weakened considerably, however, over the course of the two-year legislative struggle, and the Republican-controlled Senate predictably rejected a comparable measure five months later by a vote of 58–40.

An Incremental Policy Outcome

In Jones's public-satisfying model, the process of policy escalation culminates in a policy departure that plausibly can be characterized as nonincremental. Although the events of 1970 led to tough new emissions standards on air pollution and the creation of new line and staff agencies concerned with environmental problems, much less was achieved by the nuclear freeze movement. The House failed to pass any freeze resolution in 1982, and although a freeze resolution passed by a comfortable margin in 1983, that resolution stipulated that a freeze be followed by reductions in arms. Because the president retained clear constitutional authority to negotiate treaties, the resolution represented at best a congressional attempt to provide guidelines for that process. The language was merely advisory: The president "should" seek a negotiated freeze but was not compelled to do so. At the same time, he remained free to pursue other "complementary" arms control proposals with the Soviets. Perhaps most important of all, the resolution left deliberately ambiguous when a freeze would begin and what items ultimately would be frozen. In the meantime, the new weapons systems the president wanted would continue to go forward.

❏ THE NUCLEAR FREEZE AS DRAMATURGICAL INCREMENTALISM

The failure of the nuclear freeze case to conform to the public-satisfying model suggested the need for an alternative model to explain the events in that case. I call my model "dramaturgical incrementalism." The nuclear freeze case demonstrates that, under some circumstances at least, public arousal can produce tapering down and incremental outcomes even as the policy process departs in important ways from the pattern Jones identified as majority-building incrementalism. Why didn't public arousal, which produced a strong bandwagon effect (as predicted by the model), lead to policy escalation in the nuclear freeze case? Dramaturgical incrementalism departs from the public-satisfying model in the following ways.

Issue Area: The Pre-Formed Majority Demands Action but No Single Solution

For most issues, mass public opinion sets distinct boundaries within which policymakers must operate, although there usually is a great deal of latitude within these constraints regarding which specific policies should be pursued. On the arms control issue, for example, a succession of American presidents had retained a great deal of latitude in negotiating arms control agreements with the Soviets; the public did not demand that those agreements take a specific form or occur on a specific timetable.

President Reagan aroused public opinion in 1981, however, by declaring in very strong terms his distrust of the Soviets and his unwillingness to ratify the SALT II treaty or to engage in any new rounds of arms talks with the Soviets. This stance constituted a sharp break with previous policies dating back through several administrations; it fueled the emergence of the nuclear freeze movement and growing public support for arms control measures, such as the nuclear freeze, that would put an end to his proposed defense buildup (particularly the development of the MX missile).

Mass public arousal on the nuclear freeze issue left the president with surprising latitude, however, for although the mass public was more aware of the problem than before, there still was no agreement on any one solution. Although the public was disturbed by the Reagan administration's initial opposition to arms control, it also was concerned that the Soviet Union could not be trusted to abide by arms control agreements. Although there was very strong support in various polls for a verifiable nuclear freeze, there also was support for a wide variety of alternative approaches. To the extent that public opinion on the freeze issue failed to dictate one arms control strategy over another, the president was left with some moral high ground, enabling him to buy time for his arms buildup with a series of arms control initiatives of his own.

Moreover, the mass public exhibited all the classic characteristics of what Murray Edelman has termed "Pattern B groups": high anxiety levels, stereotypic information about the issue, and a marked susceptibility to symbolic reassurances.[31] Although nuclear freeze activists had a sophisticated grasp of highly technical information, there is little evidence that the mass public was similarly informed. Indeed, some leaders of the freeze movement supported the freeze concept less because it represented a desirable approach to arms control than because it could be made readily intelligible to an ill-informed mass public. Educational efforts by freeze groups tended to avoid technical discussions of throw-weights, numbers of warheads, or the implications of new weapons technologies; the activists chose instead to focus on the highly dramatic and less technical consequences of death by nuclear incineration.

Institutions: Conflict within the Policy Community

In dramaturgical incrementalism, the existence of an aroused mass public sets off a bandwagon effect, as a large number of policymakers who are not normally associated with an issue see political profit in identifying themselves with that issue. In distinct contrast to the public-satisfying model, however, this expansion in the number of active participants does not eliminate conflicts over important values within the "attentive public" or policy community specializing in the issue.

The rise in public concern over nuclear war forced arms control onto the legislative agenda and set off a bandwagon effect, much as Jones would have predicted. Large numbers of congresspersons who normally took little interest in such issues were attracted to the struggle by the opportunity to take highly symbolic positions in favor of arms control. Jones's model, however, would not have predicted President Reagan's determined and highly skillful opposition. The president's stubborn refusal to jump on the bandwagon reflected his recognition that a comprehensive and binding freeze resolution, passed by both houses, would have put an end to his defense buildup.

The president was not alone within the policy community in his opposition to a binding and comprehensive nuclear freeze. A substantial group of moderate Democrats within the House welcomed the opportunity to repudiate the president symbolically. Yet this group (unlike hard-core freeze proponents) saw a need for weapons modernization; to gain their support, the freeze resolution had to be amended to permit the development of at least some new weapons systems. In particular, this group favored development of the single-warhead Midgetman missile as an alternative to the existing arsenal of multiple warhead missiles. These moderate Democrats thought a return to single-warhead missiles could create a more stable deterrent posture vis-à-vis the Soviets. Although this group opposed the MX—a very powerful, accurate multiple-warhead missile with first-strike capabilities—they favored the Midgetman, with its potential to make nuclear war less likely. A binding nuclear freeze would block the Midgetman along with the MX.

Decision Making: A Dual Conflict

The persistence of significant conflicts within the policy community precludes a nonincremental outcome. The immediate result is not majority-building incrementalism, however, because the increase in mass public involvement forces any bargaining to take place before an aroused mass public that normally is inattentive to the issue. The susceptibility of this mass public to symbolic reassurances virtually guarantees that the conflict will be turned into a drama, with a wide variety of characters casting themselves as central players in a cataclysmic struggle of good versus evil.

Although mass public arousal provides real opportunities for many players who normally would take little part in the issue, the dramaturgical nature of the struggle also creates new difficulties for the major players (e.g., for those within the policy community). The aroused public has little understanding of the complex, technical issues that still divide the policy community, yet the increasingly simplistic and moralistic nature of the public debate builds pressure for policy escalation and makes necessary compromises appear to be sellouts. The major players therefore must participate in two areas of conflict. One is highly symbolic, involves a large number of players, and is played out before the mass audience. The other, which is highly technical and confined to the policy community (or even a subset within the policy community), somehow must be shifted out of public view.

For House moderates in the nuclear freeze debate, the incentives were complex. The rise of the nuclear freeze movement and the sharp increase in public concern over nuclear war provided a welcome opportunity to repudiate the president symbolically. At the same time, a binding nuclear freeze resolution would preclude what these moderates regarded as essential weapons modernization—particularly the development of the Midgetman system. A highly public and dramaturgical battle over the freeze issue enabled a wide range of moderate Democrats and moderate and liberal

Republicans to distance themselves from the president without really impinging on their own goals. Although such a resolution could never bind the president, it would enable House moderates to get on the anti-nuclear bandwagon and, at the same time, subtly change its direction.

By contrast, President Reagan had everything to lose from mass public arousal, at least initially, to the extent that it threatened his arms buildup. Eventually, however, even he succeeded in profiting electorally within this staged drama over the nuclear freeze issue by leapfrogging his opposition to propose deep cuts in U.S. and Soviet arsenals that eventually would produce nuclear parity.

At the same time, both sides needed to engage in some classic horse-trading, out of public view. In this highly technical conflict, House moderates again played a pivotal role. Support for a vaguely worded freeze resolution placed these moderates in symbolic opposition to the president's arms buildup, providing the necessary cover to engage in a *quid pro quo*. In a move that would have been unlikely before public arousal over the prospect of a renewed arms race, many of these same moderate Democrats—whose support had been essential for passage of a nuclear freeze resolution—supported development of the MX missile. Skeptical of the president's motives and doubtful about the MX's strategic value, they conditioned their support of the missile on specific changes in the president's arms control proposals and a commitment to rapid development of alternatives to the MX—particularly the Midgetman missile then under research. These conditions were calculated to make the president's arms control proposals more attractive to the Soviets while gradually modernizing the U.S. nuclear arsenal and reducing this nation's reliance on destabilizing multiple-warhead missiles.[32]

Two Conflicts and Two Sets of Outcomes

In analyzing policy outcomes under dramaturgical incrementalism, it is critically important to keep clearly in mind the dual nature of the conflict set in motion by mass public arousal. Public arousal sets in motion a highly symbolic and public conflict involving a wide variety of participants who are not normally associated with the issue. For these minor players, who are drawn to the issue by the chance to jump on a popular bandwagon, this highly symbolic struggle is essentially positive-sum. Because symbolic reassurances are intangible and because peripheral actors appeal to different audiences, everyone involved can win simultaneously; all can gain favor with their constituencies by getting on the right side of the issue. The same electoral payoffs are available to the major players, of course; in the short run, at least, they will find participating in this drama profitable (or at least unavoidable).

At the same time, however, strongly held policy views may make a number of these players reluctant to engage in policy escalation. Thus, as Edelman predicts, they will seek to restore the quiescence of the mass public through symbolic reassurances (in this instance, by passage of some kind of resolution with the word "freeze" in it). Where Edelman sees elites manipulating symbols to gain material rewards at the expense of the mass public, the motive here is to take an ongoing conflict among contending elites (or, more accurately, members of the policy community) out of public view so that necessary bargains might be struck. The outcome of this second conflict—the highly technical conflict conducted within the policy community, necessarily involving a much smaller number of participants—tends to be classically incremental, with all sides forced to compromise.

In distinct contrast to the highly symbolic struggle over passage of the nuclear freeze resolution, the moderates' MX-for-arms control deal exhibited all the classic elements of majority-building incrementalism. The issues were much more technical, and mass public involvement was virtually nonexistent. The negotiations involved a limited number of congressional actors, all of whom specialized in defense issues and had well-deserved reputations for expertise in the subject.[33] This conflict was zero-sum, necessitating hard bargaining. Ultimately, all parties were forced to compromise, yielding an incremental outcome. The president won authorization for additional MX missiles but was forced to make important modifications in his arms control proposals. Moreover, future support for his defense buildup would be held hostage to his good faith in the negotiations process.[34]

❏ THE CLEAN AIR CASE AS DRAMATURGICAL INCREMENTALISM

The clean air case suggests that mass public arousal can produce a pre-formed majority that must be satisfied, resulting in a process of policy escalation and nonincremental policy change. By contrast, the nuclear freeze case shows that mass public arousal can be very strong—even producing a strong bandwagon effect—without triggering a process of policy escalation. Although at least three potentially significant differences between the air pollution case and the nuclear freeze case may account for the different outcomes, close analysis of these apparent differences points to a different conclusion: that both cases, properly understood, represent instances of dramaturgical incrementalism.

The first apparent difference between the two cases is that public opinion may have been less directive in the nuclear freeze case. Despite the intensity of mass public concern over nuclear war, opponents of a nuclear freeze may have had more latitude to oppose a nuclear freeze without appearing to favor nuclear war. President Reagan was able to argue that a nuclear freeze would freeze U.S. and Soviet nuclear arsenals at unacceptably high levels and lock in a long-term Soviet superiority in at least some important weapons systems. Although multidimensional complexity characterized the air pollution issue as well, even in the face of mass public arousal, in 1970 arguments against a strong, technology-forcing clean air law seemed to be arguments in favor of dirty air:

> Formulation ordinarily precedes legitimation. In 1970, legitimation—public and congressional approval of policy action—came first. Public demonstrations and opinion polls projected a clear message to decision makers: "Do something dramatic about pollution." Denied the processes of filtering demands through those affected by regulation and of moderating policy choices in light of existing knowledge and capabilities, policymakers were left to speculate as intelligently as they could, both about what would satisfy the public and whether the policy devised could be enforced.[35]

Whether this distinction reflected a real difference between the two issues or merely an important difference in the political skill (or political will) between the two presidents involved is impossible to determine; perhaps if Ronald Reagan had been president in 1970, he would have found comparable ways to deflect strong pressures for policy escalation in the clean air case as well. Certainly Jones's analysis of the gap between the Clean Air Act's technology-forcing provisions and the available scientific knowledge base suggests that a president who was more strongly inclined to resist the environmental movement might have identified defensible arguments against policy escalation.

The second apparent difference centers around the degree to which each issue generated conflict within the relevant policy community. There were significant disagreements within the arms control community over the best approach to achieving nuclear stability. Bargaining and compromise were required to resolve these differences, but the presence of an aroused mass public precluded the normal process of tapering down. This dynamic created the need for policymakers to stage a drama in public while conducting serious negotiations in private.

In the clean air case, by contrast, there was no comparable conflict within the environmental policy community, at least among elected officials—all of whom wanted to be on the right side of this suddenly popular issue. As Jones observed, policy proposals were modified less in reaction to interest group positions than in response to the mass media as sounding board and surrogate for public opinion.[36] Where President Reagan was willing to oppose the nuclear freeze movement (albeit cleverly, through a spate of arms control proposals) to save his arms buildup, President Nixon was on record as favoring significant strengthening of the clean air laws, even if his reasons were at least partly political. When the Senate produced a substantially stronger bill than he had proposed, he found himself leapfrogged in the competition for credit on a popular issue, but he had no disagreements with the Senate bill that were fundamental enough to warrant a veto.

Third, the fact that the authorization of the MX missile was a separate issue moving along a separate track through entirely different committees—and that this issue was much less salient to the general public than the freeze issue—enabled policymakers to operate on two very different levels at once. Virtually everyone involved gained from having a very public conflict over the nuclear freeze issue. At the same time, the need for "tapering from the ideal down to the acceptable" created a comparable incentive not to call public attention to the MX authorization. Only in this way could the necessary bargain be struck: 50 MX missiles now and 50 later in return for a commitment to deploy the Midgetman and acquiesce to various changes in the president's arms control proposals. By contrast, the clean air fight took place on a single track: the writing of a new clean air bill.

In the longer term, however, a second track *was* available; indeed, such a track always is available in cases of domestic policymaking. Domestic policies almost always are implemented intergovernmentally; the implementation process by its very nature is a second conflict, operating out of public view and involving a much smaller number of players. In the case of the Clean Air Act of 1970, policy escalation in Washington centered exclusively around the writing of federal air quality standards into the legislation. These standards grew more stringent, and the attendant deadlines shorter, throughout the course of the legislative process in 1970, eventually producing health-based, technology-forcing standards. Although health-based, technology-forcing air quality standards served as symbolic reassurances to a mass public that was concerned with air pollution, the specific actions that would be taken in specific locations to clean the nation's air would be identified through State Implementation Plans (SIPs). This process would take place long after the legislation was signed, after public attention had waned. Although this process would be open to environmental groups, it would likely be dominated by actors with an advantage in technical expertise: bureaucrats and representatives of industry groups.

In this light, one might question whether the policy outcome in the Clean Air case really qualifies as nonincremental. After the Clean Air Act of 1970, Congress repeatedly was forced to modify standards, accept alternative technologies as the "best feasible," or extend deadlines for compliance. Mass public arousal may have created the need to satisfy a pre-formed majority, but it did not really eliminate the multidimensional complexity that had always characterized the issue. There still was a tradeoff between measures to reduce pollution and the need to generate enough energy to run our industrial economy and maintain economic growth without inflation. Referring to such tradeoffs may have been impolitic in the political climate of 1970, but they were present nevertheless. Only three years later, the first OPEC oil embargo ushered in the energy crisis, forcing policymakers to face up to these tradeoffs once again.

Moreover, although mass public concern had risen dramatically between 1967 and 1970, the scientific knowledge base had not. No breakthroughs in technology or administrative organization had emerged to warrant the dramatic leap forward in federal authority; in the absence of such breakthroughs, there was no real basis to expect anything but incremental progress in cleaning the nation's air.

In sum, notwithstanding certain apparent differences from the nuclear freeze case, the Clean Air Act of 1970 is best understood as an instance of dramaturgical incrementalism. The legislative struggle in 1970 may be regarded as an expanded and highly public conflict over intangible and highly symbolic issues in which all the participants could win together. All could be seen as "doing something dramatic about pollution" by staging a drama in which public health was given priority over economic considerations and technological feasibility.

At the same time, serious conflict remained within the policy community, especially when this policy community is defined (correctly) as including not just elected officials but bureaucrats and representatives of industry as well. This conflict necessitated a kind of tapering down from the ideal to the acceptable that simply could not take place within public view—at least not in 1970. Thus, the Clean Air Act combined highly symbolic, ostensibly technology-forcing standards with a SIP process that facilitated bargaining, compromise, and incrementalism over the long term, out of public view.

◻ PUBLIC AROUSAL AND POLICY CHANGE

Dramaturgical incrementalism is available as a response whenever legislators face a conflictual demand pattern and mass public arousal that tip the balance of forces in favor of challenging groups. There is reason to believe that the nuclear freeze and clean air issues are not isolated instances of dramaturgical incrementalism. For example, the Civil Rights Act of 1964—a major policy departure that most analysts likely would characterize as nonincremental—featured a high degree of public arousal in response to a newly mobilized interest (the civil rights movement). Challenging groups on this issue had the additional advantage of strong and skillful backing from a president who had made passage of a strong bill the centerpiece of his legislative agenda. The protracted debate over passage of the Act received enormous media attention, with the bulk of that attention focused on the highly dramatic attempt by Southern Democrats to filibuster the legislation in the Senate, attempts to invoke cloture, and so on.

Although mass public opinion had crystallized into strong support for some kind of civil rights law, serious disagreements remained within the civil rights policy community on issues such as public accommodations and equal employment opportunity. The reality was that the bipartisan coalition of civil rights liberals lacked the votes to pass a strong bill—and certainly lacked the votes to cut off a filibuster in the Senate—without winning the support of moderate, centrist Republicans. Accordingly, private negotiations were conducted between the Kennedy administration and the leader of the centrist Republicans in the House: William McCulloch, ranking Republican on the Judiciary Committee. In the final analysis, the 1964 Act represented an important breakthrough in federal authority, and the American public (then and now) was reassured that the new law addressed the major problems facing black Americans. On a wide variety of important specifics, however, the law reflected classic tapering down from the ideal to the acceptable—a process that was conducted, of necessity, almost entirely out of public view.

Republicans extracted several important concessions. The section pro-hibiting discrimination in public accommodations was amended to exempt retail stores and personal service firms such as barber shops. In various titles, the attorney general's authority to initiate suits was sharply limited. The voting rights title was limited to federal elections, and the Equal

Employment Opportunity Commission was required to pursue employment discrimination complaints in a federal district court, where defendants would be entitled to a trial. Later in the process, similar behind-the-scenes efforts by the Johnson administration to woo the critical support of Senate minority leader Everett Dirksen eventually would make possible a coalition of centrist Republicans and liberals in the Senate in spite of the highly publicized opposition to the bill by the Republican party's presidential nominee that year, Senator Barry Goldwater of Arizona.[37]

Dramaturgical incrementalism would appear to be the most likely response whenever the balance of forces shifts in favor of challenging groups, whether because of aroused public opinion, a decision by the president to make a particular reform proposal a major agenda item, or some other cause. The key here is not the source of the shift in the balance but the availability of dramaturgy as a response. The typology developed in chapter 4 should be modified accordingly. Issues for which a conflictual demand pattern gives rise to an allocative outcome are characterized as nonincremental change in chapter 4; we can now characterize such issues more properly as instances of dramaturgical incrementalism (see Figure 5-1).

This apparent tendency for policymakers to respond to mass public arousal with dramaturgy rather than nonincremental change would come as no surprise to Murray Edelman, who emphasized the vulnerability of mass publics to symbolic reassurances. Edelman distinguished between organized interests (which he termed Pattern A groups) and unorganized mass publics (which he termed Pattern B groups). Pattern A groups not only possess an important advantage in formal organization, they also are characterized by a high degree of political sophistication and an interest in tangible rewards. By contrast, Pattern B groups tend to be unorganized and are primarily interested in symbolic reassurances that policymakers will protect their interests.[38] If Edelman's analysis is correct, public arousal would be insuffi-

FIGURE 5-1. Revised Typology of Policy Processes

	Consensual Demand Pattern	Conflictual Demand Pattern
Nondecision outcome	Nondecision: Barrier I	Nondecision: Barrier II
Delegative outcome	Self-regulative issues	Normal incrementalism: Partisan mutual adjustment
Allocative outcome	Distributive issues	Dramaturgical incrementalism

cient to produce genuine policy escalation of the sort Jones identified in the Clean Air case; by contrast, dramaturgical incrementalism can be considered an elaboration of the policy process Edelman regarded as normal.

The prevalence of dramaturgical incrementalism as a response to increased issue salience is at odds with Baumgartner and Jones's thesis that seemingly stable policy areas are subject in our system to periodic bursts of nonincremental change.[39] The cases examined here affirm that policymaking takes on new and different forms when well-established issues come under increased scrutiny because of mass public arousal, increased media attention, and the mobilization of new interests. This increased attention and activity can even lead to a significant redefinition of the issue. Moreover, as Baumgartner and Jones suggest, positive feedback may result in increased attention to one issue spreading throughout the system to affect other agendas as well, although the cases I examine in this chapter do not address this phenomenon. The prevalence of incremental *outcomes* in each of these cases suggests, however, that there is a large difference between bursts of attention to issues that previously lacked salience and genuinely nonincremental change.

NOTES

1. See Charles O. Jones, "Speculative Augmentation in Federal Air Pollution Policy-Making," *Journal of Politics* 36 (May 1974): 438–64, and *Clean Air: The Policies and Politics of Pollution Control* (Pittsburgh: University of Pittsburgh Press, 1975).

2. Michael T. Hayes, "Incrementalism as Dramaturgy: The Case of the Nuclear Freeze," *Polity* 19 (Spring 1987): 443–63.

3. Jones, "Speculative Augmentation."

4. Ibid., 439.

5. Ibid.

6. Charles O. Jones, *An Introduction to the Study of Public Policy*, 3rd ed. (Monterey, Calif.: Brooks/Cole Publishing Co., 1984), 91–92.

7. Jones, "Speculative Augmentation," 439.

8. David Braybrooke and Charles E. Lindblom, *A Strategy of Decision: Policy Evaluation as Social Process* (New York: Free Press, 1963), 71, as quoted in Jones, "Speculative Augmentation," 439.

9. Jones, "Speculative Augmentation," 443; Jones, *Clean Air*, 33–37.

10. On the evolution of the 1963 Clean Air Act, see Jones, *Clean Air*, 53–76.

11. Jones, *Clean Air*, 71–73.

12. Jones, "Speculative Augmentation," 442–44.

13. Jones, *Clean Air*, 71–73.

14. Ibid., 117–20.

15. On the evolution of the Air Quality Act of 1967, see Jones, *Clean Air*, 76–84.

16. Ibid., 122.

17. Ibid., 78–79.

18. Jones, "Speculative Augmentation," 447–48, and *Clean Air*, 83–84.

19. Jones, *Clean Air*, 128.

20. Jones, *Clean Air*, 175, and "Speculative Augmentation," 449.

21. See Chapter 5, "The Rise in Public Concern for the Environment, 1969–70," in Jones, *Clean Air*, 137–55; and Jones, "Speculative Augmentation," 449–52.

22. Charles O. Jones, *An Introduction to the Study of Public Policy*, 2nd ed. (North Scituate, Mass.: Duxbury Press, 1977), 107–109.

23. Jones, "Speculative Augmentation," 455.

24. Ibid., 452–53.

25. Ibid., 453.

26. Jones, *Clean Air*, 179–83.

27. Jones, "Speculative Augmentation," 453–57, and *Clean Air*, especially 203–205.

28. R. Shep Melnick, *Regulation and the Courts: The Case of the Clean Air Act* (Washington, D.C.: Brookings Institution, 1983).

29. On the desirability of change by "large increments," see Jones, *Clean Air*, 306–309; on problems arising from "legislating beyond capability," see Chapter 8, "Implementing Policy Beyond Capability," in Jones, *Clean Air*, 211–75, and Jones, "Speculative Augmentation," 459–64.

30. This account of the evolution of the nuclear freeze issue is drawn from Hayes, "Incrementalism as Dramaturgy." The events and assertions in the discussion that follows are fully documented in that work.

31. Murray Edelman, *The Symbolic Uses of Politics* (Urbana: University of Illinois Press, 1964), 36.

32. For an account of this negotiation process, see "MX Pulls Through Turbulent Year in Congress," *Congressional Quarterly Almanac*, 1983, vol. 39 (Washington, D.C.: Congressional Quarterly, Inc., 1984), 195–205.

33. On the House side, the key participants were Les Aspin (D-Wisc.), Al Gore, Jr. (D-Tenn.), and Norman Dicks (D-Wash.). A similar group in the Senate consisted of Charles Percy (R-Ill.), Sam Nunn (D-Ga.), and William S. Cohen (R-Me.). Although these groups had somewhat different concerns, together they became known as the "gang of six." See "MX Pulls Through Turbulent Year in Congress."

34. This deal between the Reagan administration and the congressional moderates explains the otherwise mysterious outrage within Congress years later when the Bush administration announced its intention to abandon the Midgetman missile while continuing to deploy the MX, on the grounds that budgetary pressures made continued development of two redundant weapons systems impossible. Because the original agreement was reached in secret, outraged legislators could

not explain convincingly why they felt betrayed by the administration's decision. They had a deal (albeit a secret deal), and now President Reagan's successor was repudiating the deal—and there was little or nothing they could do about it.

35. Jones, "Speculative Augmentation," 463.

36. See Jones, *Clean Air*, 193–201, for a discussion of press coverage of various legislative developments. See also page 205, where Jones characterizes the climate surrounding conference committee hearings. Although normally one would expect a compromise between the House and Senate versions, leading to a weakening of the Muskie bill, "media attention, acting as a surrogate for public concern, set some limits on maneuverability, more or less forcing the conference to report a bill close to the Senate version."

37. Charles and Barbara Whalen, *The Longest Debate: A Legislative History of the 1964 Civil Rights Act* (New York: New American Library, Mentor Books, 1985).

38. Edelman, *The Symbolic Uses of Politics,* 36.

39. Frank R. Baumgartner and Bryan D. Jones, *Agendas and Instability in American Politics* (Chicago: University of Chicago Press, 1993).

CHAPTER SIX

Health Care Reform Fails in 1993–94: A Barrier II Nondecision

On September 22, 1993, President Clinton unveiled his long-awaited initiative for reforming the nation's health care system in a prime-time address to a joint session of Congress.[1] Public opinion polls conducted at the time of the president's speech showed very strong public support for the president's initiative.[2] Although no one doubted that much bargaining and compromise would have to take place before final passage, health care reform seemed like an idea whose time had come. Republicans conceded that passage of major legislation seemed almost inevitable and expressed interest in working toward a bipartisan compromise.[3]

Nevertheless, on September 26, 1994—one year and four days after the president had launched his plan—Senate Majority Leader George Mitchell held a press conference to formally announce the abandonment of efforts to pass health insurance reform in the current Congress. In November 1994, the Republicans gained control of both houses of Congress. After just two years in which the White House and Congress were controlled by the same political party, we returned to divided government—this time with a Democratic president and a Republican Congress. Although Congress passed a law in 1996 that guaranteed portability of insurance coverage,[4] Republican control of the House and Senate ensured that there would be no further attempts at comprehensive reform for the foreseeable future.

In this chapter I provide a brief case study of this issue, which was arguably the most important policy battle of Clinton's first term. In terms of the typology developed in chapter 4, health care reform represented an attempt at nonincremental policy change. Conditions seemed ripe for a departure from majority-building incrementalism, inasmuch as the issue was driven by a widespread perception among policymakers that the public was demanding strong action on the issue. Add the election of a Democratic president who was determined to make health care reform the centerpiece of his domestic agenda, and the prospects for passage seemed very promising indeed.

A full-length book would be required to do justice to this case; indeed, two full-length books have been written about it.[5] Accordingly, I make no attempt here to provide a comprehensive account of events. Instead, I limit my discussion to why this initiative failed despite strong public support for some kind of action on the issue, the apparent receptivity of major interest groups that were active on the issue, President Clinton's strong push for passage, and the return—for the first time in 12 years—of unified Democratic control of the White House and Congress.

❏ PRESIDENTIAL LEADERSHIP AND THE NEED FOR MAJORITY-BUILDING

The legislative struggle over this issue—which featured an intensely conflictual demand pattern, the utter failure of Congress to pass any health care legislation at all, and the subsequent Republican victory in the 1994 midterm elections—clearly qualifies as a Barrier II nondecision. To account for this outcome, I analyze the events of this case in light of the two models of the policy process I developed in chapter 5. In this section, I discuss why high-salience presidential items tend to be characterized by majority-building incrementalism rather than public satisfying and policy escalation. In the sections that follow, I move on to a detailed review of events, focusing on each of the four dimensions of policymaking identified by Jones: characteristics of the issue area, institutions, decision-making patterns, and policy outcomes. I conclude the chapter with an analysis of the factors that contributed to a Barrier II nondecision outcome in this case rather than an incremental policy change.

In general, the main items in any president's agenda receive a high degree of media coverage. Media coverage is particularly high, however, when presidents "go public" in an effort to secure passage of their highest priorities. Under such circumstances, the issue becomes salient for the mass public without necessarily generating mass public arousal. As predicted by the majority-building incremental model, there typically is no clearly agreed-upon public interest on these issues, and a multiplicity of interest groups are active. The president, however, plays a critical role in representing broad, national interests.

Policy subsystems no longer dominate policy development on such issues, although they remain major participants. Presidential agenda status brings in high-level actors—particularly the party leadership in both houses of Congress, who are not necessarily involved on most issues. Although presidents work with the leaders of their party in Congress to develop legislative strategies, however, they ultimately have no control over the assignment of their proposals to congressional committees, which may even include referral to multiple committees. Nor do they have any control over who the members of these committees are, or which members serve as chairs. Congressional committees are independent centers of power and expertise even where the president's own party controls Congress; where the opposing party controls Congress, the president obviously is at an even greater disadvantage.

Thus, presidential elevation of an issue in no way removes the need for majority-building and tapering down. To the contrary, the president often takes the lead in forcing the system to address issues that are characterized by a high degree of group conflict, for which the prospects for success are poor. This was certainly the case for President Clinton and health care reform. Although presidential leadership inevitably increases media coverage—making the issue salient for the public—it does not eliminate the need to persuade Congress to go along.

If presidential involvement is insufficient to produce policy escalation, incremental outcomes are the most one can realistically hope for, and outright defeat of the president's proposals—a Barrier II nondecision—becomes a very real possibility. Presidential success on such issues depends on a variety of variables that already are familiar to students of the presidency: the strength of the president's party in Congress, the president's winning margin in the previous election, the extent to which Congress believes that election yielded a strong mandate for the president's program, the length of time that has elapsed since that election, and so on.[6]

In this light, the prospects for the passage of health care reform in 1993 were not nearly as promising as they appeared to many contemporary observers. Although the Democrats did control the White House and the Congress for the first time since 1980, they had a slim majority in the House and lacked the votes to overcome a Republican filibuster in the Senate. Bill Clinton had won with 43 percent of the vote in a three-candidate race, and the ambiguities of the campaign (particularly the unpopularity of the incumbent, the emphasis on the need for "change," and the centrality of the economic issue) had combined to dilute any mandate for health care reform.

◻ ISSUE AREA CHARACTERISTICS: AN ANXIOUS PUBLIC

Jones differentiated between issues that fail to attract public attention (i.e., most issues) and issues that are characterized by a level of mass public arousal that is so high that the normal need to build a majority is simply removed (see chapter 5). Although presidential elevation of health care reform dramatically increased the level of media coverage, the issue was not characterized by mass public arousal comparable to that exhibited by either the clean air or nuclear freeze case. The issue was not triggered by a "focusing event," as that term is usually defined.

On the health care issue, the mass public was more anxious than aroused. Careful analysis of the numerous polls conducted on the issue in 1993 and 1994 reveals a public that was concerned about health care without being really directive. Although most respondents recognized a need for significant reform, they nevertheless perceived significant strengths in the existing system. Early polls that appeared to suggest very high levels of support for the Clinton plan proved to be misleading inasmuch as later polls revealed a great deal of misinformation or ignorance about precisely what was included in the Clinton plan.[7]

The Issue Arises

The issue had been forced onto the national agenda by a special election in 1991. On April 4, 1991, Senator John Heinz of Pennsylvania was killed in a collision between a small private plane and a helicopter near Philadelphia. The state's Democratic governor selected Harris Wofford to replace Heinz until a special election could be held in November. Although Wofford had a distinguished record of public service,[8] he had never run for public office and had little name recognition. To challenge Wofford in the November election, Republicans selected Richard Thornburgh—a widely known and popular former governor of the state who had served as Attorney General in George Bush's cabinet. Although most journalists and political consultants thought Wofford had little chance to win, he defeated Thornburgh by 10 percentage points—creating a political shock wave that reached all the way to Washington. Although subsequent polls suggested that economic issues had been more damaging to Thornburgh than the health care issue, in Washington politicians of both parties attributed Wofford's surprise victory to a spot commercial suggesting that adequate health care coverage should be an entitlement for all Americans: "If criminals have a right to a lawyer, I think working Americans should have the right to a doctor."[9]

Health care reform was a lively issue during the Democratic presidential primaries in 1992, although inferring any clear mandate from the final results is difficult. Senator Bob Kerry of Nebraska made health care reform the central issue of his campaign; he advocated a Canadian-style single-payer plan. Kerry's failure to win any primaries could be interpreted (and was) to suggest low public support for comprehensive national health insurance.[10]

Health care reform likewise constituted a major difference between Bill Clinton and President Bush in the fall election campaign, given Clinton's clear commitment to some kind of initiative and the president's continued opposition. Clinton's campaign, however, emphasized the economy and the general theme of the need for change; this strategy was the obvious way to exploit voter dissatisfaction with Bush's handling of the recession. (James Carville, a political consultant with the Clinton campaign, had emphasized the need to stay on message with a sign in the campaign's Little Rock "war room" reminding campaign workers: "It's the economy, stupid.") Any clear electoral mandate for health care reform was diluted by the Clinton campaign's relentless emphasis on the vaguely defined need for change, along with Clinton's proclivity to take detailed positions on a vast array of other issues through town meetings and presidential debates. Given the seriousness and apparent urgency of the problem and the clear difference between Clinton and Bush over the issue, however, in the wake of Clinton's victory health care reform clearly figured to be a major issue—perhaps the major issue—of Clinton's first year in office.

Thus, in the case of health care reform, there was no focusing event to arouse mass public opinion. Wofford's upset victory over Thornburgh was a reflection of public concern over the issue rather than a catalyst for public arousal.

An Anxious Public

Although public opinion was not aroused about health care reform comparably to the clean air or nuclear freeze cases, the public clearly was anxious about the issue.[11] The nation's health care system was failing in important respects. By some estimates, at least 35 million Americans lacked any health insurance coverage at all. For those who had coverage, insurance premiums had been rising at an alarming rate for several years. Deductibles also were rising in most conventional indemnity plans, and many corporations dealt with the problem of rising costs by scaling back the services covered under their plans. Everywhere, Americans who were lucky enough to have coverage seemed to be paying more and more for plans that covered less and less. To make matters worse, a wave of corporate downsizing created anxiety among many workers throughout the economy that they might lose not only their jobs but also their insurance coverage, which typically was provided by employers as a fringe benefit.

Although polls taken immediately after Clinton's September 1993 speech pointed to strong public approval for his efforts to overhaul health care, subsequent polls revealed that most respondents supported the president's initiative without really understanding what it was; though there was strong public support for dealing with the problem, there was less commitment to any one solution, and the existing system was perceived as having some real strengths.[12] Moreover, despite the president's promises, no one could see how any plan could bring in the 35 million people lacking coverage, eliminate insurance companies' freedom to deny coverage to people with "preexisting conditions," *and* hold down costs.

In short, although many Americans with insurance coverage felt that they were paying more and more for less and less, things could get a lot worse. Inasmuch as guaranteeing coverage to the uninsured almost surely would raise rather than lower health care costs, many people could end up paying significantly more for a standard benefits package that covered even less than their current policy and reduced their freedom to choose a physician.[13]

☐ ISSUE AREA CHARACTERISTICS: MULTIDIMENSIONAL COMPLEXITY

In majority-building incrementalism, there typically is conflict over just what constitutes the public interest. The fact that a president chooses to make an issue a major agenda item does nothing to eliminate this conflict. Although mass public arousal can create a "pre-formed majority," presidents who seek to elevate issues still confront the need to build majorities. This situation clearly was the case for health care reform.

The Interests Mobilize

Any attempt at health care reform by necessity would involve a multiplicity of organized interests mobilized on various sides of the issue. Health care is a major segment of our economy, constituting approximately one-seventh of the country's gross national product (GNP). The Clinton proposal would have affected physicians, hospitals, health maintenance organizations (HMOs), private insurance providers, pharmaceutical manufacturers, Fortune 500 companies, and small businesses, among others. It also would have affected health insurance coverage for every American. Although many Americans had health insurance coverage through their employer, about 15 percent of the population (35–40 million people) had no insurance at all. In addition, senior citizens were well represented by a variety of lobbies ready to pounce on any provision that adversely affected Medicare coverage. To the extent that abortions would be covered under the new system, the Clinton proposal also invited lobbying by pro-choice and pro-life groups.

Given this vast array of organized groups representing very disparate interests, the task of majority-building would be extremely challenging, to say the least.[14] The only major interests that were not well represented in the struggle over health care reform were the uninsured—particularly the poor, who relied heavily on emergency room care and public clinics.[15]

Many of the interests that were potentially threatened by the Clinton proposal initially acknowledged the need for reform and expressed a willingness to work with the administration to shape the legislation. Dozens of bills were introduced in Congress, and reform proposals were advanced by business groups, trade unions, insurance companies, assorted policy experts, and even the American Medical Association (AMA), which historically had been a bitter enemy of national health insurance and Medicare.[16]

Business support for some kind of reform was particularly auspicious. Unlike most Western democracies, the United States has no system of national health insurance; instead, most Americans obtain health insurance coverage through their employer. Premiums for health insurance coverage had risen alarmingly for several years, putting American firms at a competitive disadvantage vis-à-vis foreign firms, for whom national health insurance eliminated the need to provide health benefits.[17]

Policy Alternatives

These groups disagreed, however, about how serious the problem was, what its causes were, and what solutions were appropriate. Four very different approaches had attracted significant support. Some liberal Democrats favored single-payer national health insurance modeled on the Canadian system; private insurance companies would no longer have any role under this system, which would administer all claims through a federal agency. The AMA had successfully branded this approach "socialized medicine" in the late 1940s when it was advocated by President Truman; after this defeat, reformers scaled back their ambitions, opting instead for a Medicare system that provided health insurance for senior citizens.[18] This approach would be funded through a substantial payroll tax much like the Social Security tax. Because the Democrats had taken a beating on the tax issue in the 1984 and 1988 presidential elections, moderate Democrats (including Bill Clinton) regarded this alternative as particularly vulnerable to attack.[19]

Centrist Democrats therefore gravitated toward a second alternative—called "play or pay"—which would require businesses to provide health care coverage to employees or pay into a fund for a governmental program to provide coverage for those who were not covered through their place of employment. This approach would significantly expand the number of people with health insurance by forcing almost all employers to participate in one form or another. This option was quintessentially incremental, building on the existing system in which most people received health insurance coverage through their employer and leaving in place the major elements of the current system: private insurers, HMOs, and Medicare. Health policy experts, however, suspected that "play or pay" would fail to control the rise in health care costs and worried that employers might "dump" employees with chronic health problems into a public insurance program that would become increasingly expensive and second-rate.[20]

As the health care issue began to attract more interest in Washington after Wofford's victory in Pennsylvania, the Bush administration had been forced to formulate a reform package of its own.[21] Beginning in 1991 and extending into the first year of the Clinton administration, Republicans in Congress advocated market-oriented reforms that would make incremental modifications in private health insurance markets—for example, via limits on malpractice liability, requirements that insurance companies accept all applicant groups, and elimination of provisions that permitted companies to deny coverage for preexisting conditions. These reforms would promote—but not guarantee—insurance coverage through tax credits to help low-income people buy insurance.[22]

A fourth approach developed by Stanford economist Alain Enthoven, "managed competition," would rely on the market to hold down escalating costs. Congress would design a standard benefits package that would be offered through employers. Ideally, employees would be able to select from several competing providers offering the standard package. Requiring a standard benefits package would force providers to compete with one another by offering the lowest price, thus holding down premium increases. Although this approach would significantly reduce the range of choice available to consumers to one or two standard packages, that sacrifice was regarded as necessary to eliminate the product differentiation that prevented consumers from judging whether they were getting the best price for the product they were buying. Clinton found this approach particularly attractive—as a candidate and later as president—because it seemed to offer a way to hold down health care costs while avoiding the need to impose new taxes on business or employees. From the start, however, he combined managed competition with universal coverage and government-enforced cost controls; Theda Skocpol termed his plan "inclusive managed competition."[23]

Thus, with Canadian-style single-payer national health insurance ruled out by the Clinton administration from the outset, attention was confined to three major alternatives—all of which may be characterized as incremental or piecemeal social reforms, albeit of varying scope.

❑ INSTITUTIONS: POLICY COMMUNITIES AND POLICY DEVELOPMENT

According to Jones, policy communities dominate policy development in the normal process of majority-building incrementalism. These policy communities—which consist of congressional committees and subcommittees, executive agencies, and affected interest groups—ordinarily take the lead in policy development; in terms of the concentric circles discussed in chapter 5, program development typically occurs within the innermost circle, subject to ratification by the broader political system.

A variety of high-level actors will be drawn in on high-salience presidential items, however—including the president and members of his staff, as well as party leaders in Congress. Although presidents may find consultation with existing policy communities necessary (and wise) in developing major agenda items, these policy communities will no longer dominate policy formulation. To the contrary, there can be a real effort by the administration to take control of policy development away from these power centers.

The Task Force on Health Care Reform

President Clinton attempted to take control over program development by creating a health care task force—headed by his wife, Hillary—to study the issue and develop a comprehensive proposal for reform. The Task Force on Health Care Reform comprised 511 people, most of whom were executive branch employees drawn from the Departments of Health and Human Services (HHS), Labor, Treasury, and Veterans' Affairs (VA), and the Office of Management and Budget (OMB). "Stakeholder groups"—those with financial or occupational interests in the health care system—were not officially included on the task force. Although many of these stakeholders were consulted individually or invited to appear at hearings, many of these groups resented their exclusion from the task force charged with developing the administration's proposal.[24]

Members of Congress also were excluded from the task force. By concentrating policy development within the executive branch and attempting to develop a comprehensive proposal without the involvement of members of Congress and major clientele groups, Clinton was following the same path Jimmy Carter had trod in developing his comprehensive energy package in 1977—an approach that created unnecessary resentment and suspicion among powerful committee chairs.

Jones has characterized Carter's conception of his representational role as "the trusteeship presidency." In this vision, members of Congress are regarded as oriented toward reelection and excessively responsive to special interests. By contrast, the president is entrusted to represent all the people, and he must act as a counterweight to the special interests if the system is to function properly. Congress and the public rely on the president to take the lead in setting the agenda and developing comprehensive policy proposals.[25] Presidents with a trusteeship orientation, such as Carter, identify particularly thorny issues and insist that they be addressed regardless of the political costs; this approach portrays the president as morally superior to reelection-minded members of Congress.

Moreover, because trusteeship presidents regard members of Congress as more interested in reelection than in doing what is right, such presidents tend to concentrate program development in the executive branch to a greater degree than other presidents.[26] Although President Clinton's willingness to accommodate interest groups on various other issues suggests that characterizing him as a trusteeship president in the same mold as Carter may be misleading, he nevertheless acted very much like a trustee on the health care issue in early 1993—taking on a complex issue historically characterized by a high degree of interest group conflict and concentrating policy development within the executive branch, excluding members of Congress and important stakeholder groups.

Originally, the task force was pledged to produce a proposal within the first 100 days after the president took office. This deadline was repeatedly pushed back, however—largely because of the intrinsic complexity of the issues involved, but also because other issues took center stage on the national agenda. In particular, the early months of the Clinton administration were preoccupied with formulating and securing congressional passage for the budget. Having inherited federal deficits that were much larger than previously forecast, the new president faced a crisis of confidence within the bond markets. A long struggle ensued between advocates for initiatives that had been central pledges in the 1992 campaign—particularly a middle-class tax cut and new expenditures for job training and education—and those who emphasized the need to raise taxes and cut spending to restore confidence within the bond markets. Eventually, the president came down on the side of the budget balancers, abandoning his middle-class tax cut and the investments in jobs and job training that had meant so much to him. In the face of unified Republican opposition, the president had to build a majority in both houses of Congress from within his own party. Although the president eventually secured passage of his budget—which may well have had a great deal to do with the health of the economy four years later when he ran for reelection—the struggle was long and difficult.[27] Final passage in the Senate came on August 6, 1993, well after the 100-day deadline for submission of health care reform to Congress. The president's speech to Congress unveiling the long-overdue health care reform initiative followed about six weeks later, on September 22nd.

Institutional Fragmentation

Try as he might to take control of the health care issue away from the policy community that had gradually developed around the issue, President Clinton could not avoid dealing with these independent centers of power. If he had been advancing health care reform in the British parliamentary system, as prime minister he would have had the power to determine the composition of the legislative committee that would hold hearings on his proposal and to designate who the chair of that committee would be. In the British system, there are very few permanent (what we would call "standing") committees, and those that do exist have little real power. Legislative proposals emanate from the cabinet, and the party leadership creates a special committee to hold hearings on each bill; these committees go out of existence as soon as the legislation has been considered. The party leadership chooses who the members of these committees will be and designates a chair. Thus, the circumstances are ideal for passing the prime minister's legislative program.

Clinton faced a very different situation in proposing health care reform to the Congress. In the British system, the House of Commons is sovereign and can accept or reject suggestions from the House of Lords as they please. By contrast, Clinton's program would have to pass through two co-equal houses of Congress. Moreover, in the American system, legislation is referred to standing committees of the House and Senate whose membership and chairs are outside the president's control. To make matters worse, the complexity of the task force's plan, combined with reforms adopted by Congress in the 1970s, meant that health care reform was subject to multiple referrals. In the House, health care reform had to be considered by three committees: Energy and Commerce, Ways and Means, and Education and Labor. In the Senate, two committees shared jurisdiction: Education and Labor, and Finance.[28]

In 1973, an ad hoc task force had been set up in the House to manage the legislative process on the energy issue, coordinating the deliberations of the various committees that shared jurisdiction over the issue. In 1993, by contrast, Democratic members were much too independent to submit to such a device, and the Democratic leaders in the House and Senate lacked the personal or institutional clout to force the issue. As a result, the leadership in both houses deferred to these five committees for several months.[29]

Democrats on these committees were far from united in supporting the Clinton plan; members advanced a wide variety of alternatives of their own. Clinton lost perhaps his most dependable supporter when Ways and Means chairman Dan Rostenkowski was forced to step down while under indictment for financial irregularities related to the House Post Office scandal. Rostenkowski's replacement, Pete Stark, had his own plan for reform that was based on an expansion of Medicare to include uninsured Americans.[30]

Budgetary Constraints

Moreover, congressional deliberations over the Clinton proposal operated within a final institutional constraint—the fiscal legacy of the Reagan and Bush administrations. President Reagan's 1981 tax cuts, in combination with a major defense buildup, led to gigantic federal budget deficits that dominated policymaking for the remainder of his administration. In 1985, Congress enacted the Gramm-Rudman law, which set a series of steadily declining deficit targets, to be enforced by automatic sequesters in the event that Congress and the president could not agree on a budget that met the target figure for any given year. The Gramm-Rudman targets were abandoned in 1990, when President Bush broke his 1988 campaign promise by including new taxes as part of a comprehensive budget agreement approved by Congress. Although Bush's reversal on taxes may have cost him reelection in 1992, the 1990 budget agreement outperformed Gramm-Rudman as a device for gaining control over federal spending. Among other things, the 1990 agreement separated federal spending into three distinct categories. Spending levels were capped within each category, and new initiatives that cost money (such as health care reform) would have to be paid for by tax increases or by spending cuts elsewhere in the same category.

The desire to avoid new taxes led Clinton to reject single-payer national health insurance—which would have required hefty payroll tax increases—and play-or-pay, which would have imposed new taxes on businesses. Equally important, the spending caps in the 1990 budget law required the Congressional Budget Office (CBO) to "cost out" options in advance to make sure they were "deficit neutral." At a time when legislative committees most needed the flexibility to compromise to design a package capable of winning a majority on the floor, rigid requirements for CBO approval created a time-consuming process that made deals even more difficult.[31]

☐ DECISION MAKING: THE NECESSITY FOR MAJORITY-BUILDING

The strong favorable reaction to the president's proposal from virtually every quarter contributed to a sense of optimism. Even in this heady early period, however, no one expected the Clinton plan to be enacted without significant modification; tapering down from the optimal to the acceptable was part of the administration's strategy all along.[32]

Opposition from Organized Interests

Subsequent events demonstrated, however, that much of this initial optimism was misplaced. To begin with, the support of many financial and institutional interests turned out to be contingent on substantial changes in the plan. Although some of these groups eventually endorsed the Clinton plan, their initial strategy was to pay lip service to the need for reform while registering criticisms of particular provisions that needed to be amended in Congress.[33]

As time went on, intense opposition to the president's plan emerged from various quarters. The AMA challenged major elements in the plan within a week of the president's speech.[34] Small business opposition, led by the National Federation of Independent Business, was particularly intense.[35] The Health Insurance Association of America was particularly effective in its opposition, financing a series of television advertisements featuring an average American couple ("Harry and Louise") who expressed various concerns about the Clinton plan—particularly fears that the plan would take away the patient's right to choose a physician, skepticism about a health care program run by government bureaucrats, and doubts that the Clinton plan could really contain health care costs and hold down premiums.[36]

Republican Opposition Emerges

Every bit as important, Republicans in Congress backed away from their initial expressions of support for a bipartisan bill. In a memo to congressional Republicans, conservative strategist Bill Kristol urged the party to defeat health care reform outright rather than work with Democrats to produce an acceptable bill through amendments:

> It will re-legitimize middle-class dependence for "security" on government spending and regulation. It will revive the reputation of the party that spends and regulates, the Democrats, as the generous protector of middle-class interests. And it will at the same time strike a punishing blow against Republican claims to defend the middle class by restraining government.[37]

Following Kristol's advice, Republicans challenged the idea that there was a health care "crisis" and highlighted contradictions that were inherent in the Clinton plan. In a transparent reversal, Senate Minority Leader Bob Dole abandoned any effort to work with the administration and moved instead to unify his troops in opposition—forcing Clinton once again to put together a majority by drawing almost exclusively on his own fragmented party. Over the next few months, moderate Republicans who had been willing to work with the Clinton administration to produce a bipartisan bill gradually succumbed to party pressure to defeat the president's initiative.

(The one conspicuous exception was Senator John Chafee of Rhode Island, who worked to the very end to develop a bill with bipartisan support.) Eventually, Senate Republicans mounted a filibuster against health care reform, forcing Democrats to come up with 60 votes to invoke cloture.

Mobilizing Public Support for a Complex and Unprecedented Plan

As Jones observed, trusteeship presidents must go outside Congress to build coalitions in support of their programs. This strategy is dictated by earlier decisions to exclude members of Congress and key clientele groups from the process of program development; it is reinforced by the clear signal this process sends that the high-minded president is taking on the narrow, special interests.[38] In the case of health care reform, however, the necessary mobilization of public support was made unusually difficult by the sheer complexity of the administration's plan (which was 1,342 pages long)[39] and the lack of historical analogies for key elements in the plan. In particular, purchasing alliances played a central role in the president's plan; individual businesses would join these regional alliances, which would be charged with purchasing health care coverage from insurance providers. In theory, these alliances would help small businesses, whose group premiums easily could be driven up by one or two individuals with costly ailments. They also would provide greater market power in offsetting the oligopolistic power of large insurance carriers such as Prudential, Metropolitan, and The Travelers. Whereas Medicare could be sold as building on a Social Security system that most voters already understood and supported, nothing comparable to purchasing alliances had ever existed before, so explaining them was difficult.[40]

In general, the administration dealt with the complexity of the Clinton plan by focusing speeches and advertisements on program goals and avoiding discussion of how the program would work.[41] This strategy contributed to public doubts that the program could deliver on its promises. Ultimately, polls suggested, the public never understood the Clinton plan. Ironically, polls found that the public often preferred the elements of the Clinton plan to various alternatives; unfortunately for the president, however, the public did not know what the elements of his plan were.[42] Public confusion was exacerbated by the tendency of various stakeholder groups to endorse reform in principle while opposing particular provisions, as well as the tendency of individual members of Congress to introduce variants of their own that differed only slightly from the Clinton plan.[43]

❏ FINAL OUTCOME AS A BARRIER II NONDECISION

The Clinton administration and the Democratic leadership in Congress finally admitted defeat on September 26, 1994, when Senate Majority Leader George Mitchell announced that there would be no further efforts to pass health care reform in the 103rd Congress. A few weeks later, in a stunning development, the 1994 midterm election gave Republicans control of the House and the Senate, and comprehensive health care reform was effectively dead. The first year of the 103rd Congress was consumed with efforts to pass the "Contract for America" and a protracted stalemate between the president and Congress over the budget.

In 1996, Congress returned to the issue of health care reform, passing the Kennedy-Kassebaum bill (which mandated insurance portability). The incremental nature of that reform is readily apparent. Kennedy-Kassebaum does not guarantee continued insurance coverage to employees who lose their jobs. It merely guarantees employees who are fortunate enough to have coverage through their jobs the right to buy some kind of coverage from the same carrier if they change jobs or get laid off. Insurance companies are free to charge higher premiums for coverage that may very well be much less generous. Kennedy-Kassebaum does nothing to help laid-off employees pay for this new policy, and it does nothing to extend coverage to the millions of Americans who lack any insurance coverage at all.[44]

Despite the defeat of the Clinton plan, developments in the private market—particularly the rapid growth of employer-sponsored managed care via HMOs and other prepaid health plans—have prevented a return to the escalating costs that prevailed in the late 1980s. However, HMOs have accomplished these economies by reducing patients' freedom to seek the care they feel they need and a variety of other cost-cutting devices, including shorter hospital stays for various ailments. Accordingly, the health care issue has reemerged in a new form, as Congress has become preoccupied with HMO reform.[45]

Although the health care system may no longer be in "crisis," there is little evidence to suggest that the problems that forced the issue onto the agenda from 1991 to 1993 have disappeared. The number of Americans who lack health insurance coverage has risen steadily (by almost 1 million a year) and now exceeds 41 million—one-sixth of the total population. Insurance companies have found ways to circumvent the Kennedy-Kassebaum law, excluding people with preexisting conditions and charging high premiums to individuals who choose to purchase continued coverage after changing or losing their jobs. Sweeping changes in welfare policy (see chapter 7) may inadvertently increase the number of uninsured children.[46] Budgetary costs under the Medicare program, which provides health insurance through the federal government for senior citizens, have continued to rise, and reform of that program is required to stave off bankruptcy.

❏ ANATOMY OF A NONDECISION

I have identified several factors that contributed to the defeat of health care reform in 1993–94. First and foremost was the gap between broad public support for change, which was recognized and acknowledged by almost all participants in the legislative struggle on health care reform, and the kind of pre-formed majority demanding strong action that Jones observed in the clean air case in 1970.

The Limits of "Going Public"

Presidents increasingly attempt to mobilize public opinion by "going public."[47] Although Ronald Reagan may have taken this tactic to its highest level, it has long been popular with the political left. First advanced by Woodrow Wilson,[48] it was advocated more recently by Thomas Vitullo-Martin as a strategy for securing nonincremental change in pollution policy.[49] According to Vitullo-Martin, real reform—that is, radical change—requires mobilization of mass political support that is sufficient to overcome entrenched interests associated with existing policies. Indeed, mobilization of political support sufficient to overcome entrenched interests virtually requires radical policy proposals that promise meaningful change in the lives of most citizens. Only the president, speaking for a national constituency, can mobilize this political support.

Clearly, Bill Clinton hoped to mobilize public support in this way behind his proposal for comprehensive health care reform. By Vitullo-Martin's reasoning, Clinton's eventual failure can be explained easily: Only a proposal for single-payer national health insurance would have been radical enough to generate the level of mass public support necessary to overcome entrenched interests. Indeed, Clinton was criticized from the left for rejecting single-payer alternatives in favor of a centrist proposal,[50] as well as for failing to "go public" again later on in the majority-building process.[51]

Unfortunately, although presidential elevation of an issue virtually guarantees it a level of salience that is uncharacteristic of normal majority-building incrementalism, it does not necessarily produce a pre-formed majority that policymakers must satisfy. Any mandate for health care reform was muddied by the circumstances of the 1992 presidential election, which focused heavily on the economic failures of the incumbent and emphasized the need for "change," broadly defined. Moreover, Clinton was elected with only 43 percent of the vote in a three-way race, further reducing the strength of any mandate he might claim.

Although there was a kind of bandwagon effect in response to President Clinton's elevation of the issue, it was much more limited than that associated with the public-satisfying model. Although interests that potentially were threatened by the president's proposal paid lip service to the need for reform as long as broad public support seemed to dictate some kind of legislation, they were quick to mobilize in opposition as soon as public support waned.

Ironically, the tendency Jones observed for members of Congress to climb on the bandwagon by sponsoring legislation of their own worked to the president's disadvantage in this case. With multiple referrals, the Clinton plan had to move through five House and Senate committees. Initially, the president could count on support for his plan from only one of these chairs—Dan Rostenkowski of Ways and Means; the other committee chairs all advanced alternative proposals of their own. Midway through the process, Rostenkowski was forced to step down, and his successor proposed yet another alternative to the president's plan. Because public opinion was anxious rather than truly directive, the issue was characterized by multidimensional complexity and the need for tapering down—much as with majority-building incrementalism.

Nevertheless, the health care issue was a good deal more salient than most issues. Although mass public opinion was not aroused, the issue was regarded by the media as a major element in President Clinton's legislative program and perhaps the most important initiative in social policy since the New Deal. As such, it received an extraordinary degree of media coverage from beginning to end—which in itself made the issue salient for the mass public.

As Timothy Cook has shown, however, extensive media coverage of an issue changes policymaking in important ways without necessarily producing mass public arousal.[52] First, extensive media coverage certifies the importance of the issue. Furthermore, media coverage tends to frame the issue for the mass public and thus inevitably sets in motion a battle among protagonists over how the issue will be defined. Finally, extensive media coverage significantly raises the costs of doing nothing for all involved: "If elected officials are worried about angry reactions from constituents, they may feel they must deal with the problem or run the risk of being blamed for doing nothing at all."[53] This dynamic often forces reluctant legislators to address issues that are plagued by high levels of group conflict and low probability of success that they might prefer to ignore. This is undoubtedly one of the main contributions of presidential leadership within our system.

President Clinton's eventual failure on the health care reform issue—which clearly featured a high level of group conflict and a low probability of success—appears to have contributed to the public's sense that the Democrats had failed when they were given unified control of the White House and Congress, even though Clinton's first two years had resulted in important legislation on the budget, trade, crime, and governmental reorganization, among other issues. By contrast, although a defeat on a less salient issue such as the National Service Corps (a textbook example of majority-building incrementalism) would be disappointing to the president, it would not generate an electoral backlash within the mass public.

The Balance of Forces Favors Opposition Groups

Given the need to engage in normal majority-building, several additional factors came into play in this case to produce a Barrier II nondecision rather than a tapered-down incremental policy outcome. First, although Congress's failure to pass any bill reflected the equilibrium of active groups, as described in chapter 4, it also reflected the failure of important beneficiary groups to mobilize—particularly the 35–40 million people who lacked any insurance coverage under the existing system. Many of these people were desperately poor and dependent on emergency rooms or public clinics for care. Most of these poor uninsured Americans were homeless people, often gay or bisexual men of color, many of whom did not speak English or vote.[54] Even if they had succeeded in mobilizing, these groups would have been at a severe disadvantage in terms of legitimacy, strategic position, and expertise.

Second, several stakeholders who had initially endorsed reform eventually mobilized in opposition. Although a succession of events that made health care reform seem like an idea whose time had come initially forced them to pay lip service to the need for reform, they withdrew this support as soon as the president's plan began to look vulnerable. Ultimately, the plan was opposed by a variety of organized interests: small businesses, physicians' groups, insurance companies, pharmaceutical companies, and others.

In this regard, the conscious decision by congressional Republicans to work to defeat health care reform was particularly critical. According to Lawrence D. Brown, federal role breakthroughs typically are followed by a period of "agenda convergence" as previous opponents come to accept the legitimacy of the new federal activity. Policy conflicts then come to center around the best means to achieve ends that are widely shared within the population as well as within both political parties.[55] Although Medicare clearly was a Democratic initiative, its extraordinary popularity forced Republicans at least to pay lip service to the need for the program. As William Kristol convincingly argued, however, passage of the president's health security initiative had the potential to realign the electorate by relegitimizing big governmental solutions to problems and by creating a new middle-class entitlement that would draw large numbers of voters back to the Democratic party. Whatever the Republicans may have felt about Medicare (Newt Gingrich may have revealed their real feelings in 1995, when the Republicans finally controlled both houses of Congress), there surely was no agenda convergence on the need for the Democrats to be the nation's majority party.

In the realm of Barrier II nondecisions, advantaged groups effectively mobilize to defeat overt reform efforts by or on behalf of disadvantaged groups. In this case, the prime beneficiaries of the status quo—small businesses, physicians' groups, private insurance companies, pharmaceutical manufacturers, and so on—joined with Republicans to defeat the president's initiative.

Multiple Veto Points Favor Opponents of Reform

Finally, our system of checks and balances gave a decided advantage to this coalition of groups seeking to defeat health care reform by creating a system of multiple veto points (as described in chapter 2). In particular, our system—in distinct contrast to a parliamentary system—includes a genuinely independent, bicameral Congress that can say no to any president and prevail. Moreover, under our system, legislative proposals must pass through standing committees that are completely out of the president's control. The president has no say in the membership of these committees and must deal with whatever chairs he finds in place when he submits his proposals. When the legislation is particularly complex, as this proposal was, multiple referrals come into play—creating even more veto points. Although this legislative obstacle course is defensible, inasmuch as it fosters persuasion and deliberation rather than coercion, there can be no question

that it made blocking President Clinton's health care reform proposal—which, for all its expansive scope, nevertheless constituted piecemeal social reform—much easier.

President Clinton's failure to secure health care reform in 1993–94
contrasts with Richard Nixon's success in securing revenue sharing and
block grants two decades before. Nixon faced a political environment that
was every bit as bleak as that Clinton inherited. Nixon too had won by a
plurality in a three-way race. If anything, Nixon emerged from the campaign
with even less of an issue mandate than Clinton had, and with the
opposition party decisively in control of both houses of Congress. Nixon
advanced two high-salience presidential agenda items in his first year in
office: a negative income tax proposal to reform welfare and a proposal for
general revenue sharing to provide federal aid to states and localities with
a minimum of strings attached. Although Nixon failed, predictably, in his
attempts to secure passage of the negative income tax, he succeeded against
these same large odds in passing revenue sharing. The difference between
the two issues is almost surely attributable to the consensus prevailing
within the policy community in the late 1960s on the problems plaguing
categorical grant programs and the consequent need to develop a new form
of federal aid that would give states and localities more freedom of action.
As I show in chapter 7, a similar consensus within the policy community on
problems plaguing the existing welfare system contributed to the passage
of welfare reform in 1995–96.

NOTES

1. Adam Clymer, "Clinton Asks Backing for Sweeping Change in the Health
System," *New York Times*, 23 September 1993, 1.

2. See, for example, Robin Toner, "Poll on Changes in Health Care Finds
Support Amid Skepticism," *New York Times*, 22 September 1993, 1.

3. See Linda Feldmann, "Republicans Seek to Be Included In Crafting Health-
Care Reform," *Christian Science Monitor*, 19 August 1993, 1; see also Adam Clymer,
"Dole Gathering Broad Backing for a G.O.P. Health Care Plan," *New York Times*, 30
June 1994, 1.

4. Prior to the passage of the 1996 law, most employees who lost or changed
jobs could no longer be covered by the group plan offered by the firm to its employees, although some insurance providers did permit employees to retain their coverage
by continuing to pay premiums. Premiums charged to individuals purchasing coverage in this way, however, were not as low as those charged to members of the group.

The 1996 law made this portability provision universal, requiring insurance
providers to allow employees to retain their coverage after leaving the employee

group. The law continues to allow providers to charge higher rates for individuals; predictably, a new controversy has arisen over the issue as premiums charged to individuals in these circumstances have proven to be significantly higher than those charged to employees who qualify for group plans.

5. Theda Skocpol, *Boomerang: Health Care Reform and the Turn Against Government* (New York: W. W. Norton and Company, 1996), and Haynes Johnson and David S. Broder, *The System: The American Way of Politics at the Breaking Point* (Boston: Little, Brown and Co., 1996).

6. Paul C. Light, *The President's Agenda: Domestic Policy Choice from Kennedy to Carter* (Baltimore: Johns Hopkins University Press, 1982).

7. Karlyn H. Bowman, *The 1993–94 Debate on Health Care Reform: Did the Polls Mislead the Policy-Makers?* (Washington, D.C.: American Enterprise Institute for Public Policy Research, 1994).

8. Wofford had served in the Justice Department under President Kennedy and had played an important, albeit unheralded, role in the civil rights struggle of that period. He also had served, more recently, as state chairman of the Pennsylvania Democratic Party and the state's Secretary of Labor and Industry. A law school professor, he also served as founding president of the State University of New York's College at Old Westbury, and he served as president of Bryn Mawr College, near Philadelphia, for eight years. See Johnson and Broder, *The System,* 59.

9. Johnson and Broder, *The System,* 59–60. See also Skocpol, *Boomerang,* 25–30.

10. John Dillin, "Kerry's Single-Issue Bid Appears Out of Breadth," *Christian Science Monitor,* 11 February 1992, 1.

11. V. O. Key, Jr., "Patterns of Distribution," in *Public Opinion and American Democracy,* Part I (New York: Alfred A. Knopf, 1961), 27–93.

12. For a thorough treatment of the polls on this issue, see Bowman, *The 1993–1994 Debate on Health Care Reform.*

13. Bowman, *The 1993–1994 Debate on Health Care Reform,* 24–32.

14. Johnson and Broder, "The Interests," in *The System,* 194–224; Skocpol, "Mobilizing Against Government," in *Boomerang,* 133–72.

15. Johnson and Broder, *The System,* 247–48.

16. Skocpol, *Boomerang,* 30.

17. Laurent Belsie, "From Business, Urgent Cries for Reform," *Christian Science Monitor,* 21 November 1991, 6.

18. Theodore R. Marmor, *The Politics of Medicare* (Chicago: Aldine, 1970).

19. Skocpol, *Boomerang,* 32–33.

20. Ibid., 33–35.

21. Marshall Ingwerson, "Bush Plan for Health Care Market-Based," *Christian Science Monitor,* 6 February 1992, 1.

22. Skocpol, *Boomerang,* 30–31.

23. Skocpol, *Boomerang,* 39–47. See also Marshall Ingwerson, "Health Care: The Anatomy of a Reform," *Christian Science Monitor,* 22 September 1993, 1.

24. Skocpol, *Boomerang*, 56–57.

25. Charles O. Jones, *The Trusteeship Presidency: Jimmy Carter and the United States Congress* (Baton Rouge: Louisiana State University Press, 1988), 1–6.

26. Ibid., 79.

27. See Bob Woodward, *The Agenda: Inside the Clinton White House* (New York: Simon and Schuster, 1994).

28. Adam Clymer, "Long Legislative Route for Clinton Health Plan," *New York Times*, 27 February 1994, 20, and Skocpol, *Boomerang*, 100–101.

29. Skocpol, *Boomerang*, 102.

30. Ibid., 105.

31. Ibid., 102.

32. Ibid., 4–6.

33. Ibid., 95.

34. Robert Pear, "Doctors Rebel Over Health Plan in Major Challenge to President," *New York Times*, 30 September 1993, 1.

35. Robin Toner, "Small Business Is Large in Opposing Health Plan," *New York Times*, 26 April 1994, 1.

36. Skocpol, *Boomerang*, 134–39.

37. Johnson and Broder, *The System*, 234. William Kristol was and is highly influential within conservative circles. He is the son of Irving Kristol and former chief of staff for Vice President Dan Quayle. William Kristol founded a new think tank—The Project for a Republican Future—and a conservative magazine (*The Weekly Standard*).

38. Jones, *The Trusteeship Presidency*, 79.

39. Skocpol, *Boomerang*, 118.

40. Ibid., 120–25.

41. Ibid., 115–17; see also 126–27.

42. Ibid., 116–17; see also 130.

43. Ibid., 129–30.

44. Ibid., 194.

45. Ibid., 196.

46. Robert Pear, "Government Lags in Steps to Widen Health Coverage," *New York Times*, 9 August 1998, 1.

47. Samuel Kernell, *Going Public: New Strategies of Presidential Leadership*, 2nd ed. (Washington, D.C.: CQ Press, 1993).

48. Woodrow Wilson, *Congressional Government: A Study in American Politics*, 15th ed. (Boston: Houghton, Mifflin and Company, 1900), and *Constitutional Government in the United States* (New York: Columbia University Press, 1921). See also Jeffrey Tulis, *The Rhetorical Presidency* (Princeton, N.J.: Princeton University Press, 1987).

49. Thomas Vitullo-Martin, "Pollution Control Laws: The Politics of Radical Change," in *The Politics of Eco-Suicide*, ed. Leslie L. Roos, Jr. (New York: Holt, Rinehart, and Winston, 1971).

50. See, for example, David Corn, "Health Care Reform—Round I: Big Players vs. Single Payer," *The Nation*, April 26, 1993, 547–50.

51. Bernard Sanders, "Back Room Deals Won't Do It, Clinton Must Go to the People," *The Nation*, June 21, 1993, 865–67.

52. Timothy Cook, *Making Laws, Making News: Media Strategies in the U.S. House of Representatives* (Washington, D.C.: Brookings Institution, 1989), 120–25.

53. Ibid., 122.

54. Johnson and Broder, *The System*, 247–49.

55. Lawrence D. Brown, *New Policies, New Politics: Government's Response to Government's Growth* (Washington, D.C.: Brookings Institution, 1983).

Chapter Seven

Welfare Reform, 1995–96:
Self-Regulation as Calculated Risk

In August 1996, President Clinton signed the Personal Responsibility and Work Opportunity Reconciliation Act of 1996, abolishing the Aid to Families with Dependent Children (AFDC) program, which had provided monthly payments to female heads of households with dependent children for six decades. In its place, the new law provided block grants to the states. Although the amount of these block grants would be fixed in Washington—enabling Congress to get control over the costs of the program for the first time—there were few stipulations from Washington about how the states should spend the money. In particular, the states were no longer required to provide cash payments to recipients as they had done under AFDC.

The welfare reform case exhibits some characteristic features of piecemeal social engineering. Over the years, a consensus had developed within both political parties that welfare dependency was a serious problem that needed to be ameliorated. Reformers at the national level in 1995–96 built on a series of policy experiments conducted at the state level via the waiver process.[1] As a result of these experiments, policymakers possessed a good deal of information about the potential effectiveness of various strategies for moving people from welfare to work.

At the same time, there can be little doubt that the new law constituted a policy change of large scope. A federal program that had been in existence for 61 years was abolished; states were no longer required to provide monthly payments to beneficiaries. In place of AFDC, Congress enacted a block grant program that gave the states an extraordinary degree of freedom to experiment with new approaches to welfare. How can we explain this decision by Congress and the president to make such a sharp change in direction in welfare policy? Why did welfare reform succeed where health care reform failed?

In this chapter, I show that enduring policy breakthroughs typically occur—if at all—very late in the life cycle of an issue, when the conditions for rational policymaking have been satisfied after long experience with the policy. In the first section of this chapter I identify the life cycle of policies. In the second section I explore what has to happen over time for an enduring policy breakthrough to occur; in particular, these policy breakthroughs require the development of what I refer to as *consensual objectives* and *consensual expectations* regarding cause-and-effect relationships among variables that are critical to the policy area. Where neither of these conditions is satisfied, incremental policymaking is all that can be realistically attempted; Lindblom regarded this situation as the normal case. Where both of these conditions are satisfied simultaneously, however, rational decision making leading to coherent solutions to persistent public problems is possible; these policy breakthroughs, in contrast to the dramaturgical incrementalism of the clean air case, can be enduring.

Unfortunately, such breakthroughs are by no means an inevitable result of the passage of time. To the contrary, consensual objectives and consensual expectations may not develop together or at the same rates. Uneven development of these two critical variables can give rise to two new classes of policy problems, which I term pure problems of *value conflict* and pure problems of *knowledge base*. Of these two situations, pure problems of knowledge base are by far the more tractable. Where there is a consensus on objectives—and policy expansion—among participants, rapid incremental change is possible. Where the consensus is that existing policy has failed, however, warranting a sharp change in direction, major policy departures are possible even though the knowledge base remains inadequate. These sharp policy departures fall under the heading of "calculated risks," as described by Dahl and Lindblom four decades ago.

In the remainder of the chapter I focus on welfare reform in the 1990s. I argue that welfare reform is best understood as an instance of a calculated risk. A broad bipartisan consensus existed about the bankruptcy of existing welfare policy and the need for "an end to welfare as we know it." In general, policymakers agreed on the need to convert AFDC from a system of cash payments to a labor market policy aimed at moving welfare recipients from welfare to work. At the same time, however, a wealth of research suggested that no one really knew how to do this. In short, welfare reform in 1995–96 was a pure problem of knowledge base. Virtually everyone agreed that a sharp new direction was needed in welfare policy, but no one could be certain what the ultimate impact would be on poor women with dependent children.

There was little agreement on the precise direction welfare reform should take beyond this bipartisan consensus on the need to "end welfare as we know it." Welfare reform stalled repeatedly as the House, the Senate, and the president took different positions on a wide variety of issues. Throughout this protracted conflict, state governors continued to press for conversion of AFDC into a block grant that would give them broad latitude to experiment with different approaches to the challenge of moving people from welfare to work. Ultimately, conversion of AFDC into a block grant enabled politicians in both parties (and in Congress and the White House) to claim that they had dramatically changed welfare without having to come up with a clear-cut strategy for placing former recipients into jobs.

In terms of the typology I laid out in chapter 4, welfare reform in the 1990s qualifies as a self-regulatory issue inasmuch as policymakers responded to a consensual demand pattern by delegating autonomy to organized interests seeking to regulate their own behavior. Whereas most instances of self-regulatory policy involve oligopolistic industries seeking to stabilize cartels via economic regulation, welfare reform constitutes an unusual case. Here, state governors sought autonomy in the administration of welfare. Initially, they met with some resistance as various congressional factions sought to impose new and different restrictions on the administration of welfare—for example, mandating a ceiling on the number of children for which a welfare recipient could receive monthly payments. Ultimately, however, there was little everyone involved could agree on beyond the need to do something dramatic; conversion of AFDC into a block grant fit the bill in this regard, while minimizing the need for agreement in other areas.

❑ THE LIFE CYCLE OF ISSUES

The life cycle of policies I develop here builds on Lawrence Brown's distinction between "breakthrough" and "rationalizing" policies. Where breakthrough policies establish a new federal role, rationalizing policies represent efforts to fix problems arising out of experience with existing policies.[2] When Lindblom argues that policymakers typically build on existing policy, he is recognizing that most policies represent rationalizing policies. Every policy, however, must originate as a new policy.

I build on Brown's work to develop a fourfold classification of policies, from which I derive a predictable life cycle of the evolution of policies. The first dimension differentiates between breakthrough and rationalizing policies. The second dimension focuses on the state of the available knowledge base, thus building on Charles O. Jones's study of the 1970 clean air case. This dimension distinguishes between policies in which the available knowledge base is limited and those in which it has expanded significantly through the development of a policy community surrounding the issue and years of experience in implementing and reauthorizing the legislation. The resulting four categories are displayed in Figure 7-1.

Ordinarily, knowledge base tends to develop gradually, at best. As the federal government takes on new responsibilities, policy communities consisting of congressional committees and executive agencies with jurisdiction over the issue, along with any interested clientele groups, eventually develop. As these policy communities gain experience with the issue via implementation and reauthorization, the knowledge base will tend to expand. Thus, the available knowledge base almost inevitably will be limited when the federal government first takes on a new function. Accordingly, nonincremental innovations will be rare, at best—if not nonexistent.

Normally, policies will originate as federal role breakthroughs and then move into a prolonged period of incremental rationalizing policy. This situation is essentially what occurred in the clean air case: Mass public arousal gave rise to a dramatic expansion in federal authority, which was followed by a long period of incremental rationalizing policy as policymakers grappled with divisive issues such as the energy crisis, prevention of significant deterioration, and so on. Arguably, the 1990 Clean Air Act's provision for auctioning off emissions rights constituted a rationalizing breakthrough; this breakthrough occurred, however, after two decades of experience implementing the 1970 Act.

Although the clean air case eventually gave rise to a rationalizing breakthrough, such breakthroughs are not inevitable. The development of

FIGURE 7-1. Typology of Policies

	Breakthrough Policies	Rationalizing Policies
Adequate knowledge base	Nonincremental innovations	Rationalizing breakthroughs
Inadequate knowledge base	Federal role breakthroughs	Incremental rationalizing policies

coherent solutions to persistent public problems can take place only when the conditions for rationality are satisfied within the policy community after long experience with the policy. John Kingdon referred to this phenomenon as "tipping toward a solution" within the policy community.[3]

❏ RATIONALITY WITHIN THE POLICY COMMUNITY

Lindblom consistently argued that rational-comprehensive decision making requires agreement on objectives and an adequate knowledge base. I refer to these two conditions as consensual objectives and consensual expectations. Whereas Lindblom believed that these conditions will almost never be met, I argue that long experience with a policy can produce one or both of these conditions.

Consensual Objectives

Consensus on objectives is essential to rational decision making. Whenever there is no agreement on ends, means-ends analysis breaks down because determining what "best" means becomes impossible. Lindblom believed that this requirement seldom would be met inasmuch as most values come into conflict with other important values sooner or later, forcing policymakers to make tradeoffs. If nothing else, budget considerations will arise sooner or later; all public expenditures have opportunity costs.

Policymakers can agree on objectives, however, without systematically examining every alternative value mix or definition of the problem. Consensual objectives may merely reflect an inability to conceive of alternatives to the prevailing social order—as in the nondecision Barrier I cell. Alternatively, consensual objectives may merely reflect a restricted circle of decision makers; within the distributive and self-regulatory arenas in the typology in chapter 4, the consensual demand pattern typically stems from the failure of important groups affected by the policy (particularly consumers and taxpayers) to mobilize effectively.

Most important, however, is the possibility that consensual objectives may reflect what Brown termed "agenda convergence."[4] According to Brown, breakthrough policies typically are characterized by a high degree of conflict among social or economic interests; often such policies are enacted only after years of political struggle. Once these policies are in place, however, the new federal role tends to become widely accepted within the population and among policymakers. Conflict shifts from questions of ends (whether the federal government should take on a particular role) to means (how best to perform functions that are now broadly popular).

Consensual Expectations

The second dimension focuses on the extent to which decision makers understand the problem at hand. As Lindblom suggested, problems ordinarily are complex, giving rise to a variety of alternative interpretations and severely taxing policymakers' inherently limited cognitive capacities. Information costs inevitably limit the analysis of options. Important consequences are all-too-often unknown, as a complete understanding of cause-and-effect relationships would require comprehensive theories that are "greedy for facts" and "constructed only through a great collection of observations."[5]

Where problems are well-understood, however, there can be agreement—at least among specialists in the area—regarding the relevant variables for analysis, the nature of important interrelationships among these variables, and the most appropriate questions for further research. In short, there is a common language and agreement on fundamentals regarding how the world works.[6] Although the history of scientific revolutions suggests caution in imputing a high degree of objective understanding of most problems, we can distinguish between subjects characterized by substantial agreement on basic facts regarding the problem at hand and problems lacking such a paradigm. Robert Rothstein has termed such agreement on a common paradigm for understanding events "consensual knowledge": "a body of belief about cause-effect and ends-means relationships among variables (activities, aspirations, values, demands) that is widely accepted by the relevant actors, irrespective of the absolute or final 'truth' of these beliefs."[7]

It is important to stress here, as Rothstein does, the possibility that an operative consensus regarding the consequences of various alternatives may be disconfirmed by subsequent events. In 1993, for example, many health planners within the Clinton administration were confident that cost control and improved service quality could be achieved simultaneously through the operation of the marketplace in combination with managed care. Today, after several years' experience with managed care plans initiated by the private sector, much of that optimism is gone. Almost no one now believes that the health care system can offer better service to people at a lower price.[8]

Thus, this second dimension of the reformulated typology (following Lindblom) may be understood as a continuum, with the ideal situation at the far right-hand side of the continuum. To stress the fallibility and tentativeness of any such consensus, I depart slightly from Rothstein's terminology here; I refer to this situation as one of *consensual expectations*. At the other end of the continuum is the more normal case (the dominant case, according to Lindblom)—in which complex problems give rise to a variety of alternative interpretations, information costs preclude a comprehensive analysis of options, and important consequences are not known for many alternatives. Building again on Rothstein, I term this situation *conflictual expectations*.

We may combine these two continua to produce a typology of decision-making conditions, as shown in Figure 7-2.

The Realm of Normal Incrementalism

Quadrant 1 clearly is the realm of *normal incrementalism*. As Lindblom observed, problems typically are complex and poorly understood. Conflict over important values or tradeoffs among values necessitates majority-building through a process of partisan mutual adjustment. In the language of Jones's majority-building incrementalism, there is no agreement on any clearly defined conception of the public interest; instead, politics necessarily involves a clash of interests. Outcomes in this quadrant typically are incremental.

As I discuss in chapter 6, the health care policy area was (and still is) characterized by conflictual objectives and conflictual knowledge, placing it squarely within the realm of normal incrementalism. The Clinton plan in all its incarnations sought to address two mutually incompatible goals simultaneously: cost containment and extension of coverage to previously uninsured Americans. Achieving these two goals at the same time was difficult, if not impossible. The Republicans understood this difficulty and made it

FIGURE 7-2. Typology of Environments Facing Policy Communities

	Conflictual Objectives	Consensual Objectives
Conflictual Expectations	1) Normal incrementalism	4) Pure problems of knowledge base
Consensual Expectations	2) Pure problems of value conflict	3) Rationalizing breakthroughs via rational decision making

the basis of their campaign against the bill. The average family had serious complaints about their health care coverage; yet Americans also clearly recognized that they could be worse off if the government mandated a basic benefit plan that offered less complete coverage than many private plans currently on the market and then charged a high premium to subsidize the extension of coverage to the 35–40 million people who had no coverage under the present system (many of whom were either too poor to buy coverage or suffered from serious illnesses that made them unattractive to private insurers). The one alternative that might (and I emphasize the word *might* here) have attained the twin goals of expanding coverage and containing costs was a single-payer plan—and that route was ruled out from the outset.

With regard to the knowledge base, there was disagreement about how serious the problem was, what its causes were, and what solutions were appropriate—from holistic social reforms, such as single-payer plans, through the most incremental adjustments (mandating portability). Managed care and play-or-pay fell somewhere between these two extremes. Republicans, with a few isolated exceptions, showed little enthusiasm for any of these approaches but quarreled among themselves over whether to oppose the Clinton bill outright or try to work toward a bipartisan bill that would give them some share of the credit for a popular initiative.

To the extent that rationalizing breakthroughs require the development of consensual expectations and consensual objectives within the policy community, they are beyond presidential control. They depend on where an issue is in its life cycle. Although health care reform was widely understood to be the biggest and most important new program in the president's agenda, and the Clinton administration saw its proposal as the most important social policy initiative since the New Deal, the plan did not constitute a genuine rationalizing breakthrough inasmuch as the policy community was never characterized by consensual expectations or consensual objectives. To the contrary, if there had been a rationalizing breakthrough in the pipeline when Clinton took office, there would have been no need to appoint a task force to develop a solution. Nor would the administration have had to postpone the task force's report repeatedly. The Clintons were trying to formulate a rationalizing breakthrough where the policy community, in years of dealing with the issue, had failed to produce one.

President Clinton made matters worse through at least two serious mistakes that probably contributed to the defeat of the legislation. In view of the lack of any genuine rationalizing breakthrough—and the consequent need to operate within the constraints of normal incrementalism—the president can be criticized for adopting a trusteeship orientation toward his office on this issue that led him to repeat some of the same mistakes Jimmy Carter had made in dealing with Congress and important stakeholder groups. Moreover, given the broad public support that existed in 1993 for reform along the lines Clinton advocated, the administration can be faulted for failing to present the elements of the plan more clearly. The fact that public opinion polls revealed broad public support for elements of the president's plan and a widespread ignorance of the precise contents of the plan strongly suggests that there was a significant failure to educate the public. Even without these mistakes, however, the president probably could not have achieved anything more than an incremental rationalizing policy at this stage of the life cycle of the health care issue.

Pure Problems of Value Conflict

The critical importance of agreement on objectives is readily apparent from Quadrant 2, which consists of *pure problems of value conflict*. The contemporary abortion issue provides an excellent example of such a problem. Although scientists remain unable to say precisely when life begins, they know a great deal about the evolution of the fetus from conception to birth. The intense conflicts aroused by this issue are rooted in fundamental conflicts over values: At what point does a fetus become a life, and to what protections (if any) is it entitled prior to that point? Such conflicts are not likely to be resolved by new additions to the scientific knowledge base.

Within the realm of pure value disagreement, potential winners and losers from proposed policies often are acutely aware of their stake in alternative outcomes. To the extent that self-interest is self-evident for most participants, there is little to temper conflict.[9] The recurring efforts to reform Social Security financing provide an excellent example of such an issue. Social Security is a vexing issue for policymakers precisely because the underlying problem is so well understood and because any solution to it must have almost immediate redistributive consequences. Any serious attempt to reform Social Security must impose hardships on some politically aware groups; the issue, essentially, is whose ox will be gored. Politicians are understandably reluctant to impose costs that will be readily perceived by the groups involved.[10]

This situation is in distinct contrast to the realm of normal incrementalism. Where problems are subject to alternative definitions and the consequences of policies for affected groups cannot be known with certainty, policymakers possess considerable latitude. Many constituents will not be following the issue at all, and organized groups with a greater stake in the issue are vulnerable to obfuscation through vague statutes that delegate authority to administrators.[11]

The Realm of Rationalizing Breakthroughs

When consensual objectives are combined with consensual expectations, as in Quadrant 3, the minimal preconditions for *rational analysis* are met within the policy community. We must distinguish between policies that result from some form of partisan mutual adjustment (as most no doubt do) and those that emerge from a conscious process of analysis and decision, however constrained and incomplete. Rationalizing breakthroughs that yield significant and potentially enduring policy change occur here, if at all. They are most likely to occur late in the life cycle of most policies, when the policy community has become "integrated," in Kingdon's terms: when it has developed a common language and a common paradigm for understanding which variables are important and the cause-and-effect relationships among these variables. Under such circumstances, agenda convergence may combine with what Kingdon termed "tipping toward a solution" to permit a rationalizing breakthrough.

Pure Problems of Knowledge Base I: Coordination without a Coordinator

Clearly, development of the knowledge base is desirable where it produces a combination of consensual expectations and consensual objectives—as in Quadrant 3, the realm of rationalizing breakthroughs. There is no guarantee, however, that consensual objectives and consensual expectations will occur together or develop at the same rate. As the discussion of Quadrant 2 suggests, development of the knowledge base may simply accentuate conflict where objectives remain in conflict. Inaction or incremental outcomes are the most likely policy outcomes within this cell.

Significant progress in ameliorating social problems is possible, however, where there is agreement on objectives even where the knowledge base remains inadequate, as in Quadrant 4. This consensus on objectives is equally important whether it occurs as the result of a restricted circle of decision makers, a process of agenda convergence, or merely a decision by the policy community to embrace as an objective some activity that the implementing agency happens to perform particularly well.[12] Consensual objectives permit purposeful or goal-seeking behavior even if the policy area is subject to incomplete or misleading information. Cybernetic models of decision making, which emphasize the capacity for systems with stable goals to monitor information from the environment and adapt to changing circumstances through an ongoing process of feedback and adjustment, describe policymaking in this quadrant. Under such circumstances, as Karl Deutsch observed, "It might be profitable to look upon government somewhat less as a problem of power and somewhat more as a problem of steering."[13]

Under such circumstances, policymaking takes place through a process of partisan mutual adjustment—but with an important difference: Arguments tend to center around the best means to shared ends. For example, Aaron Wildavsky traced the dramatic rise in social welfare outlays from 1965 to 1975 to just such a process of partisan mutual adjustment operating within a value consensus:

> Can there be coordination without a coordinator? Yes, when interaction over policy takes place within a moral consensus specifying the rules for resolving conflicts. And I shall now specify the rules containing that consensus. Suppose a rule for making decisions in welfare policy is that no one should receive benefits who is not entitled to them. Another is that all who are entitled should receive them. Regulations meant to screen out all the undeserving will inevitably eliminate some who should be covered, and regulations designed to include all the deserving will undoubtedly catch up some who should be left out. If the injustice of excluding the deserving is considered worse than including the undeserving, coverage can be broadened (overlapping categories of recipients) without worrying about who should not qualify but do. . . . Even if such a rule is not explicitly formulated, it may be implicit in the actions of decision-makers: no law will be passed that values exclusion over inclusion of beneficiaries.[14]

This process of "coordination without a coordinator" produced a dramatic rise in outlays across the broad range of welfare policies. For example, federal outlays for AFDC rose almost 25 percent between 1965 and 1975. Supplemental Security Income (SSI) expenditures rose 19 percent over the same period; Medicare rose more than 32 percent, and Social Security increased 178 percent. According to Wildavsky, in the protracted struggle between liberals and conservatives over the relative budget shares for defense and social outlays, "the revolution we are waiting for is already here."[15] By the 1990s, however, welfare policymaking was no longer governed by the same rules.

Pure Problems of Knowledge Base II: The Calculated Risk

Welfare reform in 1995–96 is best understood as a pure problem of knowledge base. Substantial progress can be made in ameliorating social problems whenever there is a consensus on objectives even if the knowledge base is inadequate; Wildavsky termed this process "coordination without a coordinator." Policy outcomes may take another, very different form within this cell, however. Whenever policymakers agree that existing policies are so badly broken that they cannot be fixed short of radical reform, they may choose to take a "calculated risk," as defined by Dahl and Lindblom. Calculated risks may be taken, in their view, whenever the existing reality is undesirable and incremental tinkering will clearly not achieve desired goals. Legislating beyond capability is warranted under such circumstances because "in such situations, the calculated risk is the most rational action one can undertake—for all alternatives, including the alternative of simply continuing existing policies, are calculated risks."[16]

❏ WELFARE REFORM AS CALCULATED RISK

By the late 1980s a bipartisan consensus that welfare was so badly broken that it could not be fixed without a sharp change in direction was emerging. Although legislators in both political parties wanted to replace welfare with a labor market policy geared toward moving beneficiaries into private employment, nobody really knew how to move large numbers of people from welfare to work.

This consensus on objectives constitutes a critical difference between the passage of welfare reform in 1995 and the defeat of health care reform two years earlier. Any apparent agenda convergence characterizing the health care issue in the wake of the passage of Medicare in 1965 was to some degree deceptive; indiscreet comments by Newt Gingrich in 1995 suggested that Republican support for Medicare over the years reflected an unwillingness to attack a politically popular program rather than a genuine acceptance of a major federal role in health care. In any case, there could be no agenda convergence on the desirability of any major new federal initiative that had the potential to revitalize the image of big government programs and thus potentially realign the electorate to create a Democratic majority.

Agenda Convergence on Welfare Reform

In the case of welfare reform, by contrast, there was a bipartisan consensus that the existing welfare system had failed—contributing to dependency, family breakup, and crime. There also was a convergence of political interest in making a dramatic change in welfare policy. The welfare issue was an important part of President Clinton's successful effort to project himself as a "New Democrat." Clinton had campaigned on the welfare reform issue in 1992, calling for time limits on benefits and arguing that welfare should be "a second chance, not a way of life."[17] Welfare reform also offered potential political benefits to congressional Republicans. Welfare reform had been one of the items in the Contract with America, a 10-point political program on which Republicans had campaigned in winning control of the House of Representatives for the first time in 40 years.

The prospects for welfare reform appeared particularly promising during the first two years of President Clinton's first term because Democrats controlled the presidency and both houses of Congress for the first time since 1980. Unfortunately, this unique window of opportunity closed without any action on welfare reform. President Clinton's first two years in office were consumed by a series of legislative battles over the budget, NAFTA, crime, and health care reform. For tactical reasons, the president had chosen to take up health care reform before attempting welfare reform, and the Republican victory in November 1994 gave the Republicans control of the House and Senate. Thus, when the Republicans assumed control of the Congress in January 1995, no action had been taken on welfare reform. The Democrats had lost their majority in Congress, and a new breed of Republicans had ascended to power, committed to reforming welfare within the larger context of deficit reduction and tax cuts.

Divisions among Congressional Republicans

In 1993–94, Republicans responded to President Clinton's original welfare initiative with proposals of their own that called for spending even more than he had requested for job training and child support.[18] The fact that Republicans recognized the need to spend additional money on job training and child care was particularly auspicious. For all its faults, welfare is the way it is because it is cheaper than any other alternative: The negative income tax debates of the Nixon and Carter years clearly demonstrated this much. Moving people from welfare to work would be difficult at best—and impossible without spending a good deal more on welfare-related programs than we do now.

Congressional Republicans were internally divided on the welfare issue, however. The Republican victory in the 1994 midterm elections, which few observers anticipated, not only gave the Republicans control over the House and the Senate; it also shifted the balance among four Republican factions on the welfare issue. One group of Republicans emphasized the need to move people from welfare to work, even if that required increased spending on child care and job training. A second group echoed Charles Murray in regarding welfare as the primary cause of dependency and illegitimacy; this group favored major cutbacks, if not outright abolition, of welfare. A third group, led by the Republican governors, emphasized the importance of giving the states maximum flexibility for continued experimentation. The fourth faction regarded welfare reform as a way to cut spending and had little interest in the issue for its own sake.[19] In 1993–94, the first faction was dominant, producing a response to President Clinton's six points that proposed to spend more than his plan on child care and job training. After the election, however, the balance of power had shifted in favor of the "budget-cutters, the welfare-as-the-root-of-social-ills bloc, and the devolutionists."[20] Moreover, Republicans were sharply divided over whether the wiser course was to cooperate with the administration in shaping a bipartisan bill or to pass a bill the president would be compelled to veto, thus giving them a potential issue in the 1996 presidential election.

Although the president and his congressional Republican antagonists came to see the need for some kind of significant legislative achievement going into the November elections, passage of some kind of mutually acceptable bill was far from automatic. Both parties were internally divided over the issue, and the Senate was consistently more moderate than the House. During the two-year struggle, President Clinton vetoed one version of the bill and threatened to veto others. Whereas some Republicans advocated tough new strings on federal aid—particularly mandatory term limits on welfare and family caps (limiting cash payments to the first two children born to a welfare household)—governors (most of whom were Republicans) sought the broadest possible discretion to experiment with new approaches.

Welfare Reform at the State Level: The Waiver Process

Although welfare reform was a major national issue in 1995–96, it actually originated much earlier. In fact, it predated Bill Clinton's 1992 campaign pledge to "end welfare as we know it." AFDC costs are borne jointly by the federal and state governments. Contrary to popular belief, welfare programs—as distinct from universal entitlement programs such as Social Security and Medicare—represent a small portion of total federal spending; eliminating all federal spending on welfare would have made barely a dent in the mammoth budget deficits that plagued the federal government in the 1980s and early 1990s. By contrast, however, welfare benefits are a significant portion of state outlays. When welfare costs rise, states feel the pinch first.

State budgets were increasingly tight for a variety of reasons in the 1980s. Federal grants were significantly reduced for many programs in the 1980s as part of Congress's ongoing attempt to gain control over the large Reagan-era deficits. Although these budget cuts were offset, in part, by increased flexibility stemming from the replacement of cumbersome categorical grants with block grants in many instances, the bottom line still showed a significant decline in federal money. To make matters worse, Congress responded to the new austerity with "unfunded mandates"—requiring states to accomplish various social goals without providing funds to aid them in their efforts. (Repeal of unfunded mandates was one of the 10 points in the Contract with America.) In addition, the United States suffered through a series of economic recessions in the 1970s and 1980s. When each of these recessions eventually came to an end, the unemployment rate was higher than it had been going into the recession. To make matters worse, a growing number of "discouraged workers" had given up even trying to look for a job, so they were not being counted in unemployment statistics.[21] Although AFDC benefits (unlike Social Security) are not indexed for inflation—and thus declined in real value in most states during this period—welfare costs nevertheless escalated in many states, leading governors to search for ways to get control over spending.

States could experiment with AFDC under the law by petitioning the federal government for a "waiver." During the Reagan and Bush administrations, states used this waiver process to experiment with a wide variety of alternative approaches to welfare, almost all of which focused on reducing costs or making welfare less attractive. The most common approaches were work requirements ("workfare"), school attendance or grade requirements for teenage mothers ("learnfare"), family caps (denial of benefits for children conceived while their mothers are on welfare or limitations on the number of children for which benefits will be granted), family planning mandates, migration restrictions (elimination of benefits for new arrivals into a state, or "residency requirements"), and across-the-board benefit cuts.[22]

This waiver process continued under President Clinton. Although the Clinton administration introduced new procedures to speed up the consideration of waivers,[23] the process of securing federal approval remained time-consuming and frustrating—leading many governors to favor replacement of AFDC with a new block grant that would permit them to continue this process of innovation unimpeded by federal restrictions.[24] Whereas categorical grants provide federal money with a wide variety of strings attached, block grants are provided for general purposes (e.g., job training, community development, law enforcement). States and localities can spend federal block grant funds almost any way they want, as long as they spend it for the general purpose specified in the grant. Block grants originated in the 1970s as part of the political compromise that permitted passage of President Nixon's Revenue Sharing program, which provided money to states and localities with no strings attached. The use of block grants accelerated in the 1980s as the Reagan administration tried to sweeten federal aid cutbacks by granting the states more freedom of action in program design. In this context, AFDC would be merely the latest in a long line of categorical grant programs to be converted to a block grant.

Ultimately, devolution to the governors was not a rationalizing breakthrough so much as a political necessity. Welfare reform in 1996 resolved conflicts among the active players by delegating broad discretion to the states. Thus, replacing AFDC with block grants to the states constitutes an instance of self-regulation, as defined in chapter 4, inasmuch as policymakers responded to a consensual demand pattern by delegating autonomy to state governors to experiment with new approaches to welfare. Although welfare was badly broken—suggesting the need for experimentation with new approaches—devolution to the states places welfare recipients at the mercy of a new set of actors with a recurring interest in controlling welfare costs.

❑ CONFLICTUAL EXPECTATIONS AND WELFARE POLICY

The welfare policy community was "integrated" and "tipping toward a solution" by the late 1960s. Presidents Nixon and Carter sought unsuccessfully to reform welfare through proposals for a negative income tax. More important than the defeat of these two proposals was the exposure by Congress of serious dilemmas for any form of negative income tax. The negative income tax was not merely defeated but thoroughly discredited by 1978, destroying any sense of consensual objectives and consensual expectations that had existed within the welfare policy community. This development left welfare policies vulnerable to budget cutbacks in response to the massive federal deficits that plagued President Reagan's eight years in office. These budget cuts largely reflected practical politics; given the need to gain control over federal spending, attacking programs with weak or poorly organized beneficiaries, such as welfare, was easier than taking on popular middle-class entitlement programs.

As Nathan Glazer has observed, welfare policy in the Reagan years also marked a decisive rejection of the idea that intellectuals and bureaucrats could end welfare dependency by incorporating work incentives into a redesigned welfare policy:

> The most striking pattern that emerged was one that I would call the rejection of "social engineering," rejection of the capacity of human foresight, using subtly graduated incentives and disincentives and sharply focused programs, to affect human behavior and improve the human condition. This was the dominant ideology of the 1960s and 1970s; it was sharply rejected in the 1980s.[25]

This view gained visibility in 1984 with the publication of Charles Murray's *Losing Ground*.[26] Murray argued that the availability of welfare created a subculture of dependency that would be broken only if welfare were no longer available. Accordingly, Murray proposed the complete abolition of AFDC, food stamps, and other income transfer programs targeted to the poor. Although few policymakers were willing to go so far as to abolish welfare altogether, Murray's book did provide support for significant cutbacks in these programs in the Reagan years. Over the succeeding decade, a variety of additional research appeared to support this argument, including Lawrence Mead's *The New Politics of Poverty*, resulting in a kind of rewriting of social policy history.[27]

The emergence of this conservative strand within the welfare policy research community did not signal the development of consensual expectations as much as the beginnings of a lively debate over the causes of welfare dependency. In fact, Murray's argument was fairly easily refuted. For example, major works by Frank Levy and William Julius Wilson showed that the rise in welfare dependency and illegitimacy over the years had its real roots in the disappearance of work within the inner cities.[28] During the "Great Migration" of poor blacks and whites to northern cities in the 1930s and 1940s, abundant manufacturing jobs offered good wages to unskilled laborers. After World War II, the growth of the suburbs led to an outmigration of whites and jobs. With the disappearance of work in urban areas, a new culture of poverty and crime began to develop.

Dismissing attacks on welfare from the left was more difficult, however. David Ellwood—a professor at Harvard University's Kennedy School of Government who played a key role in developing the Clinton administration's welfare reform proposals—found that approximately 30 percent of AFDC recipients remain on welfare for eight years or more. This group of long-term dependents constitutes more than 65 percent of the welfare caseload at any given point in time; these long-term welfare recipients raise the average duration of a stay on welfare to 11.6 years, offsetting the large number of recipients who go on and off welfare in less than a year.[29] In Ellwood's view, reforming welfare would be counterproductive; replacing it with new programs designed to make work pay and ease the transition from welfare to work would be better. Ellwood distinguished the poverty of the ghetto poor from that affecting two-parent families and further observed that popular images of "underclass" or ghetto poverty did not accurately capture all poverty affecting single-parent families. Ellwood proposed a variety of reforms, with different policy mixes for different types of poverty.[30]

Ellwood's call for the replacement of welfare with new strategies emphasizing work was echoed by Mickey Kaus, senior editor at *The New Republic* and an avowed liberal who had served for a time in the Carter administration. In *The End of Equality*, Kaus critiqued liberals' preoccupation with income inequality—a philosophy he termed "money liberalism." This approach, Kaus argued, helped to produce the culture of welfare dependency Ellwood had so effectively identified, and it made Democrats look like soft-headed big spenders who were out of touch with prevailing American values. Kaus proposed a new philosophy for contemporary liberals, which he termed "civic liberalism."[31]

Civic liberalism would replace the traditional liberal focus on remedying income inequality with a new strategy of expanding the sphere of society in which money does not matter. This strategy would involve seizing every opportunity to nurture institutions in which people of all income classes would come into contact with one another as social equals. For example, Kaus would replace the volunteer army—which has produced a military staffed disproportionately by poor blacks—with a reinstitution of the draft, with its potential for integration of all classes and ethnic groups. He also would look for ways to revitalize public schools and move to some form of national health insurance to bring people of all social classes together in common settings. Most important for the purposes of this chapter, Kaus would abolish welfare—the most conspicuous failure of "money liberalism"—and replace it with a program of guaranteed public-service jobs. Instead of welfare, poor Americans would now be offered employment; if they refused to accept suitable work, the government would have met its obligation.[32]

Overselling the Knowledge Base

Ellwood and Kaus recognized that not all poor people are alike and proposed multifaceted strategies for dealing with the problems of poverty. Elected officials ignored the nuances of this research, however, seizing instead on the need to replace welfare with something radically different. By the 1990s, politicians of both political parties agreed that AFDC contributed significantly to a culture of dependency and that something had to be done about it. Bill Clinton called for "an end to welfare as we know it" in his 1992 campaign for the presidency, and House Republicans made sweeping welfare reform a major item in their 10-point Contract with America in 1994.[33]

As much as any other policy area, welfare policy has exhibited this tendency for elected officials to misread the available knowledge base when it suits their purposes. For example, the 1988 welfare reform law (the Family Support Act) has been characterized as an unprecedented example of how legislation can be rooted in empirical social science research when that research is characterized by consensual knowledge.[34] Yet Sanford Schram has argued that the available social science research was used to legitimate preconceived policy approaches; members of Congress perceived consensual knowledge within the welfare policy research community when the available empirical research in fact was tentative and incomplete.[35]

Much the same thing appears to have happened in 1995–96. Although there was a bipartisan consensus that welfare had failed by the early 1990s, there were no sure answers regarding how to move people from welfare to work.[36] Certainly, a considerable body of evidence suggested that assuming that large numbers of welfare recipients would find jobs as soon as welfare benefits were withdrawn, as Charles Murray argued, was extraordinarily naïve—or willfully ignorant. Moving people in large numbers from welfare to work simply could not be done without spending a good deal *more* on welfare (e.g., providing job training and child care, for starters) than we were spending in the early 1990s.

In fact, there was a great deal of evidence to suggest that many AFDC recipients tried to leave welfare through work but could not. Within a six-year period, about 40 percent of welfare recipients left welfare to enter the labor force; about 40 percent of *this* group remained below the poverty line after they left welfare. Many were forced to return to welfare because the jobs they found did not provide health care benefits, did not pay enough to enable them to support their families without welfare, or simply did not last. For the majority of recipients, AFDC was a safety net rather than a way of life, and long-term welfare dependency was the exception rather than the rule. Poor women with children were (and are) caught up in the larger problem of the decline since 1973 in real earnings for less-skilled, less-educated workers—much of which is attributable to the globalization of the economy.[37]

The fact that these approaches promised more than they could really deliver—that no one really knew how to move large numbers of people from welfare to work and that no serious attempt to accomplish this goal could be made without spending more money on welfare than we were currently spending—was well-known to all involved. At least, reliable evidence was there for anyone who cared to look.[38]

Similarly, there was plenty of evidence to suggest that terminating aid after a time limit could lead to real hardship for large numbers of children. Denial of welfare benefits after the birth of a third child—a popular reform at the state level—was advanced as a way to reduce illegitimacy and get control over welfare costs. This "family cap" was a recurring feature in welfare reform bills, and the final legislation allowed the states to cap benefits in this way (without requiring them to do so). Yet how could a family cap have a significant effect on illegitimacy rates or program costs when the size of families on AFDC had been declining for several decades? The average number of children in families on welfare is now 1.9—a figure that is actually lower than that for non-welfare families.[39] The conclusion that policymakers simply chose to ignore available evidence on several key points is difficult to avoid.

❑ WHO BEARS THE RISK?

I argue in this chapter that welfare reform in 1995–96 is best understood as a *calculated risk*, in Dahl and Lindblom's terms. A bipartisan consensus among active participants held that existing policy was badly broken, warranting a sharp change in direction. Although no one could guarantee that turning welfare into a block grant would lead to effective policies that moved poor people from welfare to work, policymakers had to acknowledge that continuing present policy was also a calculated risk.

What is striking about the calculated risk taken in welfare policy in 1996 is that so many of the risks of a failed policy would be borne by poor people. If no one really knows how to move people from welfare to work, then terminating aid for recipients who reach the time limit could result in an increase in poverty and a loss of health insurance coverage. Most poor people gain Medicaid coverage as a consequence of receiving AFDC; when they lose AFDC, they lose Medicaid as well. Moreover, most of those who do succeed in finding work obtain jobs that do not offer health benefits.[40] Preliminary evidence in the state of New York suggests that more than 200,000 children may have lost health insurance coverage within the first 10 months of experience with the state's welfare reform, for example.[41] Although several states do seem to be committed to maintaining funding levels and implementing innovative programs to help welfare recipients find good jobs, there are no guarantees under the new block grant that states will act to protect beneficiaries during economic downturns.

The shifting of risks to poor people is not surprising in view of the discussion of political inequality in chapter 4. Although all of the *active* participants in the welfare reform debate stood to gain something from passage of a new law to "end welfare as we know it," poor people were largely unmobilized and ineffective. Consensus on objectives reflected the failure of poor people to mobilize for effective political action. Even if the policy community had been characterized by consensual expectations as well as consensual objectives (thus permitting a rationalizing breakthrough as defined in this chapter), such a consensus on ends and means would have been confined to a restricted circle of decision makers—in this case, the president, members of both political parties in Congress, federal bureaucrats, and state governors.

The political weakness of poor people also helps to explain the calculated decision by policymakers not to monitor the effects of welfare reform on recipients. As Paul R. Schulman has observed, a firm public commitment to pursue a set of declared objectives can lead to a dramatic increase in research aimed at acquiring the necessary knowledge base.[42] Schulman's study focused on the Apollo program, which sought to send American astronauts to the moon and return them safely to Earth within a 10-year period. The lunar landing project was a high-salience presidential initiative by John F. Kennedy that placed the prestige of the White House on the line. A performance failure had the potential to be tragic and politically embarrassing. Accordingly, diminishing returns could not be permitted to dictate resource commitments, and any gaps in the knowledge base had to be filled as soon as possible. As NASA administrator James E.

Webb observed, "We could not stop with doing 80 or 90 or 99 percent of what we needed to do and come out reasonably well . . . a partial success was likely to be a complete failure."[43]

Although the commitment by the president and Congress in 1996 to "end welfare as we know it" was every bit as visible as President Kennedy's commitment to put a man on the moon, declining welfare rolls could be interpreted by members of both political parties as evidence of the policy's *effectiveness* regardless of the ultimate impact on poor women with children. Any performance failures resulting from the new policy probably would be invisible unless Congress took deliberate action to collect data on the effects of the policy. Yet the Senate defeated a welfare-tracking amendment that would have required the Secretary of Health and Human Services to report annually to Congress on the employment, wage, health insurance, and child-care status of welfare recipients who were terminated under the new program.[44]

As Lindblom and Popper observed, policy experiments have value only if they are designed to permit learning from inevitable mistakes. The deliberate decision not to collect data on the effects of the new welfare reform law suggests that many of its proponents were afraid of what they might learn.

NOTES

1. Joel F. Handler, "The Return to the States: Changing Social Behavior," in *The Poverty of Welfare Reform* (New Haven, Conn.: Yale University Press, 1995), 89–109.

2. Lawrence D. Brown, *New Policies, New Politics: Government's Response to Government's Growth* (Washington, D.C.: Brookings Institution, 1983), 7–11.

3. John W. Kingdon, *Agendas, Alternatives, and Public Policies* (Boston: Little, Brown, 1984). Because the conditions for rationality typically will be met only after the policy community has acquired long experience with a policy, nonincremental innovations will be virtually nonexistent. There is at least one exception to this generalization, however. The life cycle of policies that I have described here may be circumvented through the diffusion of innovations from other political systems. The adoption of Medicare in 1965 can be understood as one such instance inasmuch as policymakers were in a position to draw on the long experience of other Western democracies with various forms of national health insurance. In effect, the diffusion of innovations enables policymakers in one nation to skip stages of the life cycle by drawing on the experience other nations have gained by going through the complete life cycle. This argument is developed in Lindsay Crocker, "Medicare and Nonincremental Innovations," senior honors thesis, Colgate University, May 2000.

4. Brown, *New Policies, New Politics*, 153–54.

5. Charles E. Lindblom, "The Science of Muddling Through," *Public Administration Review* 19 (1959): 87. On these points, Lindblom's argument finds further support in the writings of Herbert Simon and Anthony Downs on information costs and bounded rationality. See Herbert A. Simon, *Models of Man, Social and Rational: Mathematical Essays on Rational Human Behavior in a Social Setting* (New York: Wiley, 1957), and Anthony Downs, *An Economic Theory of Democracy* (New York: Harper and Row, 1957). See also Charles O. Jones, *Clean Air: The Policies and Politics of Pollution Control* (Pittsburgh: University of Pittsburgh Press, 1975), on the importance of an adequate knowledge base.

6. This is what Thomas Kuhn has termed a "paradigm." Thomas S. Kuhn, *The Structure of Scientific Revolutions*, 2nd ed., enlarged (Chicago: University of Chicago Press, 1970).

7. Robert L. Rothstein, "Consensual Knowledge and International Collaboration: Some Lessons from the Commodity Negotiations," *International Organization* 38 (1984): 736. Rothstein takes this definition without change from Ernst Haas's guidelines for a panel at the American Political Science Association meeting in Chicago in September 1983.

8. The administration's most recent proposals for Medicare reform are much more modest in scope than the President's 1993 initiative. Although this modesty in large part reflects lessons learned from the disastrous defeat of that 1993 proposal and the subsequent Republican takeover of both houses of Congress in the 1994 midterm elections, it also reflects the decidedly mixed experience with managed care systems since that time. In the words of Marilyn Moon, health care analyst at the Urban Institute, at least the current Clinton proposal "doesn't lock us into big-time structural reform before we really know where we want to go." See Robin Toner, "Second Opinions: The Hard Lessons of Health Care Reform," *New York Times*, 4 July 1999, section 4, "Week in Review," 1. The quotation appears at p. 4, col. 5.

9. Theodore J. Lowi, "American Business, Public Policy, Case Studies, and Political Theory," *World Politics* 16 (July 1964): 677–715.

10. On the difficulties facing policymakers in formulating the 1978 reforms, see Joseph A. Califano, Jr., *Governing America: An Insider's Report from the White House and the Cabinet* (New York: Simon & Schuster, 1981), 368–401.

11. Raymond A. Bauer, Ithiel de Sola Pool, and Lewis Anthony Dexter, *American Business and Public Policy: The Politics of Foreign Trade*, 2nd ed. (Chicago: Aldine-Atherton, 1972). On the use of legislative delegation by legislators to obfuscate issues, see Michael T. Hayes, "The Semi-Sovereign Pressure Groups: A Critique of Current Theory and an Alternative Typology," *Journal of Politics* 40 (February 1978): 134–61.

12. Aaron Wildavsky, "Strategic Retreat on Objectives: Learning from Failure in American Public Policy," in *Speaking Truth to Power: The Art and Craft of Policy Analysis* (Boston: Little, Brown, 1979), 41–61.

13. Karl W. Deutsch, *The Nerves of Government: Models of Communication and Control* (New York: Free Press, 1966), xxvii. See also John D. Steinbruner, *The Cybernetic Theory of Decision: New Dimensions of Political Analysis* (Princeton, N.J.: Princeton University Press, 1974).

14. Other rules governing welfare policy during this period, according to Wildavsky, were "give too much rather than too little" (e.g., overpayments are preferable to underpayments), and "the need justifies the cost." Wildavsky, *Speaking Truth to Power*, 90.

15. Wildavsky, *Speaking Truth to Power*, 87–89.

16. Robert A. Dahl and Charles E. Lindblom, *Politics, Economics, and Welfare: Planning and Politico-Economic Systems Resolved into Basic Social Processes* (New York: Harper & Row, Harper Torchbooks, 1963), 85.

17. Gary Bryner, *Politics and Public Morality: The Great American Welfare Reform Debate* (New York: W. W. Norton, 1998), 77.

18. Ibid., 86.

19. Ibid., 152. Bryner cites David Ellwood, Assistant Secretary of Health and Human Services under President Clinton and co-chair of the interagency task force, on the importance of these four Republican factions.

20. Bryner, *Politics and Public Morality,* 152.

21. Lester Thurow, "The Crusade That's Killing Prosperity," in *Ticking Time Bombs: The New Conservative Assaults on Democracy,* ed. Robert Kuttner (New York: The New Press, 1996), 48–57.

22. Handler, *The Poverty of Welfare Reform,* 98.

23. Linda Feldman, "Clinton Encourages New Paths on Welfare," *Christian Science Monitor,* 23 August 1993, 1.

24. Bryner, *Politics and Public Morality,* 92–101.

25. Nathan Glazer, *The Limits of Social Policy* (Cambridge, Mass.: Harvard University Press, 1988), 42. For a fuller exposition of this view by a Reagan administration insider, see Martin Anderson, *Welfare: The Political Economy of Welfare Reform in the United States* (Stanford, Calif.: Hoover Institution Press, 1978).

26. Charles Murray, *Losing Ground: American Social Policy, 1950–1980* (New York: Basic Books, 1984).

27. Lawrence M. Mead, *The New Politics of Poverty: The Nonworking Poor in America* (New York: Basic Books, 1992). For a thorough review of this literature, see Sanford E. Schram, "Rewriting Social Policy History," in *Words of Welfare: The Poverty of Social Science and the Social Science of Poverty* (Minneapolis: University of Minnesota Press, 1995), 98–120.

28. Frank Levy, *Dollars and Dreams: The Changing American Income Distribution* (New York: W. W. Norton, 1988); William Julius Wilson, *When Work Disappears: The World of the New Urban Poor* (New York: Knopf, 1996).

29. David Ellwood, "Targeting the Would-Be Long-Term Recipient: Who Should Be Served?" Report to Department of Health and Human Services (Princeton, N.J.: Mathematica Policy Research, 1986), Table I.1.5.

30. David T. Ellwood, *Poor Support: Poverty in the American Family* (New York: Basic Books, 1988).

31. Mickey Kaus, *The End of Equality* (New York: Basic Books, 1992).

32. Mickey Kaus, "The Cure for the Culture of Poverty," in *The End of Equality*, 121–35.

33. James G. Gimpel, "Reforming Welfare," in *Fulfilling the Contract: The First 100 Days* (Boston: Allyn & Bacon, 1996), 79–94.

34. See Erica B. Baum, "When the Witch Doctors Agree: The Family Support Act and Social Science Research," *Journal of Policy Analysis and Management* 10 (fall 1991): 603–615; Ron Haskins, "Congress Writes a Law: Research and Welfare Reform," *Journal of Policy Analysis and Management* 10 (fall 1991): 616–33; Richard P. Nathan, *Social Science and Government* (New York: Basic Books, 1988), 97–121. See also Mead, *The New Politics of Poverty*, 195–98, and Schram, *Words of Welfare*, 133–37.

35. Schram, *Words of Welfare*, 133–41.

36. Handler, "Setting the Poor to Work," in *The Poverty of Welfare Reform*, 56–88.

37. Handler, "The Problem of Poverty, the Problem of Work," in *The Poverty of Welfare Reform*, 32–55. The percentages cited are from p. 50.

38. Handler, "Setting the Poor to Work."

39. Handler, *The Poverty of Welfare Reform*, 106.

40. Christopher Jencks, "The Hidden Paradox of Welfare Reform," *The American Prospect*, no. 32 (May-June 1997), 33–40. See also Mary Jo Bane, "Welfare as We Might Know It," *The American Prospect*, no. 30 (January-February 1997), 47–53.

41. Kyle Hughes, "Kids in Eye of Welfare Storm," *Utica* [N.Y.] *Observer-Dispatch*, 23 August 1998.

42. Paul R. Schulman, "Nonincremental Policy Making: Notes Toward an Alternative Paradigm," *American Political Science Review* 69 (1975): 1354–70. In the wake of the Sputnik launch by the Soviets in 1957, policymakers recognized an urgent need to upgrade existing scientific capabilities. An immediate (albeit indirect) response was the National Defense Education Act of 1958, the first major program of federal aid to education—which was fueled almost entirely by fears that the United States had fallen behind in the space race. The limited capacities and institutional rigidities of existing space agencies, however, prevented any direct action to close this perceived gap for almost four years, until President Kennedy's call in May 1961 for a massive 10-year project to put a man on the moon.

43. Quoted in Schulman, "Nonincremental Policy Making," 1362.

44. Paul Wellstone, "America's Disappeared," *The Nation* 269, no. 2 (July 12, 1999): 5–6.

CHAPTER EIGHT

Political Conflict and Policy Change

At the outset of this study I raised several questions regarding the limits of political change: To what extent is large change possible? What factors produce incrementalism under normal circumstances? Is there anything we can do to reduce the obstacles to nonincremental change? Should we at least question whether nonincremental change is in fact desirable?

The beginning of wisdom in any analysis of this sort is the recognition that different assumptions about human nature will lead to different assessments of the potential for and the desirability of policy change. Accordingly, I begin this volume by examining Friedrich Hayek's distinction between rationalist and anti-rationalist worldviews. The anti-rationalist worldview characterizes mankind as fallible and self-interested; the rationalists regard mankind as perfectible. Moreover, the rationalists place great faith in the capacity of human reason to identify comprehensive and coherent alternative visions of how the economy might be organized, how society might be remolded, even how traditional systems of morality might be improved.

By contrast, the anti-rationalists see a much more limited role for human reason. Although individuals are capable of making intelligent decisions regarding their own plans and aspirations (where to go to school, what job to take, which apartment to rent, and so on), decisions about how to organize society, the polity, or the economy are best made through a pluralistic "discovery process" of systemic rationality, according to this view. Change tends to occur via evolution and the development of traditional ways of doing things rather than through deliberate decisions to adopt well-formulated alternatives to traditional institutions and practices. Not surprisingly, anti-rationalists are much more receptive than rationalists to the two central elements in Lindblom's theory of incrementalism: policymaking through partisan mutual adjustment and the deliberate decision to focus on incremental policy alternatives. Anti-rationalists also are much more likely to see a need for checks on the exercise of political power—both to prevent tyranny and to encourage a reliance on persuasion rather than coercion in the pursuit of objectives.

In chapter 3, I asked whether acceptance of anti-rationalist premises about human nature necessarily implies acceptance of their very limited conception of the state. To answer that question, I developed a typology of four worldviews that are derived not only from the important differences between rationalist and anti-rationalist thinkers but also from an equally important distinction between those who consistently emphasize the need for economic and political reform and those who would "preserve the inheritance."

I identified four categories of political thinkers: utopian reformers, meliorative liberals, adaptive conservatives, and nostalgic conservatives. These four groups vary with regard to their receptivity to incrementalism as a method of policymaking. Utopian reformers are consistently critical of incrementalism because they can't wait to implement their holistic visions; thus, they object to any process that countenances delay and produces tapered-down and seemingly incoherent outcomes. By contrast, nostalgic conservatives are ambivalent about incrementalism. They favor any and all obstacles to rapid policy change whenever cherished values are under attack. Whenever they seek to restore the institutions or practices of an earlier age, however, they can be as impatient with incrementalism as utopian reformers. Adaptive conservatives, by contrast, recognize the necessity of adapting to changing circumstances if cherished institutions are to be preserved. Yet they do not so much embrace change as acquiesce in it. Only meliorative liberals embrace incrementalism consistently and wholeheartedly. In fact, the theory of incrementalism as a policymaking strategy was developed by two meliorative liberals: Karl Popper and Charles Lindblom. Accordingly, in chapter 3 I characterized incrementalism as a strategy for pursuing the objectives of meliorative liberalism.

The case for incrementalism *is* very strong. In the first section of this chapter I review the merits of systemic rationality, checks on political power, and a primary focus on incremental alternatives. Yet in evaluating incrementalism—and, by implication, assessing the potential for policy change under normal circumstances—the case for incrementalism must be separated from the case for meliorative liberalism as a worldview. In the second section of this chapter I focus on two critical blind spots for meliorative liberalism as an ideology or worldview. Although incrementalism was designed to pursue meliorative liberalism, it does not function effectively where the process is dominated by meliorative liberals. To the contrary, the success of incrementalism as a strategy for gradually improving public policies hinges on the ability to learn from mistakes—which, in turn, depends on the interplay of all four worldviews.

Although incrementalism offers several advantages as a policymaking strategy, it cannot be defended where it stems from significant political inequalities. As chapters 4 through 7 clearly show, there is no basis for assuming that all interests affected by any given policy proposal will be effectively represented. Many will not mobilize at all, and political resources typically will be distributed very unevenly among groups that do succeed in mobilizing. As a result, the policy process takes a variety of divergent forms. This observation suggests that the real problem is not so much with incrementalism as a way of making public policies but with the fact that the process departs from incrementalism so much of the time. Paradoxically, where the policy process most closely approximates the conditions for rational decision making, it also is most likely to benefit entrenched interests at the expense of the weak and the unorganized.

Thus, genuine policy change typically requires political conflict rather than consensus. To the extent that policy change requires conflict, any effort to make incrementalism work better must focus on ways to make the policy process more effectively conflictual.

❑ THE CASE FOR INCREMENTALISM

The case for incrementalism is very convincing on three levels. First, systemic rationality (partisan mutual adjustment) is superior to articulated rationality. Second, there are good reasons to place checks on the exercise of political power, even though these checks make achieving nonincremental policy change more difficult. Third, focusing on policies that differ only incrementally from the status quo arguably is more efficient.

The Case for Systemic Rationality

Policymaking through partisan mutual adjustment is superior to any misguided attempt at comprehensive rationality (see chapter 2). Mutual adaptation by a multiplicity of actors and institutions representing different interests and vantage points yields a form of systemic rationality, which is the best we can aspire to in a world characterized by fallibility and the pursuit of self-interest. As Hayek observed, even where the market does not function perfectly, it serves as a discovery process, making the best use of information that by its very nature is decentralized throughout the system. The political process—properly understood as a political market—serves as a discovery process in the same way, identifying and responding to a multiplicity of interests beyond the capacity of any single decision maker to identify, let alone accommodate.

The Case for Checks on Power

In a world in which political actors are fallible and prone to the pursuit of self-interest, checks on the exercise of power are essential. The issue is not whether power should be checked, but what form of check is most effective. In this regard, the debate within Western democracies focuses on the relative advantages of parliamentary systems over the American system of separation of powers. Of course, there is a major difference between multi-party parliamentary systems that feature some form of proportional representation and the strong two-party version in Great Britain.

Academic proponents of a parliamentary system for the United States—or, alternatively, reforms designed to reduce the independence of Congress vis-à-vis the presidency within our constitutional system—are drawn to the strong two-party variant. Such a system would enhance reliance on articulated rationality at the expense of systemic rationality by making it much easier for intellectuals (or experts within the bureaucracy) to obtain passage of their reformist visions essentially intact. Within this model of policymaking, political parties compete for votes by taking distinctive positions on the issues; the winning party then has a mandate for the enactment of its program—a program formulated, in advance of the election, by policy analysts associated with the winning party. Once in office, the winning party would not only have an obligation to the voters to live up to its promises; it also would have the votes to enact its program.

This system, we must acknowledge, maximizes the accountability of elected officials to voters by centralizing power and thus clarifying responsibility for results. The American system of checks and balances, by contrast, divides power among three branches of government, making for an exceedingly complex policy process in which holding anyone responsible for performance in office can be almost impossible. The extraordinary ability of congressional incumbents to secure reelection at a time when public opinion polls reveal widespread dissatisfaction with Congress and the political system generally is clear proof of this difficulty (if any were needed).

As Woodrow Wilson observed a century ago, however, the case for the British system rests on the assumption that a legislature is competent only to approve or withhold approval from initiatives emanating from the executive. Within this conception of the legislative process, parliamentary debates serve a legitimation function by providing a thorough discussion of policy issues, followed by votes on the principles and details of legislative proposals. In theory, at least, the British House of Commons makes great national decisions on behalf of the electorate when its members decide, after exhaustive and principled debate, to move in a particular direction.

Parliament is not really free to say no to the executive in such a debate, however. It *can* say no, of course, but it is not likely to. Because career advancement is controlled by party leaders, and because the failure of the party to pass its program may produce a "no-confidence" vote and a new election, majority parties in such a system tend to be cohesive. Moreover, given the majority party's ability to create new committees to consider each bill, with party leaders empowered to select committee members and designate the chair, the power of the majority to enact its program is almost overwhelming. Under such circumstances, the notion that parliamentary debates legitimate new policy directions would seem to be almost entirely dramaturgical.

The American system, for all its faults, makes for a thoroughly and genuinely independent legislature—a bicameral Congress that is able to say no to the executive and prevail. Would-be reformers—whether presidents or legislative entrepreneurs—must persuade committee chairs, party leaders, even rank-and-file members, of the virtues of their proposals because the capacity for coercion is so limited within our system. Presidents have no control whatsoever over the internal organization of Congress into permanent standing committees, and even congressional party leaders can exercise only limited control over career advancement. The American system does much more than the British system to foster genuine deliberation over the merits of public policy proposals.

Ultimately, the choice between the two systems comes down to a choice between alternative forms of majority rule, as Wilmoore Kendall recognized long ago. The presidential majority is a national majority, defined as 51 percent of the electoral college votes—which theoretically could involve less than 50 percent of the popular vote. This majority facilitates the kind of articulated rationality that intellectuals have a class interest in advancing. By contrast, the congressional majority is a national majority that comes into existence whenever majorities of the House and Senate vote in favor of a legislative proposal. This majority facilitates the kind of systemic rationality I identified in chapter 2. Within this conception of majority rule, representatives properly emerge from their elections without instructions; they are free to use their judgment to decide how to balance the views of their constituents, what they see as the interests of their constituents, and the larger interests of the nation. Whereas the presidential majority is measured once every four years and then evanesces, the congressional majority emerges every time Congress votes on a bill, and it can have an entirely different composition for each issue.

The case for the presidential majority is not as strong as it appears at first glance. To the extent that the legislature is not really free to say no to the executive within such a system, the case for the presidential majority is rooted in a false premise. Furthermore, there is little basis for inferring a mandate for the winning party's program in such a system, even where the parties actually run on issues and the voters decide between them on the issues—which is by no means guaranteed. Finally, this system provides little protection for minorities; as such, it has proven unworkable in societies characterized by intense ethnic or religious divisions. Considerable protection for minorities can be provided, within the context of a parliamentary system, by moving toward proportional representation or some form of institutionalized power sharing. Where such means are used, however, the parliamentary system loses its strong two-party character—and thus most of its appeal to rationalist reformers.

The Case for Focusing on Incremental Alternatives

Although there is a strong case for a policy process that facilitates systemic rationality while providing auxiliary checks on the power of majorities, there also is a strong case for a policy process that focuses (most of the time) on incremental, or piecemeal, social reform (see chapter 3). Holistic social reforms, which try to transform whole systems, change too many things at once, so that policymakers cannot learn from mistakes. Piecemeal social reform—*meliorative liberalism*, as I term this strategy in chapter 3—is rooted in the scientific method, inasmuch as it designs policy experiments with the idea of learning from inevitable mistakes. Piecemeal social reform also facilitates majority-building, for a variety of reasons. Incremental reforms minimize disruption of the existing system, reducing the threat to established interests. To the extent that policy outcomes are almost certain to be products of a process of "tapering down from the optimal to the acceptable," incremental reforms also merit the most attention. Finally, within a strategy of "least steps down the path of least resistance," the failure of each step can make the best case for moving on to the next step.

Thus, incrementalism in policymaking stems from a variety of sources. To the extent that incrementalism stems from limits on the use of reason and the dispersion of information throughout society (i.e., human fallibility) or from the need for checks on the exercise of political power, it is defensible. In other words, the benefits of incrementalism arguably offset the obvious costs associated with a process that, by its nature, generates tapered-down and often incoherent policy outcomes.

❑ THE LIMITED VISION OF MELIORATIVE LIBERALISM

The significant advantages stemming from incrementalism would seem to imply the superiority of the worldview of its founders, the meliorative liberals. Ironically, however, to the extent that the fallibility of mankind is an enduring condition of human nature—as the meliorative liberals argue— each of the four worldviews I identified in chapter 3 inevitably provides incomplete or erroneous guidance for policymakers. In short, meliorative liberals must be as fallible as everyone else; their chief virtue lies in their capacity to acknowledge their fallibility.

In this section I focus on two particular blind spots within meliorative liberalism. For incrementalism to work tolerably well (and tolerably well is the most we can ever expect from it), all four worldviews must be represented in a rough equilibrium.

Meliorative Liberalism's Bias toward Ever-Expanding Government

Meliorative liberals always view reform as potentially beneficial. Their critical orientation toward all social, political, and economic systems leads to a serious blind spot: a bias toward ever-expanding government. Although they emphasize the need to move gradually and learn from inevitable mistakes—thus eschewing the grandiose visions of utopian reformers—they believe they can improve on almost anything through a series of small steps.

Although Lindblom does not use the term "progress" to characterize this process, he does speak of "convergence" on solutions through "successive approximations." Although he recognizes the multiplicity of interests involved in the policy process—and in the critically important activity of learning from mistakes—he tends to view policymaking less as a power struggle than as an attempt to approximate rational decision making under severe constraints (e.g., conflictual objectives and conflictual expectations).[1] As policymakers acquire experience with policies, one would expect some kind of progress in developing workable solutions to public problems.

Unfortunately, although meliorative liberals recognize mankind's fallibility, they underestimate the human tendency to pursue self-interest; they tend to view such behavior as an occasional lapse on the part of individuals who are basically good, or the product of misguided "holistic" thinking, as Popper emphasized. By contrast, the anti-rationalist thinkers reviewed in chapter 2—including most of the framers of the U. S. Constitution—regarded the pursuit of self-interest as an enduring and inescapable element of the human condition and worried about the potential for tyranny whenever political power was left unchecked.[2]

The anti-rationalist thinkers are more realistic than the rationalists on this point (see chapter 2)—a conclusion that has only been reinforced by the case studies in chapters 5 through 7. Instances of self-interested behavior were prevalent in each of these case studies. Elected officials staged a drama to make incremental progress against air pollution look like more than it was in 1970. Republicans in Congress placed the electoral interests of their party ahead of the needs of 35–40 million people who lacked any health insurance coverage in 1993–94. Politicians of both parties (and at both ends of Pennsylvania Avenue) willfully misread the available evidence to take a politically popular calculated risk with welfare reform in 1996—a policy change that concentrated all of the risks associated with the new policy on a constituency that was economically vulnerable and politically weak.

Any time the tendency to pursue self-interest is underestimated, the result is a form of "soft utopianism," as theologian Reinhold Niebuhr observed. Niebuhr saw the modern liberal culture as rooted in the same misconceptions that gave rise to Marxism.[3] In Niebuhr's view, meliorative liberalism is saved from the excesses of communism only by the checks and balances built into democratic political systems. Democracies "check illusions by contrasting truths or errors. So the liberal world manages to achieve a tolerable life in a kind of confusion of purposes, which is better than the organization of the whole resources of the community for the achievement of false ends."[4]

In theory, incrementalism works well to the extent that it permits policymakers to learn from inevitable mistakes. Yet meliorative liberals rule out whole categories of responses to mistakes because of their incomplete analysis of human nature and their vision of steady human progress. When meliorative liberals are confronted with evidence that cherished initiatives have failed, they try to correct their mistakes by calling for a little bit more: greater federal power, additional appropriations, or earlier intervention. Thomas Sowell provides a revealing example in liberal proposals to address the rise in teenage pregnancies through programs of sex education in the schools. Where such programs fail to reduce the extent of the problem—or make the situation worse—the liberal response is not to try something different but to suggest that such programs should be started in earlier grades.[5]

Thus, meliorative liberals' chronic reformism has adverse consequences for policymaking. Left to their own devices, meliorative liberals will expand the size and power of the federal government well past any reasonable estimate of the point of diminishing returns. That kind of expansion, essentially, is what happened in the 1960s—when the Democrats controlled the White House and Congress (perhaps the zenith of meliorative liberalism)—and again in the 1970s, when an adaptive conservative Republican president (Nixon) confronted strong Democratic majorities in the House and Senate.[6]

To a substantial degree, policymaking at the federal level since the early Nixon years has been preoccupied with *decremental* policymaking: a deliberate effort to scale back the federal government and weed out programs that do not work effectively. Almost without exception, decremental policy initiatives have been introduced by adaptive conservatives (Nixon and Ford) and carried further by nostalgic conservatives (Reagan and, more recently, House Republicans). The instinctive response of meliorative liberals to decrementalism has been to deny the need for reform and to question the compassion of policymakers who seek to get control of federal spending or reemphasize traditional values.[7]

To the extent that mankind is not merely fallible but also self-interested, belief in the inevitability of human progress is naive. As Aaron Wildavsky has observed, all new policies change the mix of problems facing society—creating new problems through the very act of ameliorating old ones. "Progress" may occur, in this vision, if we find that we prefer the new set of problems to the old.[8] In some circumstances, at least, we will *not* prefer the new set of problems to the old problems. When that happens, we must first go back, at least for awhile, before we can move forward again.

Liberal Skepticism and the Need to Preserve the Inheritance

Meliorative liberals' tendency to view all reform as potentially beneficial stems from their skepticism regarding the possibility of identifying objective truth. This skepticism is a core element in the meliorative liberal worldview (see chapter 3). In Popper's terms, we learn by formulating testable hypotheses and learning from mistakes. Wheareas a hypothesis may be disconfirmed by contrary evidence, it can never really be confirmed by this process; the possibility always remains that a subsequent case will disconfirm the hypothesis.

As Popper acknowledged, however, the more often a particular hypothesis has survived these tests—that is, the more often it has not been falsified—the more confidence we can have in it. Although we may never possess absolute proof, we can proceed with some confidence by acting on the information we gain via trial and error. In chapter 7 I term this situation "consensual expectations." We may recognize that all knowledge is tentative and subject to possible revision and still have a pretty good idea from repeated trials that certain things are true. For example, in the wake of the collapse of communism in Eastern Europe, we may conclude, relatively safely, that capitalism is a superior form of economic organization—that it provides a high standard of living for a large number of people while nurturing a high degree of individual liberty. As Herbert Stein correctly observed, we have not necessarily found the best form of mixed economy; capitalism today is very different from that of the 1920s, and capitalism in the third millennium doubtless will look different again. We probably can abandon the illusion, however, that socialism provides a viable alternative, and we can recognize capitalism as a part of our inheritance that merits some preserving. (See chapter 9 for a discussion of what this might involve.)

Of course, meliorative liberals are correct in recognizing that even if there is such a thing as objective truth, people will almost inevitably disagree about what it is.[9] Should we conclude from this that nothing is worth protecting? The skepticism at the core of this worldview almost precludes the meliorative liberal from recognizing anything as worth defending—except, perhaps, a romanticized vision of the federal government as an agent for positive social change. To the meliorative liberal, experimentation and reform are always potentially beneficial; the possibility for serious harm to precious things of enduring value almost always goes unrecognized.

Nathan Glazer provides evidence on this point in an insightful work on federal social policy, in which he chronicles his own evolution from liberalism toward what some observers have termed neoconservatism.[10] According to Glazer, the liberal view that was prevalent in the 1960s held that industrialization and urbanization ultimately were forces for a better quality of life, although they produced major disruptions in traditional ways of doing things that required some kind of adaptation. Because liberals of this period believed that some policy prescription exists for every problem, they tended to view the advanced, industrialized world as having undergone progressive, if jerky, improvement primarily as a result of governmental policies adopted in response to the forces of social change.

As Glazer grappled with social policies in housing, health, education, and social welfare, however (sometimes as an academic and sometimes as a participant in the policy process), he gradually came to a different view, which he summarized in two propositions. First, our social policies deal increasingly with the breakdown of traditional ways of handling distress—particularly in the family, but also in ethnic groups, the neighborhood, and the church. Second, social policies designed to deal with the breakdown of these traditional institutions have had the unintended effect of weakening them further and thus making matters worse in at least some respects.[11] Welfare policy may be the most dramatic illustration of this phenomenon (see chapter 7), but it is by no means an isolated instance.

For Glazer as adaptive conservative, recognition of the need to adapt to the social processes of urbanization and industrialization came first. With this adaptation, he gradually came to recognize the need to preserve an inheritance (family, neighborhood, church, ethnicity) that was threatened by federal social policy. A one-time liberal such as Glazer could recognize this mistake and learn from it, but in so doing he had to abandon meliorative liberalism as a worldview.

Irving Kristol underwent a similar transformation from meliorative liberal to neoconservative. Kristol has provided an extensive autobiographical account of his intellectual evolution, making absolutely clear his perception that learning from certain kinds of mistakes requires that one cease to be a liberal. Becoming a "neoconservative" was intellectually liberating for Kristol:

> I no longer had to pretend to believe—what in my heart I could no longer believe—that liberals were wrong because they subscribe to this or that erroneous opinion on this or that topic. No—liberals were wrong, liberals are wrong, because they are liberals. What is wrong with liberalism is liberalism—a metaphysics and a mythology that is woefully blind to human and political reality.[12]

As Kristol became increasingly concerned with what he saw as "clear signs of rot and decadence germinating within American society," he came to view that decadence as not merely a consequence of meliorative liberalism but its actual agenda. He drew this conclusion because meliorative liberals share with utopian reformers a secularized vision that everything is subject to challenge and potential improvement.[13] Thus, meliorative liberals pursue the same ends as utopian reformers, albeit at a slower pace, making liberalism a form of "soft utopianism," in Niebuhr's view. Where there is nothing higher than mankind, mankind stands in judgment over everything. Under such circumstances, the state becomes a kind of secular substitute for God—the source to which people look for deliverance from worldly problems. As Glazer observed, "Central government today believes it should be capable of satisfying all human needs and all public demands, even the demand for less central government, more power to local government, local communities."[14] Niebuhr, as a Protestant theologian, characterized this misplaced faith in the state as "the sin of idolatry and pretension"—with which all government is potentially involved sooner or later, in his view.[15]

❏ SYSTEMIC RATIONALITY AND THE INTERPLAY OF WORLDVIEWS

The fact that blind spots plague meliorative liberalism does not prove that incrementalism is a bad method of making public policies. To the contrary, in this volume I suggest that nothing is to be gained by pursuing either nonincremental visions or misguided attempts at articulated rationality.

The real problem with meliorative liberalism as a worldview is its blindness to certain types of mistakes. Popper and Lindblom regarded mistakes as inevitable and advanced incrementalism (i.e., piecemeal social engineering) as the best strategy for learning from these mistakes. Indeed, this strategy is the chief contribution of democracy, in Niebuhr's view: the extraction of "a measure of truth from the contest of contrasting errors."

> It provides for checks and balances upon the pretensions of men as well as upon their lust for power; it thereby prevents truth from turning into falsehood when the modicum of error in truth is not challenged and the modicum of truth in a falsehood is not rescued and cherished.[16]

From the perspective of the anti-rationalist thinkers reviewed in chapter 2, we should not be surprised that meliorative liberalism is blind to certain categories of mistakes. Each of the four worldviews I identify in this volume has its own characteristic weaknesses, and each has its own contribution to make to "the contest of contrasting errors."

In the preceding section, I explore meliorative liberalism's blind spots in considerable detail. A fair portrait of this worldview also must identify the contributions it brings to the policy process. Meliorative liberals are a persistent force for experimentation and reform. Although they are wrong to view *all* change as potentially beneficial, their input is invaluable whenever reform is warranted, as it sometimes is. For example, if Herbert Stein is correct in arguing that capitalism survived because it adapted, surely meliorative liberals deserve a lion's share of the credit for that adaptation. Moreover, meliorative liberals, along with adaptive conservatives, inject a healthy dose of realism into the policy process through their recognition of mankind's inherent fallibility, which makes pursuing adaptations incrementally—ameliorating social problems rather than quixotically pursuing utopian visions—prudent.

Adaptive conservatives make a slightly different contribution. Like nostalgic conservatives, adaptive conservatives recognize the importance of preserving an inheritance. Therefore, they are relatively immune to this blind spot, which so debilitates meliorative liberalism. Moreover, in distinct contrast to nostalgic conservatives, adaptive conservatives recognize (correctly, in my judgment) the necessity of adjusting to changing circumstances to preserve what is truly of value in any inheritance. Although this role is very important, and my treatment of adaptive conservatives to this point makes them seem an almost perfect balance of the willingness to reform and a capacity to recognize what is worthy of preservation, adaptive conservatives may be faulted on two grounds. First, they almost never initiate reform. They may facilitate reform when it is initiated by others—sometimes by participating in the drafting of legislation and sometimes by eschewing an effort to overturn legislation associated with earlier, meliorative liberal regimes. (Many social policy analysts have remarked on the importance of Eisenhower's decision not to challenge the bulk of the New Deal in this regard.) Left to their own devices, however, they almost never instigate reform; the impetus for social or economic reform, where it really is needed, must come from meliorative liberals and utopian reformers.

Second, in their readiness to adapt to changing circumstances—the "realism" that makes them, in their own minds at least, superior to the nostalgic conservatives—adaptive conservatives may be too willing to erode what is precious in the name of adaptation. Where traditional practices or truths genuinely warrant defending (and sometimes they do), we must look to nostalgic conservatives for a vigorous, line-in-the-sand defense. Although nostalgic conservatives sometimes seem out of touch with reality—longing for a return to an idyllic earlier period that may never really have existed—they are the most dependable source of support for traditional values and institutions—Glazer's neighborhoods, families, ethnic groups, and churches—that sometimes prove to have been more effective than their modern counterparts.

Even utopian visionaries have a critical role to play in the policy process, although they have come in for more criticism than any other worldview to this point in this volume. Utopian visionaries provide most of the imagination in the policy process; they are most likely to break out of conventional modes of thinking and consider radically different alternatives to existing ways of doing things. In so doing, they provide a valuable source of inspiration and criticism for meliorative liberals, who sometimes need a nudge to consider bolder initiatives. In addition, utopian visionaries' penchant for holistic initiatives often leads them to focus on macro-level problems and macro-level solutions that policymakers otherwise would ignore—for example, the globalization of the economy and the disappearance of unskilled jobs that are the underlying causes of poverty. For the better part of three decades, as Sanford Schram has argued, research on poverty focused on the behavior of the poor as the primary cause of continued dependency. This perspective guided policymakers in the welfare reform debates of 1995–96, to the detriment of the poor. Although one need not be a utopian visionary to focus on macro-level causes of the welfare problem, they are less likely than other participants to miss such causes.

In sum, incrementalism is superior to other forms of policymaking—particularly misguided efforts at articulated rationality—because it is better equipped than any other strategy to help policymakers learn from mistakes. Each of the four worldviews I identified in chapter 3 is blind to certain kinds of mistakes, however. Although each also brings unique strengths to the policy conversation, a certain degree of humility is warranted for everyone involved. Regardless of the merits of one's particular point of view at any given moment, the policy process will function well over the long haul only if it is responsive to the full range of worldviews—which necessarily includes a lot of other people one might wish would go away.

❏ IMPROVING INCREMENTALISM: ADAPTIVE CONSERVATIVE REFORMS

In this concluding section, I suggest two reforms that are designed to make incrementalism work more effectively by ameliorating political inequalities among groups. First, I propose that the federal government explore ways to mobilize interests that currently are unorganized and thus unrepresented in the policy process. Second, I call for some form of public financing for congressional campaigns to address the problem of unequal monetary resources among political groups.

As many readers undoubtedly have guessed already, I would place myself within the adaptive conservative category in the typology I developed in chapter 3. Although readers may be surprised to find reform proposals of this sort advocated by a self-proclaimed adaptive conservative, they should not be. Earlier in this chapter I note that although adaptive conservatives recognize the need to accept change to preserve what is precious in the inheritance, they seldom initiate change themselves. This reticence is a serious fault of adaptive conservatism. Adaptive conservatives need to recognize the desirability of policy change when it is aimed at fulfilling or completing a vision of society they deem worthy of preservation.

For example, as Friedrich Hayek has argued, the real choice in economic policy is not between intervention and nonintervention. The issue is what form intervention will take. If we accept the desirability of a capitalist economy, as Hayek urges, we should confine ourselves to enhancing and protecting the market as a kind of discovery process. As I show in more detail in chapter 9, Hayek envisioned a strong, positive role for the state in promoting and maintaining competition and rejected as utopian the ideal of a self-regulating economy. Following Hayek still further, we might embrace equality under the law as a more desirable and attainable goal than equality of results. In so doing, however, we might still acknowledge a significant gap between ideal and reality, necessitating public policies to ameliorate observed inequalities in treatment of different racial or ethnic groups.

Similarly, if we accept incrementalism as the best way to make public policy under most circumstances, we should seek ways to preserve and enhance its key elements. Although the case for incrementalism is very strong, the normative case for systemic rationality rests on its ability to identify and weigh a multiplicity of contending interests and vantage points. Thus, policy change is constrained—and systemic rationality is undermined—by severe inequalities among interests.

Mobilizing the Unorganized

Unfortunately, there are distinct biases to the interest group universe (see chapter 4). Large, diffuse groups have difficulty mobilizing because of the free rider problem. Poor groups have more difficulty mobilizing than rich groups. Membership groups of all sorts have more difficulty mobilizing, and surviving, than institutions. The result—as Ralph Miliband described so well—is an imperfect competition among social interests.[17]

Thus, many groups are left out of the group equilibrium entirely on many issues. In fact, three of the six policy processes in Figure 4-1 are characterized by a consensual demand pattern in which groups seeking benefits from government encounter no effective opposition.

There is a counterintuitive lesson here regarding the desirability of rationality in policymaking. Rational decision making requires consensual objectives and consensual expectations (see chapter 7). By definition, these conditions will not be met for the three cells on the right-hand side of the typology, where the demand pattern is conflictual. In the three consensual cells, by contrast, rationality is attainable, but it is made possible by the failure of important interests to mobilize. On distributive issues, groups (e.g., sugar producers and refiners) seek and receive government subsidies, at the expense of unmobilized taxpayers. On self-regulatory issues, oligopolistic industries seek to establish and maintain cartels by securing government regulation—at the expense of unorganized consumers. Within the realm of Barrier I nondecisions, lack of demand for action may reflect widespread contentment with the status quo. On the other hand, the failure of certain issues to arise at all may just as easily reflect the privileged position of business within capitalist societies—as Lindblom and Miliband suggested—or the fact that candidates for political office, if they are to mount a campaign at all, must seek funding from wealthy contributors who don't want certain issues raised.

If the arguments in chapters 2 and 3 are correct, the task before us is not so much to circumvent incrementalism as to find ways to make incrementalism work better. Inasmuch as policy change is constrained by the failure of some groups to mobilize, the problem is not with partisan mutual adjustment as Lindblom described it (a process that is confined to the middle cell on the right-hand side of the typology in Figure 4-1). The problem is that all too often, the policy process never gets into that cell. Surprisingly, given our tendency to equate nonincremental change with some form of articulated rationality, the three policy processes associated with consensual demand patterns are all likely to benefit economically advantaged groups at the expense of unmobilized interests.

The typology I develop in chapter 4 suggests that to make incrementalism work better we must recognize the importance of political conflict and strive for a fairer equilibrium among contending groups. As Niebuhr demonstrated, social collectives (nation-states, corporations, labor unions, political interest groups, and even families) are even more inclined to pursue narrow interests than individuals are.[18] Thus, conflict is necessary if justice is to be approximated: "Conflict is necessary because relative justice depends upon setting interests against interest in the hope of achieving a degree of equality and stability between conflicting interests."[19] The kind of justice that is attainable within the political and economic world, given mankind's fallibility and the primacy of self-interest, "can be established only by a contest of power which creates a fair equilibrium of power."[20]

The health care reform and the welfare reform cases attest to the importance of such an effort. Health care reform failed, at least in part, because major beneficiary groups (particularly the uninsured) were not represented in the group struggle. Although welfare reform clearly was warranted in view of the serious problems in the existing system, it shifted all of the risks associated with the new policy to the poor. Efforts to move toward a more responsible party system will not assure a fair distribution of power. As Tom Ferguson has convincingly shown, political parties must court the support of major investors if they are to mount credible campaigns; expecting political parties to champion the causes of nonvoters over the interests of voters and campaign contributors is romantic, rather than realistic.[21]

Challenging groups might be encouraged to mobilize through direct government subsidies—as with the Community Action program of the mid-1960s[22]—or alterations in the tax code. At a minimum, actions taken by recent Republican Congresses to "defund the left" should be reversed. With each successful effort at representation, the group equilibrium should be more balanced than it was. Mobilization of challenging groups, by its very nature, encourages conflictual demand patterns—shifting the policy process into the three cells on the right-hand side of the typology in chapter 4.

Any action to mobilize the unorganized must be understood as meliorative, however, rather than utopian. Almost surely, we can never succeed in mobilizing all such interests—or even in identifying all of them. As Nathan Glazer has noted, one of the most important developments in federal social policy in the 1970s was the rise of legislative mandates that required political participation by program beneficiaries in shaping federal social policies.[23] The health care and welfare reform cases clearly show, however, how weak poor people remain, despite the prevalence of such participation mandates.

Ameliorating Disparities in Tangible Resources

Here is where the balance of forces comes into play. Mobilization of previously unrepresented interests is insufficient to guarantee a balanced process of partisan mutual adjustment, much less the achievement of nonincremental change. The major tangible resource available to political groups is money (see chapter 4). The major intangible resources are strategic position, legitimacy, and expertise. These resources are distributed unevenly among groups that succeed in mobilizing. Corporations are particularly advantaged in tangible and intangible resources, creating an imperfect competition among social interests. Although a lack of cohesion or unskilled leadership may preclude effective influence in some cases, there is little reason to expect weak groups to triumph over the strong with any regularity.

There is a limit to how much any reform can reduce the advantages that flow to special interests (especially corporations) from intangible resources. As Niebuhr observed, social scientists may succeed in pointing out that social policies do not produce the results "intended or pretended by those who champion them"—thus unmasking dishonest justifications for policies that really benefit narrow interests.[24] Certainly, that is one of my primary motivations in writing this book. Expecting too much from disinterested policy analysis is unrealistic, however; there always will be an upper limit on the role of reason in the clash of social or economic groups, as Niebuhr clearly understood:

> Men will not cease to be dishonest, merely because their dishonesties have been revealed or because they have discovered their own deceptions. Wherever men hold unequal power in society, they will strive to maintain it. They will use whatever means are most convenient to that end and will seek to justify them by the most plausible arguments they are able to devise.[25]

We can at least reduce the inequalities associated with money in politics, however. Some form of public financing of congressional elections is an indispensable element in any effort to ameliorate inequalities among political interests. Studies of congressional elections consistently suggest that money matters to challengers and incumbents in very different ways. Incumbents amass large war chests to deter strong challengers—and much of the time, they succeed. Where a strong challenger does enter the race, however, the challenger need not raise as much money as the incumbent to stand a chance of winning. Challengers need only raise enough money to gain name recognition and communicate a clear message to voters. When that happens (and it can happen at a surprisingly modest cost), the incumbent is in very serious trouble. Under such circumstances, a large war chest of campaign contributions can even become a liability for incumbents by making them appear to be captives of special interests. We can make congressional elections more competitive—and thus ameliorate the advantages currently possessed by corporations and other big donors—without limiting individual contributions to candidates or anticipating every loophole that might enable special interests to funnel soft money to candidates. It is sufficient to guarantee challengers enough money to mount serious races.[26]

Issue Movement: Conflict as a Precondition for Real Policy Change

Where challenging groups gain strength over time, there will be a tendency for issues to move down the right-hand side of the typology (see chapter 4)—beginning with Barrier II nondecisions, moving into normal incrementalism and eventually (although by no means inevitably) into the realm of nonincremental change. In this regard, the health care reform case highlights the importance of mobilization of all affected constituencies; given the failure to mobilize by uninsured and poor Americans, even vigorous presidential leadership was insufficient in this case to move the issue out of the arena of Barrier II nondecisions.

Ordinarily, mobilization of previously unrepresented interests will not lead to nonincremental legislation unless there also is an aroused mass public opinion, as in the 1970 clean air case (as well as the civil rights victories of the 1960s). Mass public arousal in the outer circle of policymaking (see chapter 5) takes the issue away from the policy community by encouraging the president or others in the broader political system to take up the issue. Mass arousal may force an issue onto the agenda or, where the issue already is on the agenda, facilitate passage of a stronger bill via policy escalation.

As the 1970 Clean Air Act amendments clearly show, however, when such legislation is a response to public arousal rather than an increase in the available knowledge base, the most likely outcome will be dramaturgical incrementalism. In the clean air case, policy escalation led to technology-forcing, health-based ambient air quality standards. At the same time, however, SIPs would determine concrete actions to be taken to clean the air; these SIPs would be the product of a second, much less salient policy process that was likely to be dominated by business interests. Thus, the product of this process of "public satisfying" was an incremental policy outcome disguised by the staging of a drama that permitted all of the active participants to claim that they were placing the public's health above economic considerations.

Dramaturgical incrementalism might seem like a good thing to the extent that the need to satisfy an aroused public pushes policymakers to pass stronger laws than they would have otherwise. Aaron Wildavsky has clearly demonstrated, however, the symbolism inherent in policy escalation through a case study of proposals to clean up the Delaware River Basin. Four proposals were considered for which estimated benefits exceeded the costs of cleanup. A proposal for which benefits barely exceeded costs was chosen over another proposal with a benefit/cost ratio that was more than twice as high. In effect, policymakers opted to maximize the absolute degree of cleanup while largely disregarding considerations of economic efficiency.

Although placing environmental considerations above economic concerns may appear courageous, the reality was that most of the participants in the decision process (particularly environmentalist and public interest groups, but also including some federal officials, members of Congress, and the governors of Pennsylvania and Delaware) would not have to bear a large share of the costs of the eventual cleanup. Given that the costs of cleaning the river basin would be borne in large part by other actors, appearing "more environmental than thou," in Wildavsky's phrase, became politically attractive. Municipal officials, whose cities would have to raise sewer rates to pay for the cleanup, were most likely to attach importance to the ratio of estimated benefits to costs.[27] Thus, as in the clean air case of 1970, what appears at first glance to be a strong commitment to the environment turns out, on closer examination, to be little more than symbolic posturing by individuals in a position to shift the costs of the policy onto others.

Although tapered-down policies may seem like very small victories within the realm of normal incrementalism, the real significance of such issues lies in the conflictual nature of the demand pattern: Challenging groups have effectively mobilized and forced some kind of federal response to their problem. An incremental outcome may be merely the first in a succession of steps that add up to significant policy change. Moreover, partisan mutual adjustment derives its value from its ability to identify and accommodate a multiplicity of interests and vantage points; challenging groups are not the only players in the game with legitimate interests to protect. As Niebuhr recognized, justice emerges, if at all, from a fair equilibrium of power rather than the ultimate triumph of the underdog.

Ultimately, however, no system that is predicated on balancing political groups each of which is concerned only with its own narrow interests can ever really achieve justice. To the extent that incrementalism effectively defines politics as being about problem solving, it implies that any problem brought to government by an organized group arguably is legitimate. Thus, the desire of sugar producers to stabilize sugar profits at a high level can be as legitimate as an attempt by environmentalists to force polluters to reduce emissions or efforts by church groups to secure aid for homeless persons. Rampant examples of "corporate welfare" show how easily special interests can equate their narrow group interests with the broader public interest.[28]

Creating a more balanced group universe is not enough—although that is a desirable objective. We also need criteria for distinguishing between legitimate and illegitimate political objectives. In chapter 9 I explore how incrementalism be governed by overarching norms that circumscribe the proper realm of politics.

NOTES

1. For a further discussion of this point, see Michael T. Hayes, "The Unequal Group Struggle," in *Incrementalism and Public Policy* (New York: Longman, 1992), 44–62.

2. See Reinhold Niebuhr, "Faith and the Empirical Method in Modern Realism," in *Christian Realism and Political Problems* (New York: Charles Scribner's Sons, 1953), 9, for an indictment of the liberal naiveté regarding selfish behavior:

> It is rather typical of the errors to which modern thought is beguiled by the tendencies of a scientific nominalism that modern psychiatry in its various schools can know so much about the complexities of the human psyche and should have such great success therapeutically, and yet should be involved in the error of assuming that the universal tendency to egocentricity must be due to faulty education; and that it could be overcome either by adequate psychiatric technic or by teaching mothers to give their children "unconditional love." The fact that the phenomenon of self-seeking may be related, not to specific forms of insecurity but to the insecurity of life itself, seems to be obscured in even the most sophisticated psychological theory.

3. Niebuhr, "Faith and the Empirical Method in Modern Realism," 5.

4. Ibid., 5–6.

5. Thomas Sowell, *The Vision of the Anointed: Self-Congratulation as a Basis for Social Policy* (New York: Basic Books, 1995), 15–21.

6. As Adam Przeworski and Michael Wallerstein have observed, the central focus within Keynesian economics on the need to maintain aggregate demand legitimized the narrow group claims of labor unions and the poor for greater shares of the national income. This dynamic set in motion a new kind of politics in which organized interests could press for greater shares of the pie while equating their narrow group interests with the broader public interest. Because Keynesianism emphasized consumption at the expense of savings and investment, however, the number of claimants inevitably outpaced the economy's capacity for growth, making a day of reckoning inevitable. When the "stagflation" of the late 1970s combined high unemployment, high inflation, and high nominal interest rates in ways the Keynesians did not anticipate and could not explain, the prevailing economic paradigm was discredited—opening the way for the triumph of supply-side economics in President Reagan's first term. See Adam Przeworski and Michael Wallerstein, "Democratic Capitalism at the Crossroads," in *The Political Economy: Readings in the Politics and Economics of American Public Policy,* ed. Thomas Ferguson and Joel Rogers (Armonk, N.Y.: M. E. Sharpe, 1984), 335–48. For a reinforcing argument, see also Claus Offe, "Competitive Party Democracy and the Keynesian Welfare State: Factors of Stability and Organization," 349–67, in the same volume.

7. Jimmy Carter, a Democratic president, also held office during this decremental era. President Carter's attempts at decremental policymaking reflected his penchant for articulated rationality. Although his centrist politics might not seem utopian, his engineering background led him to approach policy questions via the rational-comprehensive ideal of decision making. Carter's term in office is remembered less for his attempts at decrementalism than for his various attempts at comprehensive and expansionary policy initiatives in the areas of energy policy, welfare reform, health care reform, and zero-based budgeting, among others. See Aaron Wildavsky, "Skepticism and Dogma in the White House: Jimmy Carter's Theory of Governing," in *Speaking Truth to Power: The Art and Craft of Policy Analysis* (Boston: Little, Brown and Co., 1979), 238–51.

8. Wildavsky, *Speaking Truth to Power,* 83.

9. For example, as a Christian I accept the authority of Scripture. Because I believe The Bible is divinely inspired and thus God's word, I cannot agree with meliorative liberals that identifying absolute truth is impossible. I am forced to acknowledge, however, that many other religious traditions exist that claim to find absolute truth somewhere else. Moreover, Christians disagree among themselves over what The Bible means, what its practical implications are for our everyday life, and even whether the Scriptures themselves are inerrant. Politically, some Christian groups array themselves on the far right of the spectrum, whereas others join with secular liberals on the far left.

10. I do not know whether Glazer would be comfortable being classified this way or not. In terms of the typology I advanced in Chapter 3, however, Glazer would clearly seem to have evolved from meliorative liberalism toward adaptive conservatism.

11. Nathan Glazer, *The Limits of Social Policy* (Cambridge, Mass.: Harvard University Press, 1988), 2–3.

12. Irving Kristol, *Neo-Conservatism: Selected Essays, 1949–1955* (New York: Free Press, 1995), 486.

13. Kristol describes his discovery of religion—which began with a volume by Reinhold Niebuhr—and the impact it had on his evolution away from liberalism in *Neo-Conservatism*, 484–85.

14. Glazer, *The Limits of Social Policy*, 128.

15. Reinhold Niebuhr, *The Nature and Destiny of Man: A Christian Interpretation; Volume II, Human Destiny* (New York: Charles Scribner's Sons, 1964), 267.

16. Niebuhr, "Faith and the Empirical Method in Modern Realism," 14.

17. Ralph Miliband, *The State in Capitalist Society* (New York: Basic Books, Harper Colophon Books, 1969). More recently, see Ralph Miliband, *Socialism for a Skeptical Age* (London: Verso, 1994).

18. Reinhold Niebuhr, *Moral Man and Immoral Society: A Study in Ethics and Politics* (New York: Charles Scribner's Sons, 1960).

19. Reinhold Niebuhr, "Christian Politics and Communist Religion," in *Christianity and the Social Revolution,* ed. John Lewis, Karl Polanyi, and Donald K. Kitchin (London: Victor Gollancz Ltd, 1935), 446.

20. Ibid., 470.

21. Thomas Ferguson, *Golden Rule: The Investment Theory of Party Competition and the Logic of Money-Driven Political Systems* (Chicago: University of Chicago Press, 1995).

22. The Community Action program came under severe attack within two years of its initial passage; it was scaled back by President Johnson and largely (albeit not completely) dismantled under President Nixon. The Johnson administration has been justifiably criticized for caring more about passing a bill (whatever its form) that would help win the 1964 election than about how to fight poverty most effectively. Community Action was an ambiguous term, and various proponents advanced the concept for a wide variety of conflicting reasons. The result was a quintessentially ambiguous legislative mandate in which Community Action boards were charged with securing the "maximum feasible participation of all relevant community groups." This mandate left undefined which community groups were relevant, what "maximum feasible" participation meant, and just what the boards were supposed to do. From the standpoint of the analysis advanced here, however, Community Action was a failure less because of its patently political origins or its vague legislative mandate than because President Johnson weakened the program when successful efforts by local Community Action boards to mobilize blacks and poor people threatened the interests of southern Democratic congressmen and urban mayors. See John C. Donovan, *The Politics of Poverty*, 2nd ed. (Indianapolis: Bobbs-Merrill Co., Inc., Pegasus Books, 1973), and Daniel P. Moynihan, *Maximum Feasible Misunderstanding: Community Action in the War on Poverty* (New York: Free Press, 1970).

23. See Glazer, *The Limits of Social Policy*, 105–106:

> It is very hard to sum up the extent and effects of participation. It took many forms: the right to be heard, to be informed, to receive notice, to speak at public hearings, to be consulted on budgets, to sit as representatives on boards, to hold a certain percentage of seats on boards. Even without formal rights to participation, movements of the formerly unorgan-

ized or if organized not influential—such as the handicapped—have become influential in the shaping of policies that affect them, by appeal to public opinion and, at the extremes, by demonstrations blocking public offices.

24. Niebuhr, *Moral Man and Immoral Society*, 32.

25. Ibid., 34.

26. Gary C. Jacobson, *Money in Congressional Elections* (New Haven, Conn.: Yale University Press, 1980).

27. Aaron Wildavsky, "Economy and Environment: Rationality and Ritual," in *Speaking Truth to Power*, 184–88.

28. For specific and outrageous examples, see Fred R. Harris, *The New Populism* (New York: Saturday Review Press, 1973)—especially Chapter 1, "Take the Rich Off Welfare," 13–32—and Jim Hightower, *There's Nothing In the Middle of the Road but Yellow Stripes and Dead Armadillos* (New York: HarperCollins, 1997). On the tendency for public policies to provide substantial material rewards to well-organized, affluent groups while dispensing symbolic reassurances to the broader public, see Murray Edelman, *The Symbolic Uses of Politics* (Urbana: University of Illinois Press, 1964).

CHAPTER NINE

Incrementalism under the Rule of Law

In chapter 8 I identify two reforms that are designed to make incrementalism work better by ameliorating political inequality. To the extent that they are successfully implemented, those two reforms—efforts to mobilize previously unorganized groups and public funding of congressional campaigns—would make for a fairer or more balanced group equilibrium. Reforms of this sort aim at improving policy outcomes by improving policymaking; they assume, as Theodore J. Lowi observed, that "a good process means a good policy."[1]

There is an upper limit, however, to how much we can do to improve policy outcomes by focusing exclusively on the policy process. As Lowi argued, at some point we also must address the normative question of what constitutes good policy. My thesis in this concluding chapter is that incrementalism will not produce good policy outcomes unless it is constrained by some larger vision of the parts of the inheritance that are worth preserving. All such visions necessarily will be subject to considerable adaptation and change over time (see chapter 8). Nevertheless, we need to identify some criteria for distinguishing between reform proposals that are consistent with our vision of who we are as a people and those that are not.[2]

Accordingly, in this concluding chapter I focus on one final reform: Friedrich Hayek's proposal that policy outcomes conform to the rule of law. According to Hayek, incrementalism is defensible only if it operates in accordance with the rule of law. In this chapter, I define in more detail what the rule of law involves, describe what it would look like in practice, explain why it is preferable to politics as practiced now, and suggest some measures we might take to return to such a regime.

☐ INCREMENTALISM AND INSTITUTIONAL SCLEROSIS

According to Hayek, departures from the rule of law reflect the natural tendency for organized groups to pursue narrow interests at the expense of the public interest. A realistic view of politics would regard political parties as coalitions of special interests rather than as the embodiment of majority rule.[3] The proliferation of programs that benefit special interests can only be prevented, in Hayek's view, "by depriving the governing majority of the power to grant discriminatory benefits to groups or individuals."[4] Under classical liberalism, powerful norms operated to discourage such discriminatory legislation. According to Lowi, however, these norms eroded in the first part of the 20th century, giving rise to a new public philosophy of interest-group liberalism that provided an intellectual justification for the modern interest-group state.[5] In short, the new public philosophy provided a way to accommodate the multiplicity of special interests associated with modern capitalism.

Political science acted as an "unindicted co-conspirator" in this process, in Lowi's view, by developing contemporary theories of pluralism.[6] For example, the first premise of majority-building incrementalism is the lack of any agreed-upon public interest on most issues (see chapter 5). In the absence of any clear public interest, politics becomes a clash among organized interest groups. Where the public interest is equated with the equilibrium of contending interests, the rationale for interest-group liberalism is complete. There is no longer any need for lawmakers to make hard choices among contending groups; instead, they can appear to act on pressing problems while avoiding a clear decision by establishing a new game within the executive branch in which all the major interests will be players. This tactic is what Lowi called interest-group liberalism or "policy-without-law."[7]

Under the best circumstances, of course, organized interests will encounter opposition from other narrow interests, creating a conflictual pattern of demand that necessitates decision making by partisan mutual adjustment.[8] Within this realm of normal incrementalism (as identified in the typology I advanced in chapter 4), the rational approach for reelection-minded legislators is to delegate broad discretion to the bureaucracy—creating a new administrative process in which the contending interests are represented.[9] In this variant, policy-without-law institutionalizes privilege by shifting the authoritative allocation of values to bureaucratic arenas in which organized interests possess access and legitimacy but the public typically is unrepresented.

By contrast, groups seeking policies that primarily come at the expense of broad, general interests (taxpayers or consumers) often encounter no attentive or effective opposition because of the free rider problem. Under these circumstances, the rational response for self-interested legislators will be to give these organized interests whatever they are seeking: subsidies, restrictions on entry, or the right to maintain legal cartels via the regulatory process.[10]

The eventual result of a regime in which normative constraints on discriminatory legislation have broken down is a form of "institutional sclerosis," as Mancur Olson has shown.[11] Where a society's organized groups represent relatively narrow interests, broader interests become collective goods subject to the free rider problem. For example, although all groups might benefit from policies that encourage economic competition and economic growth, for each individual group the rational strategy is to pursue policies that advance their narrow economic interests.[12] The result is economic inefficiency, as the group struggle gives rise to protectionist policies that favor occupational or industry groups over broad, diffuse interests. Unfortunately, government intervention in the economy on behalf of such groups creates distortions in the market that eventually become new problems in their own right.[13] These new problems generate demands for additional interventions—which, in turn, create further distortions and pressure for additional interventions.[14]

Because decision making via bargaining among interest groups is time-consuming, interest-group liberalism is much slower to adapt to changing economic conditions than the free market—hence, institutional "sclerosis."[15] The recent rise of decremental policymaking reflects, as much as anything else, the need to put a stop to this gradual but steady drift toward larger and increasingly ineffectual government.

In sum, incrementalism leads to a steady proliferation of policies that benefit special interests and grant power to executive agencies whenever norms that support the rule of law have broken down. For incrementalism to work effectively, it must be guided by a renewed commitment to the rule of law, along with some general conception of the kind of social order we want to maintain.[16]

❏ THE RULE OF LAW DEFINED

In a society committed to the rule of law, as defined by Hayek, all laws would exhibit two qualities. First, they would be impersonal, applying equally to everyone. That is, laws would never discriminate by singling out identifiable groups for privilege or punishments. This characteristic defines equality under the law. Second, rules governing the behavior of citizens and government officials would be clear and specific. Citizens would always be able to tell what the rules are and see clear and predictable consequences for violating the rules. The arbitrary exercise of power would be minimized because administrators would have little or no discretion in enforcement.

We readily accept the need for impersonal rules in sporting events. Where rules are fair, predicting in advance who will benefit from them in specific circumstances should be impossible. We all would object to rules that were written specifically to advantage or disadvantage certain players. Moreover, good rules also are clear and specific. For example, rules that define what constitutes a foul in basketball should be clear enough that players can predict accurately which actions will be acceptable and which will not. Although referees may differ somewhat in how much contact they permit, the players can easily observe how referees differ and adjust to these minor variations because the basic definition of what constitutes a foul is written in the rule book and accepted by all. The situation would be very different if referees were granted discretion to call fouls "in the common interest." Congress essentially takes this approach when it authorizes a regulatory agency to regulate an industry "in the public interest, convenience, and necessity." Under such a broad definition, referees would have vast discretion; a foul would be whatever a referee says it is; the definition could vary from game to game or moment to moment, with no way for players to predict in advance what behaviors would qualify as fouls.

The rule of law merely extends these same two principles to the legislation that governs societies. One or both of these principles may be violated in practice for particular laws, however. Thus, these two principles may be regarded as dichotomous variables that give rise to a fourfold classification of policies, as shown in Figure 9-1. The first defining dimen-

FIGURE 9-1. Typology of Policy Outcomes

	Personal, Predictable Target	Impersonal, Unpredictable Target
Vague statute	1) Regulation of particular industries (airlines, etc.)	2) Regulation of behavior (pollution, occupational safety)
Clear and specific statute	3) Distributive policies/ particularized benefits (farm subsidies, etc.)	4) Hayek's Rule of Law (impersonal target, clear instructions)

sion focuses on the nature of the legislative mandate: The law may either issue clear and specific instructions to administrators or, through an ambiguous legislative mandate, grant administrators discretion to exercise effective power over policy outcomes.[17] The second dimension focuses on the targets of the legislation, which may be either identifiable and predictable or impersonal and abstract.[18]

The Four Quadrants

The rule of law, as defined by Hayek, is confined to Quadrant 4 of Figure 9-1. The rule of law is violated in one or more ways in all of the other cells. Within Quadrant 1, for example, regulation is applied to specific industries (railroads, airlines, radio and television broadcasters, etc.), and regulatory commissions have sweeping discretion to regulate "in the public interest, convenience, and necessity." Often, such legislation is initiated at the request of the industries themselves as a way to facilitate the maintenance of cartels.[19] In at least some instances, however, regulatory legislation represents a response to social movements or mass public arousal demanding action to regulate oligopolistic business practices. Typically, some form of regulatory capture ensues: When mass public arousal eventually subsides, the agency gives the regulated whatever they want at the expense of the broader public interest, much as Lowi argued.[20] The extraordinary discretionary power vested by these sweeping mandates is evident from the checkered history of the Civil Aeronautics Board—which shored up airline industry cartels for 40 years and then reversed course to foster procompetitive policies and eventual deregulation, all within the same ambiguous legislative mandate.[21]

Policies that fall within Quadrant 2 possess one of the qualities of good laws in Hayek's terms, inasmuch as they are not targeted at any one individual or group. The vast discretion delegated to administrators under these laws opens the door wide, however, for arbitrary, unpredictable, case-by-case decisions that preclude individuals or firms from planning their own activities.[22] Individuals and firms falling under these regulations cannot act freely, subject to rules they know in advance—because there are no rules to know in advance. Examples include business regulation that is aimed at social or economic problems that transcend any one industry (e.g., regulation of air and water pollution or occupational safety).

Policies that fall within Quadrant 3 grant benefits to narrow special interests at the expense of taxpayers or consumers. Lowi calls these policies "distributive policies." The Sugar Act, which was in effect for three decades before its defeat in 1974 (and subsequently was reenacted in similar form) provides a classic example (see chapter 4). Drafted primarily by the five largest domestic sugar producers and refiners, the Act determined how much sugar would be sold in the United States in a given year and then divided that total into domestic and foreign shares (usually about a 60–40 split). The domestic and foreign shares were then allocated to individual producers through production quotas, which served as licenses to sell specific amounts of sugar on the U.S. market. Farmers seeking to enter this profitable market could not do so without going to Congress and securing a production quota, written into the language of the statute. Any production in excess of one's quota would have to be destroyed or dumped on the international market. Thus, the Sugar Act enabled sugar producers to establish and stabilize a price for sugar that was higher than the price that would have prevailed in a free market.[23]

By contrast, policies that fall within Quadrant 4 qualify as rule of law; they combine clarity with impersonality. Unemployment compensation provides one clear instance: Beneficiaries are entitled to benefits that are determined by a clear formula (e.g., 28 weeks at 80 percent of their salary at the time they became involuntarily unemployed), thus minimizing administrative discretion. At the same time, the law was impersonal inasmuch as unemployed persons are not a static category of people who can be identified in advance. Similarly, Social Security provides benefits according to a precise—albeit complicated—formula. The program is universal in the sense that everyone who lives long enough to reach retirement age qualifies.

The federal income tax conforms to the rule of law in some aspects but not others. In general, most provisions of the tax code apply equally to all taxpayers. Although the tax code provides for various deductions and exemptions, the individuals who qualify for these provisions cannot be identified in advance. (As with unemployed persons, we might say more accurately that the specific individuals who fall within particular categories—for example, married couples with children or owners of particular types of stocks and bonds—will not always be the *same* individuals at all times.) Even special tax breaks that are designed to provide incentives to undertake particular activities (e.g., saving for retirement or medical expenses) are impersonal in much the same way speed limit laws are impersonal; individuals and firms can decide whether to undertake activities for which the special tax rates are in effect.

At the same time, however, numerous special tax provisions clearly violate the rule of law by enabling individual corporations to escape taxes that fall on everyone else in the same category. These special tax provisions are written to *appear* at least somewhat general—usually by specifying exemptions for all firms that operate within a particular line of commerce within a specified geographic region. Closer examination, however, often reveals that only one firm is engaged in that line of commerce within the area specified.

The 1986 tax reform clearly illustrates the prevalence of these special tax provisions. It eliminated a large number of deductions and exemptions, thus broadening the tax base. This reform enabled the government to raise the same amount of revenue with only two tax brackets and a maximum tax rate of 28 percent (down from about 50 percent). Although President Reagan and other proponents repeatedly characterized this tax reform as a victory for tax simplification (which in many ways it was), the statute ultimately was several hundred pages long. Clearly, several hundred pages are unnecessary to explain a tax code with a sharply reduced number of deductions and exemptions and only two tax brackets; the extraordinary length was attributible to hundreds of special tax provisions that exempted individual corporations from taxes that other firms were paying. Moreover, although the 1986 law achieved these significant rate reductions for individuals and families by ostensibly shifting a substantial share of the tax burden to corporations, corporate income taxes as a share of federal revenues in fact have declined steadily over time and now stand at about half the level in effect in the Eisenhower years—demonstrating that the *effective* rate paid by many corporations is lower than the generally applicable rate established in the 1986 law.[24]

Attempting a precise estimate of the percentages of all laws that fall within each quadrant is beyond the scope of this work. In a larger sense, however, the precise figures do not really matter. What is important (and clear) is that many policies fall outside Quadrant 4—and the number almost surely has grown over time, as Lowi suggests. The idea is not to get the balance right; each time a law that falls outside Quadrant 4 is enacted, the rule of law is further eroded, abridging liberty or violating the principle of equality under the law. Policies that fall within Quadrants 1 and 2 delegate significant discretion to administrators, preventing individuals from planning and (usually) benefiting narrow interests over consumers and taxpayers. Policies that fall in Quadrants 1 and 3 single out identifiable groups for particularized benefits,[25] violating equality under the law.

A Positive Program of Laissez Faire

The real issue in restoring the rule of law is not big government versus small government. There is no question that government must be activist.

The only issue is whether government should pursue some vision of central planning or act instead to foster and maintain a free economy. At a minimum, the state should preserve competition through vigorous and effective anti-trust policy, as well as by opposition to legislative measures (such as the Sugar Act or airline regulation) that are designed to permit oligopolistic industries to stabilize cartels. Moreover, free markets do not adequately capture spillover costs and benefits; hence, there is a clear role for government in dealing with air and water pollution and other externalities.

Contrary to popular perception, classical liberals have long advocated an extensive and important role for government. For example, in distinct contrast to contemporary libertarians—who stress the need to get government out of many policy areas entirely[26]—Hayek consistently recognized a significant role for government in assuring the proper functioning of a free economy.[27] The activities Hayek recognized as appropriate roles for government include maintenance of a reliable and efficient monetary system,[28] provision of public goods and services that otherwise would not be provided at all,[29] and facilitation of the acquisition of reliable knowledge about facts of general significance (for example, setting standards for weights and measures, gathering statistics, and providing support for education).[30] Hayek also recognized the political power of large corporations; thus, he found at least some common ground with Charles Lindblom and Ralph Miliband[31] and acknowledged an important (albeit complex) role for government in protecting against price discrimination.[32] Like all mainstream economists, Hayek recognized a governmental role in remedying externalities such as pollution.[33] Although Hayek vigorously opposed any attempt to identify and establish an ideal distribution of income in the name of "social justice," he consistently acknowledged the need to ameliorate extreme inequality of income; he supported government involvement in providing for indigent, unfortunate, and disabled persons, and he believed such policies would increase in scope with the general growth of wealth.[34]

Another self-proclaimed classical liberal, the late Henry Simons, provided what may be the best label for this vision: a "positive program for *laissez faire*."[35] The main elements of Simon's program included elimination of private monopoly in all forms, establishment of more definite and adequate "rules of the game" with respect to money, drastic reform of the tax system to reduce "unlovely" extremes in distribution of income, action to eliminate differential subsidies flowing out of the tariff system, and limitations on the squandering of resources on advertising and selling activities.[36]

Although classical liberals share the overall vision of a competitive economy, fostered and maintained as necessary by government activity, they do not agree on all points. For example, Simons advocated a progressive income tax as a means of income redistribution, whereas Hayek argued strongly for a flat tax.[37] As Hayek observed, true liberalism is not doctrinaire, and such disagreement is healthy and desirable:

> [I]t seems to me highly desirable that liberals shall strongly disagree on these topics, the more the better. What is needed more than anything else is that these questions of a policy for a competitive order should once again become live issues which are being discussed publicly; and we shall have made an important contribution if we succeed in directing interest to them.[38]

Moreover, support for this broad vision is not limited to one part of the political spectrum. Liberal Democratic Senator Fred R. Harris of Oklahoma—who also was chairman of the Democratic National Committee, grassroots political activist, and a presidential candidate in 1972—advocated a strikingly similar program, which he called a "new populism." The key elements of Harris's strategy for a return to genuinely "free" enterprise were an end to government subsidies for industries and wealthy farmers, along with antitrust measures aimed at restoring competition within a variety of increasingly oligopolistic industries.[39]

Similarly, Theodore Lowi concluded *The End of Liberalism* with a call for a "neo-liberal" program consisting of three elements.[40] First, Lowi would retain and even strengthen all nondiscretionary fiscal policies—for example, automatic stabilizers such as unemployment compensation. Because these programs are nondiscretionary, they are compatible with the rule of law; they require very little administrative apparatus and tend to be self-executing. Second, Lowi would eliminate the vast majority of "pork barrel" and subsidy programs, along with most discretionary regulation of industry by executive agencies. Finally, Lowi would replace these discretionary programs with new statutes telling the bureaucracy exactly what to do to bring about desired social or political ends.[41] For example, Keynesian demand management could be employed only if some firm and reliable rules could be established to constrain policymakers (e.g., the concept of a budget balanced at full employment).[42] Similarly, discretionary monetary policy (which vests enormous and largely unchecked power in the Federal Reserve Board) would have to be replaced by some kind of general rule, enacted by Congress, governing the conduct of monetary policy—as advocated by Simons and his most famous pupil, Milton Friedman.[43]

❏ THE RULE OF LAW AND THE POWERLESS

Whatever its precise composition, a "positive program of *laissez faire*" may appear to leave individuals defenseless against ruthless corporations driven only by the profit motive. Certainly, much of the case for big government in the modern era rests on its alleged capacity to offset the power of increasingly large corporations.

This romantic view of government as guardian of the weak against the strong ignores the privileged position of business in modern capitalistic societies, as emphasized by Lindblom and Miliband and attested by Hayek. Although modern corporations are not quite as powerful as Lindblom and Miliband suggest, they are more powerful than any other actors in the system under normal circumstances. Moreover, as Ferguson observed, politicians running for office must first obtain sufficient funds to mount competitive campaigns—which forces them into the arms of major investors. Lowi's critique of interest-group liberalism clearly reveals the naiveté of looking to the state as a source of countervailing power in a society that is organized around corporatist principles.[44]

Because the free rider problem makes it so difficult for large, diffuse groups (such as taxpayers, consumers, or poor people) to mobilize and survive, the group equilibrium almost surely will remain skewed in favor of industry and occupational groups at the expense of the larger public, despite the best efforts of the state to encourage mobilization of previously unorganized interests (as recommended in chapter 8).[45] Hayek believed that organized interests inevitably profit from government at the expense of the general public unless government is completely deprived of the power to grant discriminatory benefits to groups or individuals. Lowi echoed this sentiment when he characterized a strong commitment to the rule of law as "the only dependable defense the powerless have against the powerful."[46]

Finally, although actions that are designed to create a fairer equilibrium of contending interests can take us some distance toward a more just society, as Niebuhr suggested, in reality the balance of active groups can never represent the public's vital interest in the continuous adaptation to changing economic conditions that the market accomplishes so well—and organized interests, acting rationally, always try to prevent. A properly functioning market permits free entry by new entrepreneurs into lines of commerce that are characterized by high profits. Where the economy is planned via negotiations among organized interests that represent major sectors of the economy, existing producers have every incentive to deny access to new entrants.[47] Restrictions on entry that were built into the Sugar

Act provide one example of this phenomenon; the Civil Aeronautics Board's refusal to approve a single application for entry by a new carrier into a major interstate route for a period of nearly 40 years provides another. Lowi termed this dynamic an "iron law of decadence":

> [T]he very success of established groups is a mortgage against a future of new needs that are not yet organized or are not readily accommodated by established groups. One of modern society's great challenges is how to reap the benefits of groups and at the same time to minimize the costs. Among the costs the greatest is the "iron law of decadence," that tendency of all organizations to maintain themselves at the expense of needed change and innovation.[48]

The Special Case of the Poor

How would poor people—the most vulnerable segment of society—fare under a return to the rule of law? Hayek consistently acknowledged the need for programs to provide for the indigent, unfortunate, or disabled, although he rejected any attempt to attain an ideal distribution of income. Similarly, Simons saw extreme inequalities in income as "unlovely" and called for programs to ameliorate severe inequality. More recently, Milton Friedman has advocated a negative income tax to place a floor under incomes while preserving incentives to work.

In fact, a return to the rule of law would significantly benefit poor people in at least two ways. First, a return to the rule of law would mean an end to categorical assistance programs such as AFDC. As Sanford Schram has observed, current welfare programs stigmatize recipients; singling out certain categories of people for assistance implicitly labels the targeted groups as different, suggesting that traits specific to these groups are the primary causes of their problems. This labeling effectively places the blame for poverty on poor people themselves and focuses attention on the need for professional counseling to help individuals move from welfare to work.[49] In short, categorical programs imply that "it is the welfare recipients who need to change, and not the job market."[50]

Moreover, under existing welfare programs, bureaucrats possess enormous power over applicants for welfare—a power they often exercise arbitrarily. During the 1995–96 debate over welfare reform, politicians commonly referred to the abolition of AFDC as an effort to bring an end to welfare as an "entitlement." In reality, welfare in the United States has never been an entitlement. To the contrary, under AFDC states were given authority to determine benefit levels and set eligibility standards. Welfare workers always had considerable discretion in publicizing the availability of aid, estimating applicants' income and asset levels, making applicants wait for long periods of time or endure multiple visits before they received application forms, and accepting or rejecting individual applications as properly filled out. Applicants were subject to humiliation, delays and evasion, verbal abuse, and in some cases even physical abuse at the hands of welfare workers. Furthermore, welfare recipients had to live with the ever-present possibility that their children would be taken away from them and placed in foster care.[51]

Once applicants were accepted for aid, they could easily be thrown off the rolls even though they meet all the legal requirements, through a process known as "churning." Churning involved cutting off aid to recipients for "noncompliance"—failure to meet some legal obligation. The most common cause cited was failure to fill out and return questionnaires by specified dates. Thousands of people were eliminated from the rolls, at least temporarily, every time recertification letters went out. Studies have shown that in many of these cases of "noncompliance," clients never received mailings, the department never properly recorded correctly completed questionnaires, or English-language questionnaires were mailed to clients who didn't speak English and therefore treated the mailings like junk mail.[52] Periodic churning enabled welfare departments to cut welfare outlays significantly by randomly forcing large numbers of legally eligible recipients off the rolls, forcing them to go through a long struggle to requalify for aid. Expanding the discretion available to states and localities by replacing AFDC with a block grant program only increases the potential for such cost-cutting strategies.

By contrast, measures to alleviate poverty under the rule of law would minimize the discretion of welfare workers, thereby protecting applicants from these kinds of abuses. For example, under the negative income tax proposed by Milton Friedman, eligibility would be a function of income level as reported on federal tax forms. The amount of aid to which a particular applicant is entitled would be determined by a clear formula; Friedman's plan would guarantee a floor of half the poverty level and let recipients keep half of every dollar they earn.[53] Although the minimum benefit and the negative tax rate could be set at a wide variety of alternative levels, what matters is the underlying principle that aid should be related to income according to a clear formula that is established by law.

Moreover, under the Friedman plan, need (as measured by pretax income) would be the sole criterion for eligibility; categorical programs aimed at subpopulations deemed "worthy" would be eliminated. This reform would make aid available to groups that currently are excluded from receiving welfare (particularly able-bodied males and families headed by able-bodied males) and reduce the tendency, identified by Schram, to blame poverty on the characteristics of recipients rather than shortcomings in the job market.

Negative income tax plans advanced by Presidents Nixon and Carter were defeated in the 1970s (see chapter 7); unfortunately, the legislative struggles surrounding these proposals uncovered internal contradictions within the plans that discredited the negative income tax as a potential rationalizing breakthrough. The Nixon plan was plagued by serious "notch effects" resulting from the interaction of the negative income tax with existing welfare programs—all of which were left in place to avoid a political battle over abolition of popular programs. Where the negative income tax replaces existing programs, as envisioned by Friedman, these notch effects disappear.

President Carter proposed to substitute the negative income tax for existing welfare programs, but his initiative was doomed by his unwilling-ness to commit any additional funds to welfare reform beyond those already devoted to welfare programs. Although a workable negative income tax could have been adequately funded through the elimination of preexisting welfare programs, as Carter envisioned, doing so while holding harmless welfare recipients in states paying the most generous benefits proved impos-sible. To fund the negative income tax this way, the basic benefit level would have to be set somewhere near the median AFDC benefit level. Although this formula would have lowered monthly payments for recipients in high-bene-fit states (who were, unfortunately, the only welfare recipients successfully mobilized by the National Welfare Rights Organization in the Nixon and Carter years), it would have left the vast majority of welfare recipients better off than they were under AFDC. Thus, the defeat of the Carter plan does not really demonstrate the unworkability of a negative income tax.[54]

Moreover, we are not bound as a society by Carter's zero cost constraint. Welfare—with all its disincentives to work and alleged incentives to have children out of wedlock—is the least expensive way to deal with the problem of poverty; welfare is structured the way it is because it is cheap (see chapter 7). There can be no real reform of welfare that does not involve spending more money than we do now. As soon as we recognize this fact and commit ourselves as a society to spend more to alleviate poverty, the minimum benefit level can be set above the AFDC median at any level we choose, enabling us to hold harmless as many welfare recipients as we are willing to pay for.

In short, there is nothing inherent in the negative income tax that precludes its adoption as a program to alleviate poverty while maintaining a firm commitment to the rule of law. A negative income tax would make welfare recipients better off by basing eligibility for welfare solely on need and by establishing a clear legislative formula linking benefit levels to pretax income, thereby minimizing the near life-and-death discretion available to bureaucrats. It would do so without attempting to identify and implement an ideal conception of social justice.

The Special Problem of Medicaid

In general, there is a strong case to be made for giving recipients cash in lieu of goods, services, or food stamps, and letting them decide how to allocate their own resources. Although almost all existing welfare programs could be replaced by a negative income tax, the most difficult program to "cash out" would be Medicaid. For all of its faults and abuses, Medicaid is an extraordinarily generous benefit, providing free medical care to those who qualify. Medicaid recipients do not pay premiums for this coverage, and they are not subject to copayments or deductibles. Nor do they bear responsibility for any portion of expenses after the deductible is met, as is the case under conventional indemnity plans. Providing a cash equivalent for Medicaid benefits, if the program were abolished as part of a comprehensive negative income tax, would dramatically increase the minimum benefit and the overall costs of the program. Leaving Medicaid in place, however, retains the greatest notch effect of all: the severe disincentive to work beyond the earnings limit for Medicaid.

This disincentive is not a problem only for the negative income tax. As long as Medicaid exists as a separate program that provides free medical care to a means-tested population, recipients will never have a rational incentive to move from welfare to work unless they can find a job that pays substantially more than welfare, provides health insurance coverage as a fringe benefit, or both. The overwhelming majority of jobs available to people with low skills and little prior work experience fail on both counts.

Clearly, poor people must be incorporated into the larger health insurance system. Whether this reform takes the form of a comprehensive, single-payer national health insurance plan covering all Americans, some variant of the Clinton plan, a market-based program of medical savings accounts, or some other scheme, the key principle must be elimination of Medicaid as a targeted program of free health care for the poor. Alternatively, if we leave Medicaid in place, we should expect poor people to choose welfare over work. All the talk in the world about the breakdown of morality and the demise of the work ethic cannot change the simple fact that few welfare recipients will forfeit health care coverage for their families to take low-wage employment.

Disconnecting health care for the poor from welfare would eliminate the most serious disincentive to work in the present system. It also would remove the most serious notch effect in the negative income tax as an alternative to the present system. Equally important, it would eliminate a major source of insecurity for welfare recipients. Because eligibility for Medicaid was tied to eligibility for AFDC in most states, the loss of AFDC meant the loss of Medicaid as well. Welfare bureaucrats had extraordinary discretion under AFDC to deny assistance to eligible applicants and to remove recipients from the rolls via churning. This power of the state over its most vulnerable citizens is multiplied when access to health care is tied to eligibility for welfare.

❏ RESTORING THE RULE OF LAW

In this chapter, I review what the rule of law is and why it is so important. I also explore in some detail what a return to the rule of law would look like. I now examine various ways in which the rule of law might be restored.

The key to restoring and maintaining the rule of law, according to Hayek, is to deny legislators the authority to grant discriminatory benefits to groups or individuals.[55] Hayek proposed to accomplish this prohibition through a model constitution. The "basic clause" of such a constitution

> would have to require that the rules should be intended to apply to an indefinite number of unknown future instances, to serve the formation and preservation of an abstract order whose concrete contents were unforeseeable, but not the achievement of particular concrete purposes, and finally to exclude all provisions intended or known to affect principally particular identifiable individuals or groups.[56]

Except in times of war or national emergency, coercion would be used only to enforce the universal rules of just conduct and to raise revenues to support the services provided by government.[57]

A further safeguard would be provided by a bicameral legislature in which an upper house would be charged with developing general rules of just conduct and the lower house would focus on the day-to-day affairs of government within the framework of the general rules developed by the upper house. Members of the lower house would be prevented by the constitution from enacting discretionary legislation; they also would be subject to frequent elections and would be expected to be responsive to constituents and organized interests. By contrast, the upper house would consist of men and women between the ages of 45 and 60 who would be elected for 15-year terms (with one-fifteenth replaced each year), to encourage both experience and detachment.[58]

One can hardly imagine a circumstance under which Americans would amend the Constitution to replace the House and Senate with a new bicameral legislature along the lines Hayek envisions. Conceivably, however, the basic clause of Hayek's model constitution, requiring that all laws issue clear and specific instructions to administrators while conforming to the principles of impersonality and equality under the law, might be adopted as a constitutional amendment. If such an amendment were adopted, incrementalism would function as envisioned by Lindblom and Popper—but subject to an overarching vision of a free society governed by laws rather than people.

Short of a constitutional amendment, each of the major institutions of government could take steps to reinvigorate the rule of law, as Lowi made clear in concluding *The End of Liberalism*. The courts could force a return to juridical democracy by overturning acts of Congress whenever they grant sweeping delegations of legislative authority to the executive branch. Presidents could veto legislation that violates the principles of rule of law. Congress could periodically undertake codification of existing laws. Executive agencies could stop making idiosyncratic and arbitrary case-by-case decisions and instead develop formal rules that scholars of administrative law have long advocated.[59]

Although these actions by the major institutions of our government would go a long way toward restoring the rule of law, each requires a degree of self-abnegation—a willingness to subordinate short-term political interest to long-term principle—that is unlikely to occur spontaneously. As Lowi acknowledged:

> [T]hese changes will have to be guided by a new public philosophy, and a new public philosophy does not come out of a package. It will emerge from a kind of political discourse in which few of us have engaged during the false consensus of our generation.[60]

Presidents historically have played a critical role in redefining who we are as a people in relation to one another or the outside world. Most of the time, politics operates within prevailing definitions of who we are and what we are about, but circumstances or an accumulation of important trends periodically force us to reexamine these definitions. The New Deal, the Marshall Plan, and the Containment Doctrine, for example, were moments in our history in which we redefined our national identity. As the sole elected official with a national constituency, the president ordinarily must articulate these new visions if they are to be accepted by the broader public.[61] The failure of Newt Gingrich's attempt at such a redefinition in 1995–96 is testimony to the almost insurmountable advantages any president possesses in such a contest; President Clinton could hardly have been weaker entering that showdown, yet he prevailed decisively, virtually assuring his reelection almost a year in advance.

In this regard, Jeffrey Tulis concluded his study of the "rhetorical presidency" with a call for a return to what he called "constitutional speech."[62] The analysis in this chapter suggests that what is needed is a return to a particular form of constitutional speech that redefines who we are as a people by educating the public on the nature and importance of the rule of law. Historically, presidents have often championed what they regarded as the broader public interest against narrow special interests. In calling for a return to the rule of law, future presidents would be defending the public's interest in predictable and impersonal statutes against the demands of narrow interests for discriminatory benefits and the electoral incentive for members of Congress to maintain themselves in office by providing particularized benefits to constituencies.[63] As the only elected official within our system with a national constituency, the president is more likely to champion this cause than any other actor, and there is no question that a president who chooses to use the bully pulpit of the presidency for this purpose could do more to educate the public than any other public official.

In the meantime, political scientists can make a critical contribution to the development of a new public philosophy. This volume represents one attempt to advance that conversation. As Hayek observed, we have moved so far away from the rule of law as a society that few people today can even define the concept.[64] Lowi's experience in writing *The End of Liberalism* illustrates this observation well. Lowi did not elaborate on the meaning of juridical democracy in that work because he felt the term would be readily understood by all of his readers and thus could be used without definition. When he subsequently realized that this expectation was unfounded, Lowi wrote a sequel, *The Politics of Disorder*, to flesh out the concept: "It is a measure of the decline of law and legitimate government that I needed more elaboration."[65]

We also need—from members of Congress as well as the president—a rhetoric that educates the public about what they can realistically expect from politics. In recent years, successful presidential candidates have campaigned against the very government they hope to lead, and members of Congress have found running *against* Congress almost irresistible. Few incumbents do a good job of explaining to their constituents what Congress does, and how.[66]

Here again, political science can make a major contribution through the preparation and education of responsible citizens. As Frank Knight observed, respect for authority is undermined as much by romantic illusions concerning the capacity of government as it is by corrupt politicians. There remains a pressing need to educate the public—specialists and nonspecialists alike—on what politics can accomplish, and at what speed.

NOTES

1. Theodore J. Lowi, "Decision-Making vs. Policy Making: Toward an Antidote for Technocracy," *Public Administration Review* (May/June 1970), 319.

2. See Friedrich Hayek, *Law, Legislation, and Liberty, Vol. 1: Rules and Order* (Chicago: University of Chicago Press, 1973), 62–65 for a discussion of the role of "utopias" in guiding and constraining policymaking. In view of Hayek's strong critique of rationalist thought (see Chapter 2 of this volume), he introduces some confusion by emphasizing the indispensability of utopias as heuristic devices in policymaking. Hayek does differentiate between utopias that "aim at radically redesigning society and suffer from internal contradictions which make their realization impossible" and those that serve merely as a "guiding model of the overall order" that will only be approximated and never fully achieved. Developing a utopian vision in the rationalist sense is not necessary to have some sense of who we are as a people or what part of our inheritance is worth preserving. For Hayek (as the discussion in this chapter shows), the key issue is whether government activism will reinforce free markets by fostering and preserving competition or undermine and distort markets via a succession of pragmatic concessions to expediency that are unguided by any clear vision of the nature of the larger economic order.

3. "What today we call democratic government serves, as a result of its construction, not the opinion of the majority but the varied interests of a conglomerate of pressure groups whose support the government must buy by the grant of special benefits, simply because it cannot retain its supporters when it refuses to give them something it has the power to give." Friedrich A. Hayek, *Law, Legislation and Liberty, Volume 3: The Political Order of a Free People* (Chicago: University of Chicago Press, 1979), 129. This view is echoed by Lowi, who argues in *The End of Liberalism: The Second Republic of the United States*, 2nd ed. (New York: W. W. Norton & Co., 1979), that "the most important difference between liberals and conservatives, Republicans and Democrats, is to be found in the interest groups they identify with" (p. 51). See also Tom Ferguson, *Golden Rule: The Investment Theory of Party Competition and the Logic of Money-Driven Political Systems* (Chicago: University of Chicago Press, 1995); Ferguson argues that political parties must be viewed as coalitions of major investors rather than coalitions of voters.

4. Hayek, *Political Order of a Free People*, 128–29.

5. Lowi, *The End of Liberalism*, Chapter 3, "The New Public Philosophy: Interest Group Liberalism," 42–63, and Chapter 5, "Liberal Jurisprudence: Policy without Law," 92–126.

6. Lowi, *The End of Liberalism*, 31–41.

7. Ibid., 54–55.

8. This is most likely to occur on issues for which both the benefits and costs of legislation are concentrated on narrow interests rather than broadly distributed. See James Q. Wilson, "The Politics of Regulation," in *The Political Economy: Readings in the Politics and Economics of American Public Policy*, ed. Thomas Ferguson and Joel Rogers (Armonk, N.Y.: M. E. Sharpe, Inc., 1984), 87–89.

9. Michael T. Hayes, *Lobbyists and Legislators: A Theory of Political Markets* (New Brunswick, N.J.: Rutgers University Press, 1981), 93–127, and "The Semi-Sovereign Pressure Groups: A Critique of Current Theory and an Alternative Typology," *Journal of Politics* 40 (February 1978): 134–61.

10. See James L. Payne, *The Culture of Spending: Why Congress Lives Beyond Our Means* (San Francisco: ICS Press, 1991).

11. Mancur Olson, Jr., *The Rise and Decline of Nations: Economic Growth, Stagflation, and Social Rigidities* (New Haven, Conn.: Yale University Press, 1982). On this same theme, see also Jonathan Rauch, *Demosclerosis: The Silent Killer of American Government* (New York: Random House, Times Books, 1994).

12. For a thorough explanation of the free rider problem, see Mancur Olson, Jr., *The Logic of Collective Action: Public Goods and the Theory of Groups* (New York: Schocken Books, 1970).

13. For depressing examples, see Irving Welfeld, *HUD Scandals: Howling Headlines and Silent Fiascos* (New Brunswick, N.J.: Transaction Publishers, 1992). For a more sanguine view of the tradeoff between equity and efficiency, see Arthur S. Okun, *Equality and Efficiency: The Big Tradeoff* (Washington, D.C.: Brookings Institution, 1975).

14. Friedrich A. Hayek, *The Road to Serfdom* (Chicago: University of Chicago Press, 1994). See also Hayek, *Rules and Order*, 59–61; Ludwig von Mises, *Planning for Freedom: And Twelve Other Essays and Addresses* (South Holland, Ill.: Libertarian Press, 1974), 18–35, and "The Failure of Interventionism," in *Socialism* (Indianapolis: Liberty Fund, 1981), 483–88.

15. On the economic inefficiency resulting from the investment of resources by groups seeking discriminatory benefits from government, see James M. Buchanan and Roger D. Congleton, *Politics by Principle, Not Interest: Toward Nondiscriminatory Democracy* (New York: Cambridge University Press, 1998).

16. "Except on rare occasions, such as constitutional conventions, the democratic process of discussion and majority decision is necessarily confined to part of the whole system of law and government. The piecemeal change which this involves will produce desirable and workable results only if it is guided by some general conception of the social order desired, some coherent image of the kind of world in which the people want to live." Friedrich A. Hayek, *The Constitution of Liberty* (Chicago: University of Chicago Press, 1960), 113–14.

17. This is the same distinction I drew in an earlier policy typology between delegation and allocation. See Hayes, "The Semi-Sovereign Pressure Groups," and *Lobbyists and Legislators*. In developing the earlier typology, I emphasized the equivalence between this delegation/allocation distinction and Lowi's distinction between policy-without-law and rule of law. In building on Hayek's definition, I now see clear instructions to administrators (which I earlier termed allocation) as only one of the two qualities involved in true rule of law.

18. Although the typology I am presenting here differs on both dimensions from Lowi's earlier four-cell effort, my thinking was very much aided by his work; see Theodore J. Lowi, "Decision Making vs. Policy Making: Toward an Antidote for Technocracy," *Public Administration Review* (May/June 1970), 314–25. The two defining dimensions of that typology focused on the likelihood of coercion (immediate or remote) and the application of coercion (to individual conduct or through an environment of conduct).

19. George J. Stigler, "The Theory of Economic Regulation," *Bell Journal of Economics and Management Science* 2 (spring 1971): 359–65.

20. Marver P. Bernstein, *Regulating Business by Independent Commission* (Princeton, N.J.: Princeton University Press, 1955).

21. See Martha Derthick and Paul J. Quirk, *The Politics of Deregulation* (Washington, D.C.: Brookings Institution, 1985).

22. The Occupational Safety and Health Administration (OSHA) came under strong criticism for issuing an overwhelming volume of highly detailed regulations. Although the very specificity of these rules might appear likely to bring about the predictability Hayek associated with rule of law, many OSHA regulations were widely regarded as arbitrary and inapplicable to particular situations and were selectively enforced, which resulted in administrative discretion.

23. On the Sugar Act, see Hayes, *Lobbyists and Legislators*, 12–14, and sources cited therein.

24. See Dan Clawson, Alan Neustadtl, and Denise Scott, *Money Talks: Corporate PACs and Political Influence* (New York: Basic Books, 1992), and Barber B. Conable, Jr., *Congress and the Income Tax* (Norman: University of Oklahoma Press, 1989). On the decline of corporate tax revenues as a share of total federal revenues, see: Donald L. Bartlett and James B. Steele, *America: Who Really Payes the Taxes?* (New York: Touchstone Books, 1994), 23–24. Bartlett and Steele estimate that if corporations paid taxes at the same rate in the 1990s that they paid in the 1950s—taking into account all tax preferences business received then and now—the

U.S. Treasury would have collected $250 billion more each year in revenues. That figure is about two and one-half times as much revenues as corporations actually paid in taxes in 1994; it would have been almost sufficient to eliminate the federal deficit by itself. Alternatively, this amount would have been sufficient to provide health care coverage for the 35–40 million people who were uninsured, with money left over for a tax cut (see Bartlett and Steele, *America*, 140).

25. The term "particularized benefits" was coined by David Mayhew in *Congress: The Electoral Connection* (New Haven, Conn.: Yale University Press, 1974).

26. Charles Murray, *What It Means to Be a Libertarian: A Personal Interpretation* (New York: Broadway Books, 1997).

27. "The range and variety of government action that is, at least in principle, reconcilable with a free system is thus considerable. The old formulae of *laissez faire* or nonintervention do not provide us with an adequate criterion for distinguishing between what is and what is not admissible in a free system. There is ample room for experimentation and improvement within that permanent legal framework which makes it possible for a free society to operate most efficiently." Hayek, *The Constitution of Liberty*, 231. For Hayek's views on the proper role of government in the economy, see "Economic Policy and the Rule of Law," in *The Constitution of Liberty*, 220–33, as well as the case studies of specific policy areas in Part III of the same volume; "Government Policy and the Market," in *Political Order of a Free People*, 65–97; and *Road to Serfdom*, 89*ff.*

28. Hayek, *The Constitution of Liberty*, 223.

29. Ibid., 222–23.

30. Ibid., 223 and 365.

31. Hayek, *Political Order of a Free People*, 84. On the privileged position of business within capitalist societies, see Charles E. Lindblom, *Politics and Markets: The World's Political-Economic Systems* (New York: Basic Books, 1977); Charles E. Lindblom, "The Market as Prison," *Journal of Politics* 44 (May 1982): 324–36; and Ralph Miliband, *The State in Capitalist Society* (New York: Basic Books/Harper Colophon Books, 1969).

32. Hayek, *Political Order of a Free People*, 85–88.

33. Hayek, *The Constitution of Liberty*, 365.

34. Ibid., 257. Hayek's most comprehensive critique of the ideal of social justice is contained in *Law, Legislation and Liberty, Volume 2: The Mirage of Social Justice* (Chicago: University of Chicago Press, 1976).

35. Henry Simons, "A Positive Program for Laissez Faire: Some Proposals for a Liberal Economic Policy," in *Economic Policy for a Free Society* (Chicago: University of Chicago Press, 1948), 40–77.

36. For a concise intellectual biography of Simons, see Herbert Stein, "Henry Calvert Simons," in *On the Other Hand: Essays on Economics, Economists, and Politics* (Washington, D.C.: AEI Press, 1995), 240–46.

37. Simons advocated a progressive income tax as a means of redistributing income. See Simons, "A Positive Program for Laissez Faire," 65*ff.* By contrast, Hayek believed that steeply progressive taxes encouraged the mass of citizens to think they could advocate public policies that would be substantially paid for by someone else. See Hayek, "Taxation and Redistribution," in *The Constitution of Liberty*, 306–323. For differences between Simons and his students Friedman and Stigler, see Stein, *On the Other Hand*, 245–46.

38. Friedrich A. Hayek, "'Free' Enterprise and Competitive Order," in *Individualism and Economic Order* (Chicago: University of Chicago Press, 1948), 108.

39. For example, there is a remarkable similarity between the "positive program of *laissez faire*" advanced here and the "new populism" advocated by former Senator Fred R. Harris, a liberal Democrat, in *The New Populism* (New York: Saturday Review Press, 1973).

40. Lowi, *The End of Liberalism*, 292–93.

41. As Lowi observed, critics who contend that legislating clear rules for administrators is impossible implicitly concede the impossibility of economic planning:

> [E]verything that is said against precision in regulatory laws applies with even greater cogency to the still more complicated and interdependent activity that makes up planning. All the economy or society really needs is a specification of bad conduct whose consequences justify restriction or elimination. These bad behaviors could range from particular instances of unfair competition all the way across to particular types of racial discrimination. *But they can be specified.* (Lowi, *The End of Liberalism*, 293; emphasis in original)

42. Although there was some attempt to identify such a rule in the postwar period, Keynesian economists of the Kennedy era and afterward did not want to limit their flexibility in responding to changing economic circumstances through any such rules. See Stein, *On the Other Hand*, 156.

43. Simons was a major proponent of such a rule. See "Rules versus Authorities in Monetary Policy," *Journal of Political Economy* 54 (February 1936): 1–30. More recently, the foremost advocate of such a rule has been Milton Friedman. See Milton Friedman, "The Control of Money," in *Capitalism and Freedom* (Chicago: University of Chicago Press, 1962), especially 51*ff.* This strategy would restore rule of law by having Congress pass a law directing monetary authorities to achieve a specified rate of growth in the stock of money. See also Milton Friedman, *A Program for Monetary Stability* (New York: Fordham University Press, 1959).

44. The concept of countervailing power is John Kenneth Galbraith's; see *American Capitalism: The Concept of Countervailing Power* (Boston: Houghton Mifflin, 1952).

45. The proliferation of citizen groups that mobilized in the 1960s and 1970s, in spite of the free rider problem, is attributable to the availability of alternative funding sources outside the groups' memberships. Yet the explosion in group activity during this period did not produce a more balanced group universe; it featured mobilization by more groups of all kinds—thus preserving the bias in favor of narrow interests over the broader public interest. See Jack L. Walker, "The Origin and Maintenance of Interest Groups in America," *American Political Science Review* 77 (June 1983): 390–406, and Kay Lehman Schlozman and John T. Tierney, *Organized Interests and American Democracy* (New York: Harper and Row, 1986).

46. Lowi, *The End of Liberalism*, 298.

47. "[T]he interests of those who bring about the required adjustments to changes, namely those who could improve their position by moving from one group to another, are systematically disregarded. So far as the group to which they wish to move is concerned, it will be its chief aim to keep them out." Hayek, *Political Order of a Free People*, 92.

48. Theodore J. Lowi, *The Politics of Disorder* (New York: Basic Books, Inc., 1971), 5.

49. Sanford F. Schram, *Words of Welfare: The Poverty of Social Science and the Social Science of Poverty* (Minneapolis: University of Minnesota Press, 1995), 139.

50. Ibid., 139.

51. For a first-person account of what applying for welfare is like, see Theresa Funicello, *Tyranny of Kindness: Dismantling the Welfare System to End Poverty in America* (New York: Atlantic Monthly Press, 1993), especially Chapter 2, "The Brutality of the Bureaucracy," 24–53. See also Frances Fox Piven and Richard A. Cloward, *Regulating the Poor: The Functions of Public Welfare* (New York: Pantheon, 1971).

52. Schram, *Words of Welfare*, 92–93.

53. Milton Friedman, "The Alleviation of Poverty," in *Capitalism and Freedom*, 190–95.

54. On the Carter welfare reform proposal, see Laurence E. Lynn, Jr., and David deF. Whitman, *The President as Policymaker: Jimmy Carter and Welfare Reform* (Philadelphia: Temple University Press, 1981). On the Nixon proposals, see Daniel P. Moynihan, *The Politics of a Guaranteed Income: The Nixon Administration and the Family Assistance Plan* (New York: Random House, Vintage Books, 1973), and Vincent J. Burke and Vee Burke, *Nixon's Good Deed: Welfare Reform* (New York: Columbia University Press, 1974).

55. Hayek, *Political Order of a Free People*, 128–29.

56. Ibid., 109.

57. Ibid., 111.

58. Ibid., 109–117.

59. Lowi, *The End of Liberalism*, 298–309.

60. Ibid., 298.

61. Tom Cronin, "The Cult of the Presidency: A Halo for the Chief," in *The State of the Presidency* (Boston: Little, Brown, 1975), 23–51. On the advantages any president possesses over potential rivals (including the Speaker of the House) in a battle to mold public opinion, see Woodrow Wilson, *Constitutional Government in the United States* (New York: Columbia University Press, 1921), 127*ff*.

62. Jeffrey Tulis, *The Rhetorical Presidency* (Princeton, N.J.: Princeton University Press, 1987).

63. David Mayhew, *Congress: The Electoral Connection* (New Haven, Conn.: Yale University Press, 1974).

64. See Philip Norton, *The British Polity*, 3rd ed. (New York: Longman, 1994), 64–65, for an excellent discussion of how elusive the concept has become even in Britain, where rule of law is considered a central element of the uncodified constitution.

65. Lowi, *The Politics of Disorder*, 184.

66. Richard F. Fenno, Jr., *Home Style: House Members in Their Districts* (Boston: Little, Brown, 1978).

Index